SMP AS/A2 Mathematics

Mechanics 1
for Edexcel

CAMBRIDGE
UNIVERSITY PRESS

The School Mathematics Project

SMP AS/A2 Mathematics writing team David Cassell, Spencer Instone, John Ling, Paul Scruton, Susan Shilton, Heather West

SMP design and administration Melanie Bull, Pam Keetch, Nicky Lake, Cathy Syred, Ann White

The authors thank Sue Glover for the technical advice she gave when this AS/A2 project began and for her detailed editorial contribution to this book. The authors are also very grateful to those teachers who commented in detail on draft chapters.

PUBLISHED BY THE PRESS SYNDICATE OF THE UNIVERSITY OF CAMBRIDGE
The Pitt Building, Trumpington Street, Cambridge, United Kingdom

CAMBRIDGE UNIVERSITY PRESS
The Edinburgh Building, Cambridge CB2 2RU, UK
40 West 20th Street, New York NY 10011–4211, USA
477 Williamstown Road, Port Melbourne, VIC 3207, Australia
Ruiz de Alarcón 13, 28014 Madrid, Spain
Dock House, The Waterfront, Cape Town 8001, South Africa

http://www.cambridge.org/

© The School Mathematics Project 2005
First published 2005

Printed in the United Kingdom at the University Press, Cambridge

Typeface Minion   *System* QuarkXPress®

A catalogue record for this book is available from the British Library

ISBN 0 521 60536 9 paperback

Typesetting and technical illustrations by The School Mathematics Project
Illustrations on pages 52, 79–80, 125 and 135 by Chris Evans

The authors and publisher thank the Lynton and Lynmouth Cliff Railway, Devon, for supplying the photograph on page 106.

The authors and publisher are grateful to London Qualifications Limited for permission to reproduce questions from past Edexcel examination papers. Individual questions are marked Edexcel. London Qualifications Limited accepts no responsibility whatsoever for the accuracy or method of working in the answers given.

Using this book

Each chapter begins with a **summary** of what the student is expected to learn.

The chapter then has sections lettered A, B, C, … (see the contents overleaf). In most cases a section consists of development material, worked examples and an exercise.

The **development material** interweaves explanation with questions that involve the student in making sense of ideas and techniques. Development questions are labelled according to their section letter (A1, A2, …, B1, B2, …) and answers to them are provided.

D Some development questions are particularly suitable for discussion – either by the whole class or by smaller groups – because they have the potential to bring out a key issue or clarify a technique. Such **discussion questions** are marked with a bar, as here.

K **Key points** established in the development material are marked with a bar as here, so the student may readily refer to them during later work or revision. Each chapter's key points are also gathered together in a panel after the last lettered section.

The **worked examples** have been chosen to clarify ideas and techniques, and as models for students to follow in setting out their own work. Guidance for the student is in italic.

The **exercise** at the end of each lettered section is designed to consolidate the skills and understanding acquired earlier in the section. Unlike those in the development material, questions in the exercise are denoted by a number only.

Starred questions are more demanding.

After the lettered sections and the key points panel there may be a set of **mixed questions**, combining ideas from several sections in the chapter; these may also involve topics from earlier chapters.

Every chapter ends with a selection of **questions for self-assessment** ('Test yourself').

Included in the mixed questions and 'Test yourself' are **past Edexcel exam questions**, to give the student an idea of the style and standard that may be expected, and to build confidence.

Contents

1 Kinematics in one dimension

In this chapter you will learn how to
• draw and interpret kinematics graphs
• use the constant acceleration equations to solve problems in one dimension

A Velocity and displacement (answers p 136)

Mechanics is about **forces** and **motion**.

We will start by looking at motion itself, leaving aside questions about how the motion is produced. This part of mechanics is called **kinematics**. Key ideas in kinematics include distance, displacement, time, speed, velocity, acceleration and deceleration.

This chapter will deal with motion in a straight line only.

A1 Jack walks along a straight road at a constant speed of 2 metres per second.

(a) How far has Jack walked after 30 s?

(b) What other information do you need to know in order to fully define his final position?

Many of the situations studied in mechanics are in reality quite complicated. The first step is usually to simplify the situation so as to focus on the most important aspects. For example, Jack's size is ignored and he is assumed to be a moving point. His motion is considered to be in a precise straight line, with any small deviations ignored. The scale of the problem allows these assumptions to be made: Jack is small compared with the distance he has walked, as are any deviations from the straight line.

Notation: 'metres per second' may be written as m/s or as m s^{-1}. The latter notation will be used in this book.

A2 Jack and Kim start walking from the same point on a straight road at a constant speed of 2 m s^{-1}.

(a) How far have they walked after 1 minute?

(b) Jack and Kim are not at the same place after 1 minute. Can you explain this?

In question A2, although Jack and Kim started from the same place and walked at the same speed for the same length of time, they ended up in different places. This is because their speeds were the same but their directions were opposite.

The quantity which includes both speed and direction is called **velocity**.

If Jack's direction is taken as the positive direction then his velocity is 2 m s^{-1} and Kim's velocity is -2 m s^{-1}.

K The quantity which includes both distance and direction is called **displacement**.

After 1 minute, Jack's displacement is 120 m from the start and Kim's displacement is –120 m.

```
  −120 m        0        120 m
 ├──────────────┼──────────────┤
   Kim        start        Jack
```

A3 (a) Write down Jack's displacement from the starting point after 2 minutes.

    (b) Write down Kim's displacement from the starting point after 2 minutes.

    (c) How far apart are they after this time?

A4 Fran walks 3 km due east and then 1 km due west.

    (a) How far did she walk?

    (b) Taking east as positive, what is Fran's final displacement?

A5 Jack now runs along the straight road in the positive direction at a constant speed of $3.5\,\text{m s}^{-1}$ for 2 minutes. He turns around and walks in the opposite direction at a constant speed of $2\,\text{m s}^{-1}$ for another 2 minutes.

    (a) For what distance did Jack run?

    (b) For what distance did he walk?

    (c) What was his displacement from his starting position after 4 minutes?

A6 This **displacement–time** graph shows the motion of a vehicle travelling at a constant velocity along a straight road.

    (a) What is the velocity of the vehicle?

    (b) What feature of the graph tells you the velocity?

    (c) What feature shows that the velocity is constant?

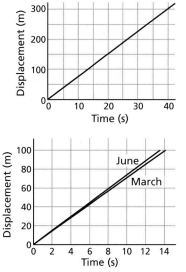

A7 An athlete was in training for the 100 metre sprint. In March her best time was 14.1 seconds. By June she had reduced her best time to 13.5 seconds. She draws this displacement–time graph.

    (a) Calculate the gradient of each line. What are the units for the gradients?

    (b) What quantity does each gradient represent?

    (c) How does the graph for June show that the athlete had improved her performance?

    (d) The graphs are both straight lines. What does this say about her motion?

    (e) Are straight line graphs realistic here? Sketch a more realistic graph for the motion of an athlete in a 100 m sprint.

K The gradient of a displacement–time graph gives the velocity.

If the displacement–time graph is a straight line then the motion is at constant velocity.

In the previous question, the athlete **modelled** her motion as a straight line graph. This model, which implies a constant velocity, does not fit the motion exactly.

For example, in the first few fractions of a second, the athlete's velocity increases from zero. So a close-up of the start of the graph would look something like this.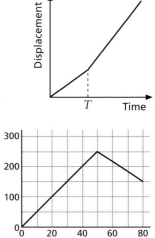

Also it is unlikely that the athlete's velocity would be constant for the whole sprint. She may increase her velocity near the finishing line.

However, the straight line model is still a good approximation for a sprinter. For a much longer race it would be less realistic.

Displacement–time graphs often simplify a real situation. For example, this graph shows a vehicle whose velocity increases instantaneously at time T. In reality, it would take some time for the velocity to change. But if this time is short in comparison with the journey as a whole, then it can be ignored and the change treated as instantaneous.

A8 Dan went for a short run.
This displacement–time graph shows his run.

(a) What was his velocity for the first part of the run?

(b) What was his velocity for the last part of the run?

(c) What was his displacement at the end of the run?

K The **average velocity** is the constant velocity at which a journey of the same overall **displacement** could have been completed in the same total time.

$$\text{Average velocity} = \frac{\text{displacement from starting point}}{\text{time taken}}$$

Notation: The letter s is used for displacement and t for time.

A9 What was Dan's average velocity?

A10 What distance did Dan run altogether?

K The **average speed** is the constant speed at which a journey of the same overall **distance** could have been completed in the same total time.

$$\text{Average speed} = \frac{\text{total distance travelled}}{\text{time taken}}$$

A11 What was Dan's average speed?

Example 1

A car travels along a straight road at a constant velocity of $70\,\mathrm{km\,h^{-1}}$.
How far does it travel in 45 seconds?

Solution

First convert the velocity into $\mathrm{m\,s^{-1}}$.

$$70\,\mathrm{km\,h^{-1}} = 70 \times \frac{1000}{3600}\,\mathrm{m\,s^{-1}} = \frac{175}{9}\,\mathrm{m\,s^{-1}}$$

Leave the velocity as an exact value.

$$\text{Displacement} = \frac{175}{9} \times 45 = 875\,\mathrm{m}$$

The car travels $875\,\mathrm{m}$ in $45\,\mathrm{s}$.

Example 2

A jogger runs for $100\,\mathrm{m}$ at a speed of $4\,\mathrm{m\,s^{-1}}$ and then walks the same distance at a speed of $2\,\mathrm{m\,s^{-1}}$. What is his average speed?

Solution

Calculate the time spent running.

$$\text{Time running} = \frac{100}{4} = 25\,\mathrm{s}$$

Calculate the time spent walking.

$$\text{Time walking} = \frac{100}{2} = 50\,\mathrm{s}$$

Average speed $= \dfrac{\text{total distance travelled}}{\text{time taken}}$

$$\text{Average speed} = \frac{200}{75} = 2.7\,\mathrm{m\,s^{-1}} \text{ to 1 d.p.}$$

Example 3

This displacement–time graph represents a short cycle ride.

Find the velocity for each part of the journey.

Solution

Find the gradient of each line segment.

For $0 < t < 120$, velocity $= \dfrac{500}{120} = 4.2\,\mathrm{m\,s^{-1}}$ to 1 d.p.

For $120 < t < 180$, velocity $= \dfrac{500}{60} = 8.3\,\mathrm{m\,s^{-1}}$ to 1 d.p.

For $180 < t < 240$, velocity $= -\dfrac{1000}{60} = -16.7\,\mathrm{m\,s^{-1}}$ to 1 d.p.

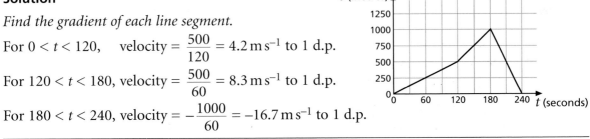

Exercise A (answers p 136)

1 Convert the following speeds into metres per second.

(a) $36\,\text{km}\,\text{h}^{-1}$ (b) $45\,\text{km}\,\text{h}^{-1}$ (c) $54\,\text{km}\,\text{h}^{-1}$ (d) $75\,\text{km}\,\text{h}^{-1}$

2 A jogger runs for 30 seconds at $5\,\text{m}\,\text{s}^{-1}$ and then walks an equal distance at $2\,\text{m}\,\text{s}^{-1}$. What is her average speed?

3 Find the average speed of a jogger who runs for 30 seconds at $5\,\text{m}\,\text{s}^{-1}$ and then walks at $2\,\text{m}\,\text{s}^{-1}$ for an equal period of time.

4 Tom walks on a treadmill at $2.5\,\text{m}\,\text{s}^{-1}$ for 60 seconds followed by 120 seconds at $1.7\,\text{m}\,\text{s}^{-1}$. What distance has he walked altogether?

5 A cyclist travels due west for 45 seconds at $10\,\text{m}\,\text{s}^{-1}$ and then turns and cycles due east for 30 seconds at $12\,\text{m}\,\text{s}^{-1}$. Take east as the positive direction.

(a) What distance has the cyclist travelled?

(b) What is the cyclist's final displacement?

(c) What is his average speed?

(d) What is his average velocity?

6 Michelle runs along a long straight road at $4\,\text{m}\,\text{s}^{-1}$ for 2 minutes. She turns around and runs in the opposite direction at $5\,\text{m}\,\text{s}^{-1}$ for 1 minute.

(a) What is her average speed?

(b) What is her average velocity?

7 A car completed a journey of $360\,\text{km}$ at an average speed of $80\,\text{km}\,\text{h}^{-1}$. The average speed for the first half of the journey's distance was $75\,\text{km}\,\text{h}^{-1}$. What was the average speed for the second half of the journey?

8 Marlon went for a walk. This displacement–time graph represents the first part of his walk.

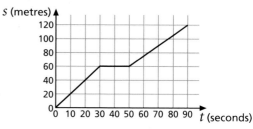

(a) What happened at time 30 seconds?

(b) Find Marlon's velocity for the first 30 seconds.

(c) What was Marlon's velocity at time 80 seconds?

(d) Find Marlon's average velocity.

9 Paige jogged along a 100 metre straight track in 20 seconds. She then rested for 10 seconds before walking back to the start in 45 seconds.

(a) Sketch a displacement–time graph to represent Paige's motion.

(b) Find Paige's average speed.

(c) What was her average velocity?

10 Tracy cycles from Aycliffe to Beford, a distance of 3 miles, in 16 minutes.
She rests for 10 minutes before continuing to Ceville, a further distance
of 4 miles, which takes 20 minutes.
Simon walks the same journey, does not stop to rest and takes 2 hours.

If Tracy starts out 50 minutes after Simon, when and where will she overtake him?

11 It is 10 km from Blakesfield to Norton Pond.
Maisie cycles from Blakesfield to Norton Pond, starting at 12 noon,
at a steady speed of 15 km h^{-1} and then immediately turns and
comes back to Blakesfield at a speed of $7\frac{1}{2}$ km h^{-1}.
John sets off on foot from Norton Pond at noon and walks at a steady
speed of 3 km h^{-1} to Blakesfield.

(a) Draw displacement–time graphs of their motion on the same diagram.

(b) At what times t_1 and t_2 do Maisie and John pass each other and
how far are they from Blakesfield at these times?

(c) At what time between t_1 and t_2 are they the greatest distance apart?

B Graphs of motion (answers p 137)

A car travels along a straight road with increasing velocity.
The table shows its velocity at different times.

Time (seconds)	0	10	20	30	40	50	60
Velocity (m s^{-1})	0	2.5	5	7.5	10	12.5	15

This **velocity–time** graph shows the motion of the car.

B1 (a) What is the gradient of the graph?

(b) What are the units of the gradient?

(c) What do you think this gradient represents?

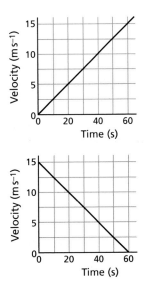

B2 If the velocity of the car were decreasing
from 15 m s^{-1}, the velocity–time graph
would be as shown.

What do you think the gradient represents
in this case?

K The rate of change of velocity with respect to time is the **acceleration**. The units of acceleration are metres per second per second, m/s^2 or $m\,s^{-2}$.

The gradient of a velocity–time graph gives the acceleration. If the velocity–time graph is a straight line, then the acceleration is constant.

$$\text{Acceleration} = \frac{\text{change in velocity}}{\text{time}}$$

Negative acceleration is sometimes described as **deceleration** or **retardation**. For example, an acceleration of $-3\,m\,s^{-2}$ can also be described as a deceleration of $3\,m\,s^{-2}$.

Notation: the letter v is used for velocity and a for acceleration.

To find acceleration in this way the motion must be in a straight line. So the graph may also be called a speed–time graph.

B3 A car starts moving from rest with a constant acceleration of $2\,m\,s^{-2}$. Find its velocity after

(a) 1 second **(b)** 2 seconds **(c)** 10 seconds **(d)** 20 seconds

B4 A car moving at $25\,m\,s^{-1}$ starts to decelerate at $1\,m\,s^{-2}$. What is its velocity after 10 seconds?

B5 This velocity–time graph shows the motion of a cyclist along a straight track. Find the acceleration of the cyclist.

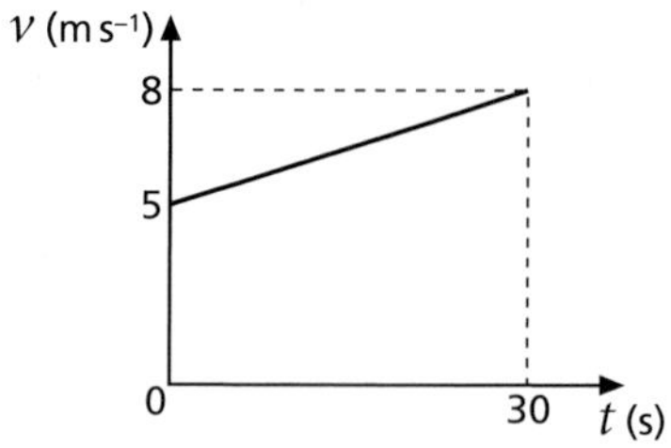

This displacement–time graph shows the motion of a cyclist who cycles at constant velocity until time t_1, then cycles at a greater constant velocity until t_2 and then comes to rest.

The graph simplifies the motion, assuming that the velocity changes instantaneously and the cyclist comes to rest instantaneously.

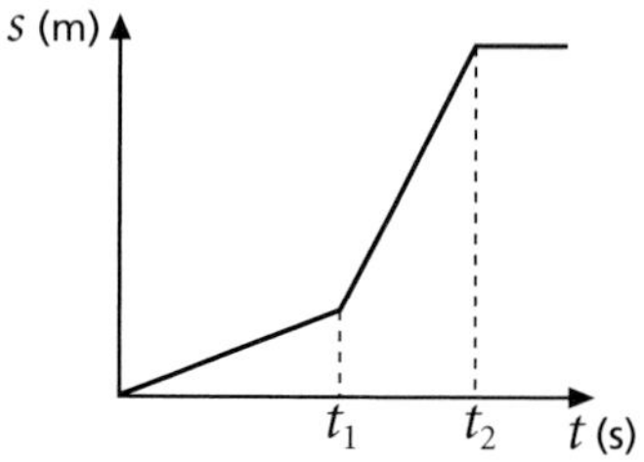

The motion of the cyclist can also be shown in this velocity–time graph.

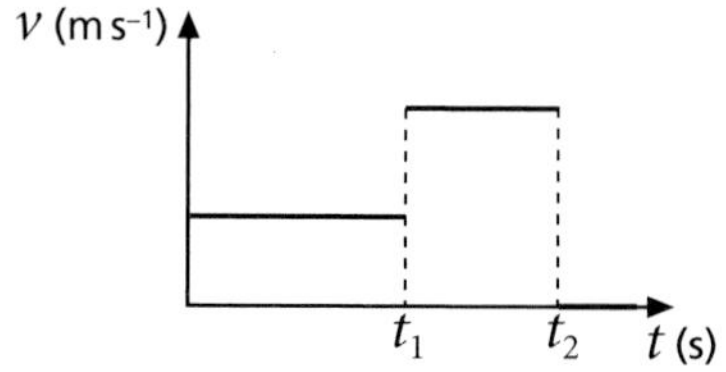

D **B6** How are the following represented on

(i) the displacement–time graph

(ii) the velocity–time graph

(a) the initial constant velocity

(b) the greater velocity

(c) the cyclist at rest

D | **B7** An acceleration–time graph could be drawn for the motion of the cyclist. Would it give any useful information about the motion of the cyclist?

B8 (a) This velocity–time graph shows the motion of a car along a straight road. Describe the motion of the car.

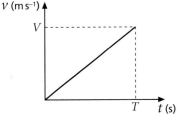

(b) Sketch the corresponding acceleration–time graph.

(c) How is the displacement of the car changing? Sketch a displacement–time graph for the car.

B9 This velocity–time graph shows the motion of a cyclist along a straight track.
Describe the motion of the cyclist at each of the labelled points.

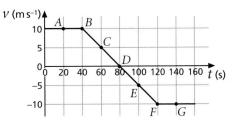

Example 4

A train travelling along a straight track accelerates uniformly from rest for 30 seconds until it reaches a velocity of $20\,\mathrm{m\,s^{-1}}$.
It then travels at this constant velocity for 120 seconds.
Finally it travels with constant deceleration for 45 seconds until coming to rest.

Sketch a velocity–time graph to show this motion.
Calculate the acceleration in the first 30 seconds and the deceleration in coming to rest.

Solution

Uniform acceleration means that the first part of the graph is a straight line with positive gradient.
Constant deceleration means that the last part of the graph is a straight line with negative gradient.
Sketch the graph, indicating the key points.

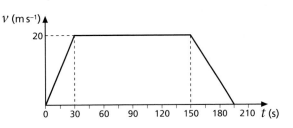

$$Acceleration = \frac{change\ in\ velocity}{time}$$

In the first 30 s, $a = \dfrac{20}{30} = 0.7\,\mathrm{m\,s^{-2}}$ to 1 d.p.

In the last 45 s, $a = \dfrac{-20}{45} = -0.4\,\mathrm{m\,s^{-2}}$ to 1 d.p.

The acceleration in the first 30 s is $0.7\,\mathrm{m\,s^{-2}}$ and the deceleration in coming to rest is $0.4\,\mathrm{m\,s^{-2}}$.

Exercise B (answers p 137)

1 A cyclist sets off from rest with a constant acceleration of $0.2 \, \mathrm{m\,s^{-2}}$.
Find his velocity after

   (a) 1 second   **(b)** 2 seconds   **(c)** 10 seconds   **(d)** 1 minute

2 A car decelerates uniformly from a velocity of $30 \, \mathrm{m\,s^{-1}}$ to a velocity of $20 \, \mathrm{m\,s^{-1}}$ in 20 seconds. Calculate the deceleration of the car.

3 This velocity–time graph represents the motion of a cyclist. Find

   (a) the acceleration between A and B

   (b) the acceleration between B and C

   (c) the acceleration between C and D

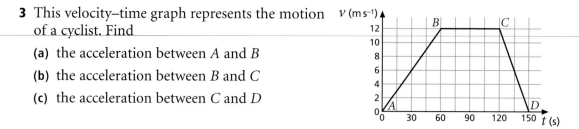

4 For each of the following graphs describe the motion shown and sketch the corresponding velocity–time graph.

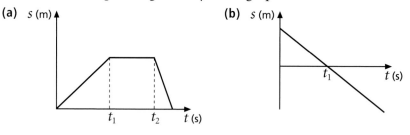

5 For each of the following graphs describe the motion shown and sketch the corresponding acceleration–time graph.

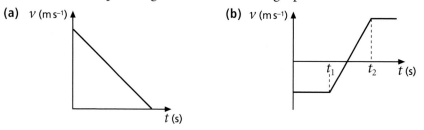

6 A car joins a straight road travelling at a velocity of $12 \, \mathrm{m\,s^{-1}}$ and accelerates uniformly for 20 seconds until it reaches a velocity of $18 \, \mathrm{m\,s^{-1}}$. It travels at this constant velocity for 2 minutes until it slows down with constant deceleration, coming to rest after a further 40 seconds.

   (a) Sketch a velocity–time graph for this motion.

   (b) Calculate the acceleration in the first 20 seconds.

   (c) Calculate the acceleration in the last 40 seconds.

   (d) Sketch an acceleration–time graph for this motion.

C Area under a velocity–time graph (answers p 138)

D **C1** Aisha runs along a straight road at $4\,\text{m\,s}^{-1}$ for 45 s and then jogs at $3\,\text{m\,s}^{-1}$ for 60 s. This is the velocity–time graph for her run.

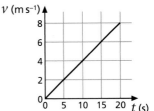

(a) Calculate the area under the graph for $0 < t < 45$.

(b) Calculate the area under the graph for $45 < t < 105$.

(c) What are the units of these areas?

(d) What do you think these areas represent?

Consider a cyclist who accelerates uniformly along a straight road from rest to a velocity of $8\,\text{m\,s}^{-1}$ in 20 seconds. His velocity is continuously increasing as shown in this velocity–time graph.

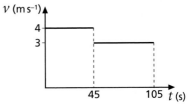

To find his displacement we can simplify the situation by assuming that he has cycled at constant velocity for short periods of time, as shown in this graph.
The displacement can then be found by summing the areas under each part of the graph.

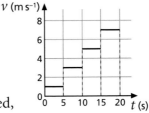

As the times that he cycles at constant velocity are reduced, the simplified graph becomes closer to the actual graph, and the displacement can be found by calculating the area under the true velocity–time graph.

K The area under a velocity–time graph gives the displacement.

D **C2** Mike runs along a straight track. This is the velocity–time graph for his run.

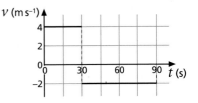

(a) What is the area under the graph for $0 < t < 30$?

(b) What is the area under the graph for $30 < t < 90$?

(c) What is Mike's displacement at time 90 s?

C3 This velocity–time graph shows the motion of a cyclist along a straight track.

Calculate the displacement of the cyclist at time 30 s.

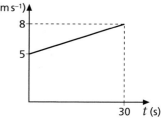

C4 The graph shows the velocity of a car for a short time after it starts from rest at a set of traffic lights.

(a) Describe what is happening to the velocity of the car during the journey.

(b) Find the distance travelled by the car in the first 45 seconds of the journey.

(c) What is the total distance travelled by the car in the 120 s?

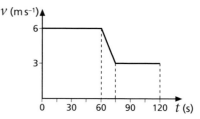

Example 5

The graph shows part of a cyclist's journey.

(a) What is the cyclist's acceleration between $t = 60$ and $t = 75$?

(b) Find the total distance travelled by the cyclist.

Solution

(a) *The required acceleration is the gradient of the graph between $t = 60$ and $t = 75$.*

$$\text{Acceleration} = \frac{3-6}{75-60} = \frac{-3}{15} = -0.2\,\text{m s}^{-2}$$

Negative acceleration means the velocity of the cyclist is decreasing.

(b) *To find the total distance, find the sum of the areas under the sections of the graph.*

For $0 < t < 60$, distance $= 6 \times 60 = 360\,\text{m}$

For $60 < t < 75$, distance $= \frac{1}{2} \times (6 + 3) \times 15 = 67.5\,\text{m}$

For $75 < t < 120$, distance $= 3 \times 45 = 135\,\text{m}$

So total distance travelled $= 360 + 67.5 + 135 = 562.5\,\text{m}$

A graph used in this way may be called a speed–time graph. A speed–time graph may be used for a journey along a route that is not straight, but the area below the graph gives the distance, which in that case will be different from the displacement.

Exercise C (answers p 138)

1 This velocity–time graph represents an athlete's pre-race warm up.
Calculate the distance she covered in her warm up.

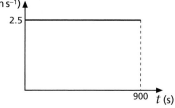

2 This velocity–time graph represents the motion of a cyclist.

(a) Find the displacement of the cyclist at $t = 20$.

(b) Find the displacement of the cyclist at $t = 60$.

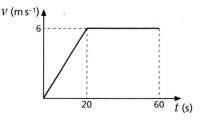

3 As part of his training schedule, Chris runs for 60 seconds at $4.4\,\mathrm{m\,s^{-1}}$ followed by 90 seconds jogging at $3\,\mathrm{m\,s^{-1}}$ in the same direction.
He repeats this 3 times.

(a) Draw a velocity–time graph for Chris's motion.

(b) Find his total displacement.

4 A car decelerates uniformly from a velocity of $20\,\mathrm{m\,s^{-1}}$ to a velocity of $13\,\mathrm{m\,s^{-1}}$ 20 seconds later. It then continues at this velocity for a further 30 seconds.

(a) Sketch a velocity–time graph for this motion.

(b) Find the total distance travelled by the car.

5 A train accelerates uniformly for 20 seconds from rest to a velocity of $9\,\mathrm{m\,s^{-1}}$.
It then travels at this constant velocity for 2 minutes.
Find its total displacement.

*6 These velocity–time graphs show the motion of a car and a van moving from rest along a straight road.

The van accelerates for 30 seconds and then continues on at a steady speed.
The car accelerates at a constant rate.

Find the time when the car overtakes the van.

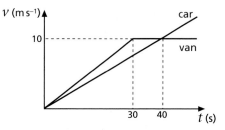

*7 The motion of an object is represented by the graphs shown below.

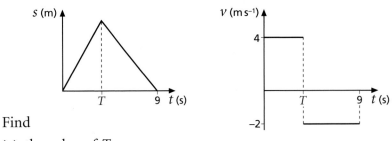

Find

(a) the value of T

(b) the distance covered during the 9 seconds

D Motion with constant acceleration (answers p 139)

A standard set of letters (u, v, a, t, s) is used for the motion of an object moving in a straight line with constant acceleration:

u m s^{-1} is the initial velocity of the object.

v m s^{-1} is the final velocity.

a m s^{-2} is the constant acceleration.

t s is the time for which the object is accelerating.

s m, is the displacement during the time the object is accelerating.

The motion is shown in this velocity–time graph.

The constant acceleration, a m s^{-2}, is equal to the gradient of the graph.

So $a = \dfrac{v - u}{t}$

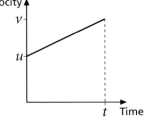

D1 Show that the above equation can be rewritten as $v = u + at$.

This equation can be applied to any situation with **constant** acceleration.
If the initial velocity u m s^{-1} is known, the velocity v m s^{-1} at time t s can be calculated.

D2 A tram initially travelling at 10 m s^{-1} accelerates at 0.5 m s^{-2} for 10 seconds.
Calculate its final velocity.

D3 A car's initial velocity is 20 m s^{-1}.
It decelerates at 0.4 m s^{-2} for 15 seconds.
Calculate its final velocity.

When an object is decelerating, it has negative acceleration.
The same constant acceleration equations can be applied, but remember
to substitute a negative value for the acceleration.

The area under the velocity–time graph at the start of this section gives the
displacement, s m.

The area is a trapezium, so

$$s = \tfrac{1}{2}(u + v)t$$

Again, this equation can be applied to any situation with **constant** acceleration.
If the initial and final velocities are known, the displacement s m at time t s
can be calculated.

D4 A car travelling with constant acceleration increases its velocity from $15\,\mathrm{m\,s^{-1}}$
to $22\,\mathrm{m\,s^{-1}}$ in 15 seconds.
Calculate the car's displacement.

D5 A train decelerating at a constant rate travels between two marker posts
a distance of 250 metres apart.
When it passes the first post, the velocity of the train is $15\,\mathrm{m\,s^{-1}}$.
When it passes the second post, its velocity is $10\,\mathrm{m\,s^{-1}}$.
Calculate the time taken for the train to travel between the two posts.

K For an object moving with constant acceleration,

$$v = u + at$$
$$s = \tfrac{1}{2}(u + v)t$$

Example 6

A car travelling along a straight road at $20\,\mathrm{m\,s^{-1}}$ accelerates at $0.4\,\mathrm{m\,s^{-2}}$ for 25 seconds.
Find the final velocity of the car.

Solution

First list the known values and the unknown. $u = 20,\ a = 0.4,\ t = 25,\ v = ?$

Select the equation that links the letters you have listed.

Use $v = u + at$ to find the final velocity. $v = 20 + 0.4 \times 25$

$v = 30$

The final velocity of the car is $30\,\mathrm{m\,s^{-1}}$.

Example 7

A cyclist applies his brakes for 20 seconds, reducing his speed from $10\,\mathrm{m\,s^{-1}}$ to $6\,\mathrm{m\,s^{-1}}$.
Calculate his deceleration and the distance travelled while braking.

Solution

First list the known values and the unknowns. $t = 20, \; u = 10, \; v = 6, \; a = ?, \; s = ?$

Note that $u > v$ as the cyclist is decelerating.

Substitute known values into $v = u + at$. $\qquad 6 = 10 + a \times 20$

Rearrange to find a. $\qquad\qquad\qquad a = \dfrac{6 - 10}{20} = -0.2$

The acceleration is negative indicating that the cyclist is slowing down.

Use $s = \frac{1}{2}(u + v)t$ to find the distance. $\qquad s = \frac{1}{2}(10 + 6) \times 20 = 160$

$\qquad\qquad\qquad\qquad\qquad\qquad$ He was decelerating at $0.2\,\mathrm{m\,s^{-2}}$ for $160\,\mathrm{m}$.

Exercise D (answers p 139)

1 A motorbike accelerates at a constant rate of $0.5\,\mathrm{m\,s^{-2}}$ from rest.
Calculate its velocity after 20 seconds.

2 A train accelerates at $0.2\,\mathrm{m\,s^{-2}}$ for 45 seconds to a velocity of $21\,\mathrm{m\,s^{-1}}$.
Calculate its initial velocity.

3 A cyclist accelerates uniformly from $5\,\mathrm{m\,s^{-1}}$ to $9\,\mathrm{m\,s^{-1}}$ in 30 seconds.
Calculate the distance the cyclist travels during this time.

4 A car accelerates uniformly from $20\,\mathrm{m\,s^{-1}}$ to $28\,\mathrm{m\,s^{-1}}$ in 40 seconds.
Calculate its acceleration.

5 A car initially travelling at $15\,\mathrm{m\,s^{-1}}$ accelerates uniformly for 16 seconds
covering a distance of $280\,\mathrm{m}$. Calculate its final velocity.

6 A cyclist accelerates uniformly along a straight track.
She takes 20 seconds to cover a distance of $100\,\mathrm{m}$.
Given that her final velocity is $6\,\mathrm{m\,s^{-1}}$, calculate her initial velocity.

7 A train decelerates at a rate of $0.1\,\mathrm{m\,s^{-2}}$ for 30 seconds.
Its initial velocity is $14\,\mathrm{m\,s^{-1}}$.

(a) Calculate its final velocity.

(b) How far has it travelled in this time?

8 A cable car accelerates from rest to its maximum speed of $4\,\mathrm{m\,s^{-1}}$ in one minute.

(a) How far has it travelled in this time?

(b) What is its acceleration?

9 A car decelerates uniformly at $0.4\,\mathrm{m\,s^{-2}}$ from $16\,\mathrm{m\,s^{-1}}$ to rest.

   (a) Calculate the time it takes to come to rest.

   (b) How far has the car travelled while decelerating?

E Constant acceleration equations (answers p 139)

The equation $s = \frac{1}{2}(u + v)t$ derived in the previous section can be used
to calculate the displacement only if the final velocity is known.
In some cases, only the initial velocity and the acceleration are known and
it would be useful to have an equation for displacement using these two quantities.

E1 Show that $s = ut + \frac{1}{2}at^2$ by substituting $v = u + at$ into $s = \frac{1}{2}(u + v)t$.

E2 A cyclist travelling at an initial velocity of $5\,\mathrm{m\,s^{-1}}$ accelerates at $0.1\,\mathrm{m\,s^{-2}}$.
Calculate the distance she travels in 20 seconds.

E3 **(a)** Make u the subject of $v = u + at$.

   (b) By substituting the expression for u found in (a) into $s = \frac{1}{2}(u + v)t$,
show that $s = vt - \frac{1}{2}at^2$.

The equation $v = u + at$ can be used to calculate the final velocity only if
the time is known. It would be useful to have an equation that can be applied
in cases where the displacement rather than the time is known.

E4 **(a)** Make t the subject of $v = u + at$.

   (b) By substituting the expression for t found in (a) into $s = \frac{1}{2}(u + v)t$,
show that $v^2 = u^2 + 2as$.

E5 A car accelerates at a constant rate of $0.25\,\mathrm{m\,s^{-2}}$ over a distance of $400\,\mathrm{m}$.
If it was initially travelling at $15\,\mathrm{m\,s^{-1}}$, calculate its final velocity.

E6 A train decelerates at a constant rate of $0.15\,\mathrm{m\,s^{-2}}$ for $500\,\mathrm{m}$.
Initially the train was travelling at $20\,\mathrm{m\,s^{-1}}$.
Calculate its final velocity.

K The constant acceleration equations for motion in one dimension are

$$v = u + at$$
$$s = \tfrac{1}{2}(u + v)t$$
$$s = ut + \tfrac{1}{2}at^2$$
$$s = vt - \tfrac{1}{2}at^2$$
$$v^2 = u^2 + 2as$$

These five equations can be applied to any situation involving motion in a
straight line with constant acceleration. In order to decide which equation
should be applied, start by listing the known and unknown values.

Example 8

A car travelling along a straight road at $20\,\mathrm{m\,s^{-1}}$ accelerates at $0.4\,\mathrm{m\,s^{-2}}$ for $625\,\mathrm{m}$.
Find the final velocity of the car.

Solution

First list the known values and the unknown. $u = 20,\ a = 0.4,\ s = 625,\ v = ?$

Select the equation that links the letters you have listed.

Use $v^2 = u^2 + 2as$ to find the final velocity. $v^2 = 20^2 + 2 \times 0.4 \times 625 = 900$

The velocity will be positive. $v = \sqrt{900} = 30$

The final velocity is $30\,\mathrm{m\,s^{-1}}$.

Example 9

A car drives with a constant acceleration of $0.5\,\mathrm{m\,s^{-2}}$ between two marker posts $500\,\mathrm{m}$ apart. It is travelling at $15\,\mathrm{m\,s^{-1}}$ when it passes the first post.
Find the time taken to travel between the posts.

Solution

First list the known values and the unknown. $u = 15,\ a = 0.5,\ s = 500,\ t = ?$

Substitute known values into $s = ut + \frac{1}{2}at^2$. $500 = 15t + \frac{1}{2} \times 0.5 \times t^2$

$$\Rightarrow\ 0.25t^2 + 15t - 500 = 0$$

This quadratic does not factorise, so use the formula to solve the equation.

$$t = \frac{-15 \pm \sqrt{15^2 - 4 \times 0.25 \times -500}}{2 \times 0.25}$$

$$= \frac{-15 \pm \sqrt{725}}{0.5}$$

$$= 23.85\ldots \text{ or } -83.85\ldots$$

We know the time is positive, so ignore the negative root.

The time taken for the car to travel between the two posts is $23.9\,\mathrm{s}$ (to 1 d.p.).

An alternative method is as follows.

Use $v^2 = u^2 + 2as$ to find v. $v^2 = 15^2 + 2 \times 0.5 \times 500 = 725$

Substitute into $v = u + at$ to find t. $\sqrt{725} = 15 + 0.5 \times t$

$$t = \frac{\sqrt{725} - 15}{0.5} = 23.85\ldots$$

Exercise E (answers p 139)

1 A cyclist starts from rest and accelerates at $0.25\,\mathrm{m\,s^{-2}}$.
What is his speed after 30 seconds?

2 A train travelling at $15\,\mathrm{m\,s^{-1}}$ accelerates at $0.3\,\mathrm{m\,s^{-2}}$ over a distance of $750\,\mathrm{m}$. What is its final velocity?

3 A car moves with constant acceleration from rest to $30\,\mathrm{m\,s^{-1}}$ in 12.6 seconds. Find the acceleration and the distance travelled.

4 A car joins a motorway travelling at $14\,\mathrm{m\,s^{-1}}$ and then accelerates at $0.8\,\mathrm{m\,s^{-2}}$ for 20 seconds.
Find the distance travelled and the final speed.

5 A car brakes from $31\,\mathrm{m\,s^{-1}}$ to $10\,\mathrm{m\,s^{-1}}$ under constant deceleration while travelling $250\,\mathrm{m}$. Find the deceleration and the time taken to slow down.

6 The motion of an object moving in a straight line with constant acceleration a is shown in this velocity–time graph. The area under the graph represents the displacement of the object.

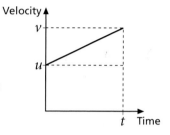

(a) By splitting the area into a rectangle and a triangle as shown, show that $s = ut + \frac{1}{2}at^2$.

(b) Use the graph to show that $s = vt - \frac{1}{2}at^2$.

7 A motorcyclist travelling at $24\,\mathrm{m\,s^{-1}}$ accelerates uniformly for 30 seconds over a distance of 900 metres.

(a) Calculate the acceleration of the motorcyclist.

(b) What is his final velocity?

8 A train travels with constant acceleration along a straight horizontal track.
It passes point O with speed $5\,\mathrm{m\,s^{-1}}$.
It passes point A 25 seconds later with speed $18\,\mathrm{m\,s^{-1}}$.

(a) Show that the acceleration of the train is $0.52\,\mathrm{m\,s^{-2}}$.

(b) Find the distance OA.

(c) The point B is the mid-point of OA.
Find, to three significant figures, the speed of the train when it passes B.

9 A train travelling at $9\,\mathrm{m\,s^{-1}}$ enters a straight stretch of track of length $1000\,\mathrm{m}$. It immediately accelerates at $0.24\,\mathrm{m\,s^{-2}}$ and maintains this acceleration until the end of the straight stretch.
Find the time taken for the train to cover this distance.

10 (a) A snooker ball hit at $1.8\,\mathrm{m\,s^{-1}}$ stops after travelling $3.2\,\mathrm{m}$ with constant retardation. Find the speed with which the ball would have hit a second ball $1.6\,\mathrm{m}$ from the starting point if it had been in the way.

(b) A ball is struck at $u\ \mathrm{m\,s^{-1}}$ and travels with constant retardation, stopping after s metres.
What was its velocity after going $\frac{1}{2}s$ metres?

F Vertical motion under gravity (answers p 139)

D

F1 Sarah is standing at a cliff edge. She drops a stone over the edge.

  (a) Describe the motion of the stone from the time it leaves Sarah's hand until it hits the water.

  (b) Sarah now drops a stone that is twice as heavy.
  How do you think the motion of this stone will differ from that of the previous stone?

K

The acceleration of a falling object is caused by gravity. This acceleration is known as the **acceleration due to gravity**, g, and is approximately equal to $9.8\,\text{m s}^{-2}$.

The motion of the object is in a vertical straight line with constant downwards acceleration, so the constant acceleration equations can be applied.

This assumes that the object is falling freely and air resistance can be ignored.

F2 Assuming that Sarah's stone started from rest, what would its velocity be after 2 seconds?

F3 Sarah throws the stone with an initial **upward** velocity of $15\,\text{m s}^{-1}$.
Calculate the velocity of the stone after

  (a) 1 second   (b) 2 seconds   (c) 3 seconds   (d) 4 seconds

D

F4 Leroy throws a ball vertically upwards and catches it when it returns.

  (a) Describe how the velocity of the ball changes during its motion.

  (b) What is the velocity of the ball when it is at its maximum height?

  (c) How does the velocity of the ball when Leroy catches it relate to its velocity when he threw it?

  (d) Sketch a velocity–time graph for the motion of the ball after it leaves Leroy's hand.

  (e) Sketch a displacement–time graph for the motion of the ball, where displacement is measured upwards from Leroy's hand.

Example 10

A stone is dropped off the edge of a cliff. It hits the water after 4 seconds.
Calculate the height of the cliff above the water.

Solution

First list the known values and the unknown. Note that the stone is moving downwards so the downwards direction will be taken as positive and hence the acceleration due to gravity is positive. $u = 0,\ t = 4,\ a = 9.8,\ s = \,?$

Use $s = ut + \frac{1}{2}at^2$ *to find the displacement.* $s = 0 \times 4 + \frac{1}{2} \times 9.8 \times 4^2 = 78.4$

The height of the cliff is $78.4\,\text{m}$.

Example 11

A ball is thrown vertically upwards from ground level with initial speed $20\,\mathrm{m\,s^{-1}}$. Calculate the maximum height of the ball and the time it takes to reach this height.

Solution

At its maximum height the velocity of the ball is zero. It is moving upwards, so the upwards direction will be taken as positive and hence the acceleration due to gravity is negative.

$$u = 20, \ v = 0, \ a = -9.8, \ s = ?, \ t = ?$$

Use $v^2 = u^2 + 2as$ to find the displacement.

$$0 = 20^2 - 2 \times 9.8 \times s$$
$$\Rightarrow \ 0 = 400 - 19.6\,s$$
$$\Rightarrow \ s = \frac{400}{19.6} = 20.4 \text{ to 1 d.p.}$$

Use $v = u + at$ to find the time.

$$0 = 20 - 9.8 \times t$$
$$\Rightarrow \ t = \frac{20}{9.8} = 2.0 \text{ to 1 d.p.}$$

The ball reaches its maximum height of $20.4\,\mathrm{m}$ after $2.0\,\mathrm{s}$.

Example 12

A ball is thrown vertically upwards from ground level with an initial speed of $12\,\mathrm{m\,s^{-1}}$. Find the total time the ball is in the air.

Solution

During its motion the ball moves from ground level, where $s = 0$, to its maximum height and back to ground level. Substituting the known values into $s = ut + \frac{1}{2}at^2$ will give a quadratic equation which can be solved to find the times when the ball is at ground level.

$$u = 12, \ a = -9.8, \ s = 0, \ t = ?$$
$$s = ut + \tfrac{1}{2}at^2$$
$$\Rightarrow \quad 0 = 12t - \tfrac{1}{2} \times 9.8 \times t^2$$
$$\Rightarrow \quad 0 = 12t - 4.9t^2$$
$$\Rightarrow \quad 0 = t(12 - 4.9t)$$
$$\Rightarrow \quad t = 0 \text{ or } 2.448\ldots$$

The ball is thrown when $t = 0$, so $t = 2.448\ldots$ when the ball hits the ground.

The ball is in the air for 2.45 seconds (to 2 d.p.).

Exercise F (answers p 140)

1 A ball is dropped from a balcony. It hits the ground after 2 seconds. What is the velocity of the ball when it hits the ground?

2 A coin is dropped from the top of a high tower.

(a) Find its velocity after 3 seconds.

(b) How far has it fallen in this time?

(c) It takes 5 seconds for the coin to hit the ground.
How high is the top of the tower above the ground?

3 A stone is thrown off a cliff with an initial speed of $5\,\mathrm{m\,s^{-1}}$ downwards.
The stone falls vertically downwards until it hits the water.
If the top of the cliff is 30 metres above the water, find the speed of the stone
when it hits the water.

4 A stone is thrown vertically upwards from ground level to dislodge a conker on a tree.
The maximum speed the stone can be thrown with is $14.8\,\mathrm{m\,s^{-1}}$ and it must hit the
conker with a speed of at least $5\,\mathrm{m\,s^{-1}}$ to dislodge it.
What is the height of the highest conker the stone can dislodge?

5 A ball is thrown vertically upwards with an initial speed of $10\,\mathrm{m\,s^{-1}}$.
Assume the ball is thrown from ground level and air resistance can be ignored.

(a) Find the maximum height of the ball.

(b) Find the total time the ball is in the air.

6 A toy rocket is catapulted vertically upwards from ground level and reaches
a maximum height of 30 metres before returning to its starting position.

(a) Find the initial speed of the rocket.

(b) Find the total time the rocket is in the air.

7 A stone is thrown vertically upwards from ground level with initial speed $18\,\mathrm{m\,s^{-1}}$.

(a) Find the times when it is 5 m above ground level.

(b) For how long is the stone more than 5 m above ground level?

8 A cricket ball is thrown vertically upwards from ground level with a speed of $25\,\mathrm{m\,s^{-1}}$.
For how long is the ball more than 20 metres above the ground?

9 A ball is thrown vertically upwards from ground level with an initial speed $u\,\mathrm{m\,s^{-1}}$.

(a) Sketch a velocity–time graph for the motion of the ball.

(b) Find an expression, in terms of u, for the maximum height reached by the ball.

(c) Find an expression for the time when the ball is at its maximum height.

(d) State one modelling assumption you have made regarding the motion of the ball.

*10 A man throws a coin vertically upwards with a speed of $2\,\mathrm{m\,s^{-1}}$.
His hand is initially 1.2 metres above the ground.

(a) Find the time taken for the coin to hit the ground.

(b) Find the speed with which the coin hits the ground.

Key points

- Average speed $= \dfrac{\text{total distance travelled}}{\text{time taken}}$

  Average velocity $= \dfrac{\text{displacement from starting point}}{\text{time taken}}$ (p 8)

- The gradient of a displacement–time graph gives the velocity. (p 8)

- The gradient of a velocity–time graph gives the acceleration. (p 12)

- The area under a velocity–time graph gives the displacement. (p 15)

- The constant acceleration equations for motion in one dimension are

  $v = u + at$

  $s = \frac{1}{2}(u + v)t$

  $s = ut + \frac{1}{2}at^2$

  $s = vt - \frac{1}{2}at^2$

  $v^2 = u^2 + 2as$ (pp 18–19, 21)

- The acceleration due to gravity is approximately equal to $9.8\,\text{m s}^{-2}$ (p 24)

Mixed questions (answers p 140)

1 A car travels along a straight horizontal road on which there are some roadworks
  with a speed restriction in force. The brakes are applied for 5 seconds on the
  approach to the roadworks, reducing the car's speed from $28\,\text{m s}^{-1}$ to $22\,\text{m s}^{-1}$.
  The brakes are released and the car continues at a constant speed of $22\,\text{m s}^{-1}$
  for a further 10 seconds.

  The speed–time graph for this motion is shown.

  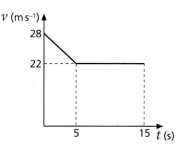

  (a) Explain how the speed–time graph shows that when
      the brakes are applied the car undergoes constant
      deceleration.

  (b) Calculate the car's deceleration in the first 5 seconds
      of the motion.

  (c) Find the total distance covered by the car during
      the 15 seconds.

  (d) What is the car's average speed during the 15 seconds?

2 A tram moves with constant acceleration along a straight horizontal track.
  It passes point A with speed $4\,\text{m s}^{-1}$ and 10 seconds later passes point B
  where $AB = 80\,\text{m}$.

  (a) Find the acceleration of the tram.

  (b) When the tram passes point C its speed is $16\,\text{m s}^{-1}$. Find the distance AC.

3 A stone is thrown vertically upwards at a speed of $5\,\mathrm{m\,s}^{-1}$ from the edge of a cliff 15 m above the water. Assume that air resistance can be ignored and the stone does not hit the cliff.

(a) Find the maximum height of the stone above the water.

(b) Find the speed of the stone when it hits the water.

(c) Find the time taken for the stone to hit the water.

4 A lift can travel at a maximum speed of $1.6\,\mathrm{m\,s}^{-1}$.

The lift accelerates at a constant rate from rest and reaches its maximum velocity after 10 seconds. It continues at this constant velocity then finally decelerates at a constant rate for 12 seconds before coming to rest.

The lift has travelled a total distance of 40 metres.

(a) Find the initial acceleration of the lift.

(b) Find the deceleration of the lift.

(c) Find the time taken for the lift to travel 40 m.

5 A toy rocket is fired vertically upwards using a catapult. A student attempts to model the motion of the rocket using the velocity–time graph shown.

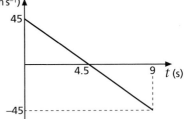

(a) At what time is the velocity of the rocket zero?

(b) Find the acceleration of the rocket.

(c) Find the total distance travelled by the rocket during its flight.

6 A truck and a car are at rest and level with each other at a set of traffic lights on a straight road. When the lights change they move off at the same time.

The truck accelerates with constant acceleration until it reaches a top speed of $15\,\mathrm{m\,s}^{-1}$. It then continues at this constant speed.

The car accelerates with constant acceleration for 20 seconds until it reaches a top speed $V\,\mathrm{m\,s}^{-1}$, where $V > 15\,\mathrm{m\,s}^{-1}$. It then continues at this constant speed. The car draws level with the truck when the truck has been travelling for 30 seconds at its top speed.

The distance travelled by each vehicle is then 525 m.

(a) Find the time for which the truck is accelerating.

(b) On the same diagram sketch velocity–time graphs to illustrate the motion of the two vehicles from the time they start to the time when the car overtakes the truck.

(c) Find the top speed of the car.

7 A parachutist drops from a helicopter H and falls vertically from rest towards the ground. Her parachute opens 2 s after she leaves H and her speed then reduces to $4\,\mathrm{m\,s^{-1}}$. For the first 2 s her motion is modelled as that of a particle falling freely under gravity. For the next 5 s the model is motion with constant deceleration, so that her speed is $4\,\mathrm{m\,s^{-1}}$ at the end of this period. For the rest of the time before she reaches the ground, the model is motion with constant speed of $4\,\mathrm{m\,s^{-1}}$.

(a) Sketch a speed–time graph to illustrate her motion from H to the ground.

(b) Find her speed when the parachute opens.

A safety rule states that the helicopter must be high enough to allow the parachute to open and for the speed of a parachutist to reduce to $4\,\mathrm{m\,s^{-1}}$ before reaching the ground. Using the assumptions made in the above model,

(c) find the minimum height of H for which the woman can make a drop without breaking this safety rule.

Given that H is 125 m above the ground when the woman starts her drop,

(d) find the total time taken for her to reach the ground.

(e) State one way in which the model could be refined to make it more realistic.   Edexcel

*8 A lorry of length 16 m is travelling at a constant speed of $12\,\mathrm{m\,s^{-1}}$ in the inside lane of a straight road. A car of length 4 m is initially travelling in the outside lane in the same direction as the lorry and at the same speed. The gap between the two vehicles is 50 m.

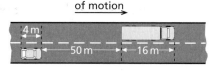

The car accelerates at $2\,\mathrm{m\,s^{-2}}$ for 5 seconds, then travels at constant speed for a time and finally decelerates at $2\,\mathrm{m\,s^{-2}}$ for 5 seconds. Now the car is travelling at the same speed as before, but in front of the lorry and the gap is the same as it was before.

How long did the car take to get from its initial to its final position?
How far did the car travel in this time?

Test yourself (answers p 141)

1 A particle is released and falls vertically for 4 seconds before hitting the ground.

(a) Find the speed at which the particle hits the ground.

(b) From what height above the ground was the particle released?

2 A cyclist moves with constant acceleration along a straight horizontal road. She passes point A with speed $4\,\mathrm{m\,s^{-1}}$ and 10 seconds later she passes point B, where $AB = 60\,\mathrm{m}$.

(a) Find the acceleration of the cyclist.

(b) Find the speed of the cyclist after 15 seconds.

3 The graph shows how the velocity, v m s^{-1}, of a car varies with time, t seconds, as it moves along a straight horizontal road.

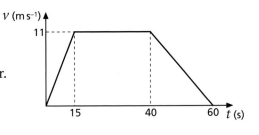

(a) Calculate the total distance travelled by the car.

(b) Find the acceleration of the car between

    (i) $t = 0$ and $t = 15$ (ii) $t = 15$ and $t = 40$

    (iii) $t = 40$ and $t = 60$

4 A train travels along a straight horizontal track at a speed of 20 m s^{-1}. The brakes are applied when it passes a signal causing the train to move with a constant deceleration. After 3 seconds the train is moving at a speed of 5 m s^{-1}.

(a) Find the deceleration of the train.

(b) The train comes to rest at a station. Find the distance from the signal to the station.

5 A cyclist accelerates uniformly from rest to a speed of 6 m s^{-1} in T seconds. He then travels at a constant speed of 6 m s^{-1} for $2T$ seconds and finally decelerates at a constant rate of 0.4 m s^{-2} before coming to rest.

(a) Sketch a speed–time graph for the motion of the cyclist.

(b) The total distance travelled by the cyclist is 225 m. Find the value of T.

(c) Find the initial acceleration of the cyclist.

6 A train starts from rest at a station A and moves along a straight horizontal track. For the first 10 s, the train moves with constant acceleration 1.2 m s^{-2}. For the next 24 s it moves with constant acceleration 0.75 m s^{-2}. It then moves with constant speed for T seconds. Finally it slows down with constant deceleration 3 m s^{-2} until it comes to rest at a station B.

(a) Show that, 34 s after leaving A, the speed of the train is 30 m s^{-1}.

(b) Sketch a speed–time graph to illustrate the motion of the train as it moves from A to B.

(c) Find the distance moved by the train during the first 34 s of its journey from A.

The distance from A to B is 3 km.

(d) Find the value of T.

Edexcel

7 The speed–time graphs show the motion of a car and a bicycle along a straight horizontal road. The cyclist is travelling at a constant speed of 7 m s^{-1}. When $t = 0$, the cyclist passes the car which accelerates from rest to a speed of 12 m s^{-1} in 5 seconds then continues at this constant speed. When $t = T$ the car overtakes the cyclist. Find the value of T.

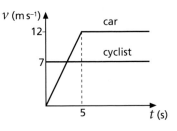

2 Kinematics in two dimensions

In this chapter you will learn how to
- use vectors to represent displacement, velocity and acceleration
- use the unit vectors **i** and **j**
- find the magnitude and direction of a vector
- solve problems involving resultant vectors

A Displacement (answers p 141)

A1 Alexia is standing in the centre of a large field.
She walks in a straight line for a distance of 50 metres.
Sketch her possible finishing points.

From the information given above it is not possible to find a single finishing point for Alexia. The distance she covers has been given, but in order to decide where she finishes you need to know in which direction she has walked.

If you know that Alexia has walked 50 m north-east, then her finishing point is fully defined.

This vector represents her walk.

The quantity that includes both distance and direction is the **displacement**.

The **magnitude** or size of the displacement is the distance.

Displacement is a **vector** quantity, a quantity that has both magnitude and direction.

Distance is a **scalar** quantity; it has magnitude but not direction.

Displacement can be given as a distance and a direction – for example, Alexia's displacement can be defined by giving a distance (50 m) and a direction (NE) – but it can also be represented as a column vector.

Alexia's displacement can also be described using the distance she could have walked east followed by the distance she could have walked north to give the same total displacement.

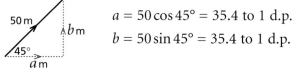

$a = 50 \cos 45° = 35.4$ to 1 d.p.

$b = 50 \sin 45° = 35.4$ to 1 d.p.

So Alexia could have walked 35.4 m east followed by 35.4 m north to give the same total displacement.

These distances are the **components** of her displacement in the east and north directions.

If east is taken as the *x*-direction and north as the *y*-direction, then a displacement can be described as a column vector using the *x*- and *y*-**components** of the displacement.

Alexia's displacement can be written $\begin{bmatrix} 35.4 \\ 35.4 \end{bmatrix}$ m.

K   If a vector is given as a magnitude and direction, expressing it as a pair of components in two perpendicular directions is called **resolving** the vector into components.

A2 A model plane flies 36 m on a bearing of 030°.

    (a) Resolve the displacement into *x*- and *y*-components.

    (b) Write the displacement as a column vector.

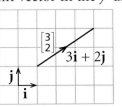

Instead of using a column vector, a vector can be written in terms of **i** and **j**, where **i** is the unit vector in the *x*-direction and **j** is the unit vector in the *y*-direction.

$$\mathbf{i} = \begin{bmatrix} 1 \\ 0 \end{bmatrix}, \mathbf{j} = \begin{bmatrix} 0 \\ 1 \end{bmatrix}$$

The vector shown on the grid can be written

$$3\begin{bmatrix} 1 \\ 0 \end{bmatrix} + 2\begin{bmatrix} 0 \\ 1 \end{bmatrix} \text{ or } 3\mathbf{i} + 2\mathbf{j}.$$

Using this notation the vector $\begin{bmatrix} 20 \\ -30 \end{bmatrix}$ is equivalent to $20\begin{bmatrix} 1 \\ 0 \end{bmatrix} - 30\begin{bmatrix} 0 \\ 1 \end{bmatrix}$ or $20\mathbf{i} - 30\mathbf{j}$.

Note that vector quantities are represented by bold type in this book.

In written work underlining can be used, for example i̲ and j̲, or ḭ and j̰.

A displacement given as a column vector or in terms of **i** and **j** can be converted into distance and direction form.

Example 1

The displacement of a model boat is given by $(-10\mathbf{i} + 15\mathbf{j})$ m.
Write the displacement in distance and direction form.

Solution

Sketch the vector.

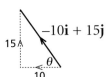

Use Pythagoras's theorem to calculate the magnitude, d, of the displacement.

$$d = \sqrt{15^2 + 10^2} = \sqrt{325} = 18.0 \text{ to 1 d.p.}$$

The vector makes an angle θ° with the negative x-direction.

$$\tan \theta = \tfrac{15}{10} = 1.5, \text{ from which } \theta = 56.3° \text{ to 1 d.p.}$$

The displacement is 18.0 m at 56.3° to the negative *x*-direction.

A3 Gina walks in a straight line. Her final displacement is $(60\mathbf{i} + 80\mathbf{j})$ m.

    (a) Sketch a vector to represent her walk.

    (b) Use Pythagoras's theorem to calculate the distance she walks.

    (c) Use trigonometry to calculate the angle the vector makes with the *x*-direction.

Mike walks 30 m on a bearing of 110°.

The sketch shows his displacement.

The dotted lines show the components of his displacement in the *x*- and *y*-directions.

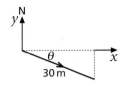

In order to write the displacement in terms of **i** and **j** or as a column vector these components need to be calculated.

In this case the displacement is positive in the *x*-direction and negative in the *y*-direction.

A4 **(a)** Find angle θ.

    (b) Calculate the *x*- and *y*-components of this displacement.

    (c) Write the displacement in terms of **i** and **j**.

K Displacement can be

  (1) given as a magnitude and direction, or

  (2) resolved into two components at right angles to each other and

      represented as either a column vector $\begin{bmatrix} a \\ b \end{bmatrix}$ or in the form $a\mathbf{i} + b\mathbf{j}$,

      where **i** and **j** are unit vectors at right angles to each other.

Example 2

Keith walks 75 m on a bearing of 040°.
Taking **i** and **j** as the unit vectors in the directions east and north respectively, find his displacement in terms of **i** and **j**.

Solution

Sketch the vector.

*The displacement is a**i** + b**j**.*

Use trigonometry to find a and b.

                $a = 75 \sin 40° = 48.2$ to 1 d.p.

                $b = 75 \cos 40° = 57.5$ to 1 d.p.

                Keith's displacement is $(48.2\mathbf{i} + 57.5\mathbf{j})$ m.

Exercise A (answers p 141)

1 Taking **i** and **j** as the unit vectors in the directions east and north respectively, write each of the following displacements in terms of **i** and **j**.

(a) 20 km east and 15 km north   (b) 20 km west

(c) 18 km east and 6 km south   (d) 5 km west and 10 km north

2 (a) Sketch the vector 8**i** + 3**j**.

(b) Find its magnitude and direction.

3 Darren walks in a straight line, so that his displacement is (15**i** − 12**j**) m.

(a) How far does he walk?

(b) What angle does his displacement make with the vector **i**?

4 Fran walks 100 m on a bearing of 070°. Taking **i** and **j** as the unit vectors in the directions east and north respectively, find her displacement in terms of **i** and **j**.

5 A model plane flies 50 m south-east. Taking **i** and **j** as the unit vectors in the directions east and north respectively, write its displacement in terms of **i** and **j**.

6 A ship moves so that its displacement is given by (−15**i** + 20**j**) m. Find the distance and bearing from its starting point.

B Resultant displacement (answers p 142)

Vic has a model car. He drives it from point *A*, around a marker at *B*, to point *C*.

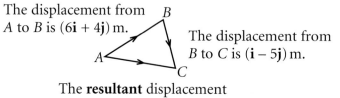

The displacement from *A* to *B* is (6**i** + 4**j**) m.

The displacement from *B* to *C* is (**i** − 5**j**) m.

The **resultant** displacement is from *A* to *C*.

The resultant can be found by adding the vectors $\overrightarrow{AB}$ and $\overrightarrow{BC}$. This is the **vector sum** or just sum of $\overrightarrow{AB}$ and $\overrightarrow{BC}$.

These vectors can be added 'tail to head' using a 'triangle rule'.

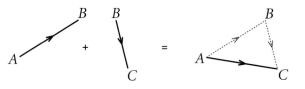

B1 Draw the triangle *ABC* on squared paper.
Write down the resultant displacement from *A* to *C*.

Vectors given in component form can be added by adding the *x*-components and adding the *y*-components.

B2 (a) Add together the vectors $(6\mathbf{i} + 4\mathbf{j})$ and $(\mathbf{i} - 5\mathbf{j})$.
Check that your answer is the same as for B1.

(b) Use a vector diagram to explain why this method works.

The displacement from *A* to *C* can be represented as $\overrightarrow{AC}$.
The magnitude, or size, of the displacement $\overrightarrow{AC}$ can be represented as $|\overrightarrow{AC}|$.

D **B3 (a)** Calculate $|\overrightarrow{AC}|$.

(b) Calculate the distance the car has travelled to get from point *A* to point *C*.

Example 3

A yacht sails from *P*, around a buoy at *Q*, to a buoy at *R*.

The displacement from *P* to *Q* is $8\mathbf{i} - 2\mathbf{j}$. The displacement from *Q* to *R* is $4\mathbf{i} + 4\mathbf{j}$.

Find the displacement of *R* from *P*.

Solution

*Add **i** terms; add **j** terms.*
$$(8\mathbf{i} - 2\mathbf{j}) + (4\mathbf{i} + 4\mathbf{j}) = (8 + 4)\mathbf{i} + (-2 + 4)\mathbf{j}$$
$$= 12\mathbf{i} + 2\mathbf{j}$$

Example 4

A displacement of $(3\mathbf{i} + 2\mathbf{j})\,\text{m}$ is followed by a displacement of $(7\mathbf{i} - 6\mathbf{j})\,\text{m}$.
Find the magnitude and direction of the resultant displacement.

Solution

Find the resultant displacement by adding.
$$\text{Resultant} = (3\mathbf{i} + 2\mathbf{j}) + (7\mathbf{i} - 6\mathbf{j})$$

*Rearrange to separate the terms in **i** and **j**.*
$$= (3 + 7)\mathbf{i} + (2 - 6)\mathbf{j}$$
$$= 10\mathbf{i} - 4\mathbf{j}$$

Sketch the resultant vector.

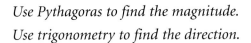 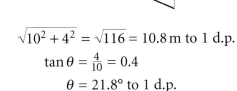

Use Pythagoras to find the magnitude. $\sqrt{10^2 + 4^2} = \sqrt{116} = 10.8\,\text{m}$ to 1 d.p.

Use trigonometry to find the direction. $\tan\theta = \frac{4}{10} = 0.4$

$$\theta = 21.8° \text{ to 1 d.p.}$$

The resultant is a displacement of $10.8\,\text{m}$ at $21.8°$ below the vector $\mathbf{i}$.

Exercise B (answers p 142)

1 A displacement of $30\mathbf{i} + 40\mathbf{j}$ is followed by a displacement of $120\mathbf{i} - 70\mathbf{j}$.
Find the resultant displacement.

2 A displacement of $6\mathbf{i} - 2\mathbf{j}$ is followed by a displacement of $-4\mathbf{i} + 4\mathbf{j}$.
  (a) Find the resultant displacement.
  (b) Find the magnitude and direction of the resultant displacement.

3 Four displacement vectors have a resultant of $10\mathbf{i} - 2\mathbf{j}$.
Given that three of them are $-2\mathbf{i} - 3\mathbf{j}$, $5\mathbf{i} - 7\mathbf{j}$ and $16\mathbf{i} + 4\mathbf{j}$, find the fourth vector.

4 A model car drives from point A to point B with a displacement of $(8\mathbf{i} - 2\mathbf{j})\,\text{m}$.
It then drives from point B to point C with a displacement of $(-3\mathbf{i} + 10\mathbf{j})\,\text{m}$.
  (a) Find its resultant displacement.
  (b) Calculate the direct distance from point A to point C.
  (c) Calculate the total distance travelled by the car.

5 A hiker walks from marker post P to post Q and then to post R.
The displacement from P to Q is $(30\mathbf{i} + 20\mathbf{j})\,\text{m}$ and the displacement from Q to R is $(50\mathbf{i} - 10\mathbf{j})\,\text{m}$, where $\mathbf{i}$ and $\mathbf{j}$ are unit vectors in the directions east and north respectively.

Find the magnitude of the displacement from P to R and the angle this displacement makes with the vector $\mathbf{i}$.

C Position vector (answers p 142)

The displacement of an object is the distance moved in a certain direction.

K The position of an object is defined by its displacement from a fixed origin.
This displacement is called the **position vector** of the object.

Notation: the letter $\mathbf{r}$ is used for position vector;
the letter $\mathbf{s}$ is used for displacement.
The unit vectors $\mathbf{i}$ and $\mathbf{j}$ are at right angles to each other.

The position vector of the point A with respect to the origin O
is given by $\mathbf{r}_A = 4\mathbf{i} + 2\mathbf{j}$.

C1 Write down the position vector of point B.

C2 An object moves from A to B.
Write down its displacement $\mathbf{s}$.

If the original position vector of an object and its displacement are known,
its final position vector can be found by adding the two vectors.

$$\mathbf{r}_A + \mathbf{s} = \mathbf{r}_B$$

C3 An object with position vector $(6\mathbf{i} - 2\mathbf{j})$ is displaced by $(-3\mathbf{i} + \mathbf{j})$. What is its final position vector?

C4 (a) Write down the position vectors of points C and D.

(b) Write down the displacement from C to D.

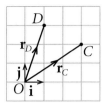

The displacement of the object is the difference between the position vector of D and the position vector of C.

Vectors given in component form can be subtracted by subtracting the x-components and subtracting the y-components.

C5 Find $\mathbf{r}_D - \mathbf{r}_C$. Check that your answer is the same as in C4(b).

C6 An object moves from the point $(-2\mathbf{i} + 5\mathbf{j})$ to the point $(4\mathbf{i} + 3\mathbf{j})$. What is its displacement?

K The final position vector of an object is the sum of its initial position vector and its displacement.

$$\mathbf{r}_B = \mathbf{r}_A + \mathbf{s}$$

To find the displacement of an object, subtract the initial position vector from the final position vector.

$$\mathbf{s} = \mathbf{r}_B - \mathbf{r}_A$$

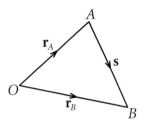

C7 The position vector, in metres, of a speedboat at time t seconds relative to a fixed point O is given by $\mathbf{r} = 30t\mathbf{i} + (20 - 4t)\mathbf{j}$, where $\mathbf{i}$ and $\mathbf{j}$ are unit vectors in the directions east and north respectively.

(a) Find the position vectors of the ship when $t = 0$ and $t = 10$. Plot these positions on a grid.

(b) Find the displacement of the speedboat between $t = 0$ and $t = 10$.

(c) What distance has the speedboat travelled between $t = 0$ and $t = 10$?

(d) At what time is the speedboat due east of its starting point?

Example 5

The position vector, in metres, of an object at time t seconds is given by $\mathbf{r} = t^2\mathbf{i} + (4 - 5t)\mathbf{j}$.
Find its displacement between $t = 5$ and $t = 10$.

Solution

Find the position vectors at the two times.

When $t = 5$ $\quad$ $\mathbf{r} = 5^2\mathbf{i} + (4 - 5\times5)\mathbf{j} = 25\mathbf{i} - 21\mathbf{j}$

When $t = 10$ $\quad$ $\mathbf{r} = 10^2\mathbf{i} + (4 - 5\times10)\mathbf{j} = 100\mathbf{i} - 46\mathbf{j}$

Subtract to find the displacement.

$\mathbf{s} = (100\mathbf{i} - 46\mathbf{j}) - (25\mathbf{i} - 21\mathbf{j})$

$\mathbf{s} = 75\mathbf{i} - 25\mathbf{j}$

Example 6

An object moves so that its position vector, in metres, relative to the origin O at time t seconds $(t \geq 0)$ is given by $\mathbf{r} = (200 + 10t)\mathbf{i} + t^2\mathbf{j}$, where $\mathbf{i}$ and $\mathbf{j}$ are unit vectors in the directions east and north respectively.
At what time is the object north-east of the origin?

Solution

The object is north-east of the origin when the $\mathbf{i}$- and $\mathbf{j}$-components of the position vector are equal and both positive.

$$200 + 10t = t^2$$

$$t^2 - 10t - 200 = 0$$

$$(t + 10)(t - 20) = 0$$

$$t = -10 \text{ or } 20$$

Take the positive value for the time.

The object is north-east of the origin when $t = 20$.

Exercise C (answers p 142)

1 An object with position vector $4\mathbf{i} + 2\mathbf{j}$ is displaced by $8\mathbf{i} - 3\mathbf{j}$.
What is its new position vector?

2 A hot air balloon has position vector $(6\mathbf{i} - \mathbf{j})\,\text{km}$ relative to its launch site.
It moves by $(-2\mathbf{i} + 3\mathbf{j})\,\text{km}$. The unit vectors $\mathbf{i}$ and $\mathbf{j}$ are directed east and north respectively.

(a) What is its new position vector?

(b) What distance is the balloon from its launch site?

3 An object moves from A with position vector $-3\mathbf{i} + 6\mathbf{j}$ to B with position vector $4\mathbf{i} - 2\mathbf{j}$.
Find the displacement from A to B.

4 A yacht is at the point with position vector $(25\mathbf{i} - 40\mathbf{j})\,\text{m}$.
A lifeboat is at the point with position vector $(40\mathbf{i} - 30\mathbf{j})\,\text{m}$.
Find the displacement of the yacht from the lifeboat.

5 The position vector, in metres, of an object at time t seconds is given by
$\mathbf{r} = 3t^2\mathbf{i} + (4t - 2)\mathbf{j}$.

(a) Find the position vector of the object at $t = 0$.

(b) Find the position vector of the object at $t = 10$.

(c) Sketch a diagram to show the positions of the object at $t = 0$ and $t = 10$.

(d) What is the displacement of the object between $t = 0$ and $t = 10$?

6 A ball is kicked so that its position vector, in metres, after time t seconds is given by $\mathbf{r} = 18t\mathbf{i} + (8t - 4.9t^2)\mathbf{j}$, where $\mathbf{i}$ and $\mathbf{j}$ are horizontal and vertical unit vectors respectively.

(a) Find the position of the ball when $t = 1$.

(b) Find the time when the ball hits the ground.

(c) What horizontal distance has the ball covered in this time?

7 The position vector, in metres, of a particle relative to the origin at time t seconds is given by $\mathbf{r} = (2t - 10)\mathbf{i} + (t^2 + 6)\mathbf{j}$, where $\mathbf{i}$ and $\mathbf{j}$ are unit vectors in the directions east and north respectively.

(a) At what time is the particle due north of the origin?

(b) How far is the particle from its starting point at this time?

8 The position vector, in km, of an object relative to the origin at time t hours is given by $\mathbf{r} = (8t - 12)\mathbf{i} + (t^2 - 8)\mathbf{j}$, where $\mathbf{i}$ and $\mathbf{j}$ are unit vectors in the directions east and north respectively.

(a) At what time is the object south-east of the origin?

(b) What distance is the object from the origin at this time?

D Velocity (answers p 143)

In the previous chapter we dealt with objects moving in one dimension. Here we will consider objects moving in two dimensions.

> Velocity is a vector quantity, a quantity with both magnitude and direction.
>
> The magnitude of the velocity is the speed.
>
> Speed is a scalar quantity; it has magnitude but not direction.

A ship moves with constant velocity $(4\mathbf{i} + 2\mathbf{j})\,\mathrm{m\,s^{-1}}$.

Velocity is the increase in displacement per second, so a velocity of $(4\mathbf{i} + 2\mathbf{j})\,\mathrm{m\,s^{-1}}$ means that the displacement of the ship increases by $(4\mathbf{i} + 2\mathbf{j})\,\mathrm{m}$ each second.

The position of the ship will be as shown in the diagram.

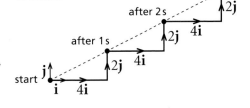

D1 The ship starts from the origin O when $t = 0$.

(a) Write down the position vector of the ship when $t = 1$.

(b) Write down the position vector of the ship when $t = 5$.

(c) Write down the position vector of the ship when $t = 2.5$.

(d) Write down an expression for the position vector of the ship at time t seconds.

D2 The diagram shows the velocity vector for the ship.

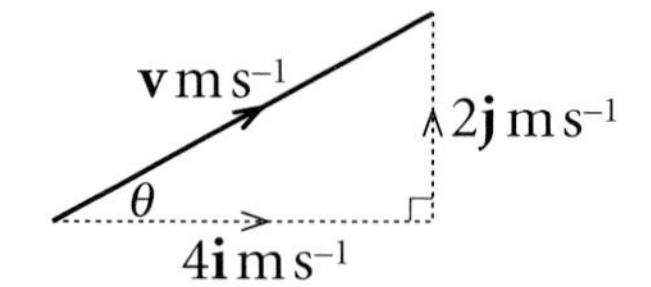

(a) What is the magnitude of the velocity?

(b) Find θ, the angle that the velocity makes with the vector **i**.

D3 A helicopter flies south-east at a constant speed of $55\,\mathrm{m\,s^{-1}}$.
Take **i** and **j** as the unit vectors directed east and north respectively.

(a) Sketch the velocity vector for the helicopter.

(b) What angle does the velocity make with the vector **i**?

(c) Use trigonometry to work out the components of the velocity in the **i**- and **j**-directions.

(d) Write the velocity of the helicopter in terms of **i** and **j**.

In one-dimensional motion the **average velocity** was defined as the constant velocity at which a journey of the same overall displacement could have been completed in the same total time. This also applies to two-dimensional motion.

If the position vector of an object at two different times is known, then the displacement is the change in position vector.

$$\text{Average velocity} = \frac{\text{change in position vector}}{\text{time taken}}$$

For an object moving with constant velocity,

$$\text{velocity} = \frac{\text{change in position vector}}{\text{time taken}}$$

D4 The position vector of a ship moving at a constant velocity is $(7\mathbf{i} - 8\mathbf{j})\,\mathrm{m}$. Five seconds later it is at point B with position vector $(22\mathbf{i} + 17\mathbf{j})\,\mathrm{m}$.

(a) Write down the displacement of the ship.

(b) What is the velocity of the ship?

D5 The position vector, in metres, of a model plane at time t seconds is given by $\mathbf{r} = (2t + 3)\mathbf{i} + 8t\mathbf{j}$, where **i** and **j** are unit vectors in the directions east and north respectively.

(a) Write down the plane's position when $t = 0$.

(b) Write down its position when $t = 30$.

(c) Find the displacement of the plane in the first 30 seconds of the flight.

(d) What is the average velocity of the plane for the first 30 seconds?

D6 A ship moves with constant velocity $(5\mathbf{i} - 2\mathbf{j})\,\mathrm{m\,s^{-1}}$. Its initial position vector is $(-10\mathbf{i} + 4\mathbf{j})\,\mathrm{m}$.

(a) Find an expression for the displacement of the ship, **s**, after t seconds.

(b) Find an expression for the position vector of the ship, **r**, after t seconds.

Example 7

At noon a ship S is at the point with position vector $(50\mathbf{i} - 20\mathbf{j})$ km with respect to a fixed origin O, where $\mathbf{i}$ and $\mathbf{j}$ are unit vectors in the directions east and north respectively. At time t hours after noon the position vector of S is $\mathbf{r}$ km. The velocity of S is constant and has magnitude 20 km h^{-1} in the direction of $(-3\mathbf{i} + 4\mathbf{j})$.

(a) Find an expression for $\mathbf{r}$ in terms of t.

(b) At what time is S is due east of O?

Solution

(a) *If the velocity vector is in the direction of $(-3\mathbf{i} + 4\mathbf{j})$, then it must be $k \times (-3\mathbf{i} + 4\mathbf{j})$ where k is a constant. The magnitude of this vector is 20.*

$$\text{Velocity} = -3k\mathbf{i} + 4k\mathbf{j}$$
$$\text{Magnitude of velocity} = \sqrt{(-3k)^2 + (4k)^2} = 20$$
$$\Rightarrow \quad \sqrt{25k^2} = 20$$
$$\Rightarrow \quad 5k = 20$$
$$\Rightarrow \quad k = 4$$
$$\Rightarrow \text{Velocity} = -12\mathbf{i} + 16\mathbf{j}$$

Position vector at time t = initial position vector + displacement at time t, and the displacement is velocity multiplied by time.

$$\mathbf{r} = (50\mathbf{i} - 20\mathbf{j}) + (-12\mathbf{i} + 16\mathbf{j}) \times t$$
$$\mathbf{r} = (50 - 12t)\mathbf{i} + (16t - 20)\mathbf{j}$$

(b) S is due east of O when the $\mathbf{j}$-component of the position is zero.

$$16t - 20 = 0$$
$$\Rightarrow \quad t = 1.25$$

S is due east of O after 1.25 hours.

Exercise D (answers p 143)

1 Write these velocities in terms of $\mathbf{i}$ and $\mathbf{j}$, where $\mathbf{i}$ and $\mathbf{j}$ are unit vectors in the directions east and north respectively.

(a) 20 m s^{-1} due north   (b) 5 m s^{-1} due west

2 A model plane moves with constant velocity $(3\mathbf{i} + \mathbf{j})$ m s^{-1}, where $\mathbf{i}$ and $\mathbf{j}$ are unit vectors in the directions east and north respectively.

(a) Write down its displacement after 1 second.

(b) Write down its displacement after 10 seconds.

(c) Write down an expression for its displacement after t seconds.

3 A ship moves with velocity $(12\mathbf{i} - 8\mathbf{j})\,\mathrm{m\,s^{-1}}$.

(a) Find the magnitude of the velocity.

(b) Find the angle that the motion makes with the vector $\mathbf{i}$.

4 A ship moves at $20\,\mathrm{m\,s^{-1}}$ on a bearing of $065°$.
Find the velocity in terms of $\mathbf{i}$ and $\mathbf{j}$, where $\mathbf{i}$ and $\mathbf{j}$ are unit vectors in the directions east and north respectively.

5 A golf ball is hit so that it moves off at a speed of $15\,\mathrm{m\,s^{-1}}$ in the direction of $(4\mathbf{i} + 3\mathbf{j})$, where $\mathbf{i}$ and $\mathbf{j}$ are horizontal and vertical unit vectors respectively.
Find the initial velocity of the golf ball in terms of $\mathbf{i}$ and $\mathbf{j}$.

6 The position vector of a helicopter is $(70\mathbf{i} + 30\mathbf{j})\,\mathrm{m}$, where $\mathbf{i}$ and $\mathbf{j}$ are unit vectors in the directions east and north respectively.
After 60 seconds moving at constant velocity it is at the point with position vector $(40\mathbf{i} + 270\mathbf{j})\,\mathrm{m}$.

(a) Find the displacement of the helicopter.

(b) What is the velocity of the helicopter?

7 The position vector, in metres, of a ship at time t seconds is given by
$\mathbf{r} = (10 - 3t)\mathbf{i} + (5t + 1)\mathbf{j}$.
Find the average velocity of the ship in the first 30 seconds of its motion.

8 The position vector, in metres, of a particle at time t seconds is given by
$\mathbf{r} = 2t^2\mathbf{i} + (8 - 3t)\mathbf{j}$.

(a) Find the position of the particle when $t = 10$.

(b) Find the position of the particle when $t = 20$.

(c) Find the average velocity of the particle between $t = 10$ and $t = 20$.

9 The initial position vector of a ship, in metres, is $(20\mathbf{i} + 30\mathbf{j})$, where $\mathbf{i}$ and $\mathbf{j}$ are unit vectors in the directions east and north respectively.
The ship moves with a constant velocity $(4\mathbf{i} - 3\mathbf{j})\,\mathrm{m\,s^{-1}}$ for t seconds.

(a) Find an expression for the displacement, $\mathbf{s}$, of the ship after t seconds.

(b) Find an expression for the position vector, $\mathbf{r}$, of the ship after t seconds.

(c) What is the position vector of the ship when $t = 60$?

10 An object moves with velocity $(10\mathbf{i} - 3\mathbf{j})\,\mathrm{m\,s^{-1}}$.
Initially it is at the point with position vector $(-30\mathbf{i} + 12\mathbf{j})\,\mathrm{m}$.
Find its position vector after 20 seconds.

11 The initial position vector of a particle is $(6\mathbf{i} + 10\mathbf{j})\,\mathrm{m}$. The particle moves with velocity $(-2\mathbf{i} + 3\mathbf{j})\,\mathrm{m\,s^{-1}}$.

(a) Find an expression for the position vector, $\mathbf{r}$, of the particle at time t seconds.

(b) Find the time when the particle is moving parallel to the vector $\mathbf{j}$.

E Resultant velocity (answers p 143)

A motorised toy duck walks at a speed of $0.3\,\mathrm{m\,s}^{-1}$. It walks on a tray, as shown in this diagram.

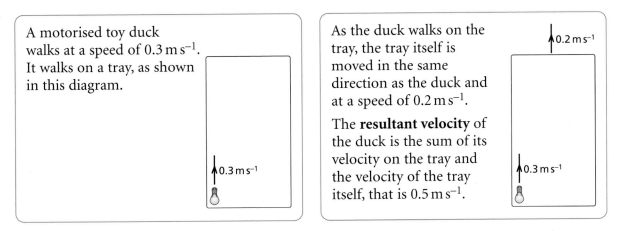

As the duck walks on the tray, the tray itself is moved in the same direction as the duck and at a speed of $0.2\,\mathrm{m\,s}^{-1}$.

The **resultant velocity** of the duck is the sum of its velocity on the tray and the velocity of the tray itself, that is $0.5\,\mathrm{m\,s}^{-1}$.

E1 Suppose that the tray moves at $0.2\,\mathrm{m\,s}^{-1}$ but in the opposite direction to the duck. What is the resultant velocity of the duck?

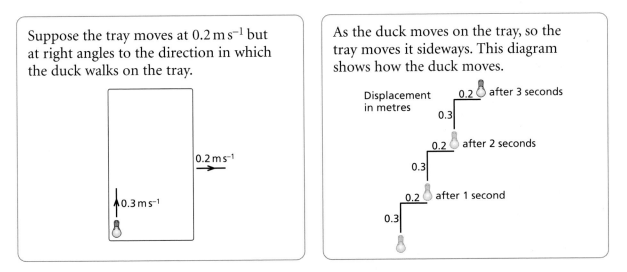

Suppose the tray moves at $0.2\,\mathrm{m\,s}^{-1}$ but at right angles to the direction in which the duck walks on the tray.

As the duck moves on the tray, so the tray moves it sideways. This diagram shows how the duck moves.

The duck's resultant velocity is found by adding the velocity vectors 'tail to head' using a vector triangle.

The resultant velocity is denoted by a double-headed arrow.

> Resultant velocity = velocity of duck on tray + velocity of tray

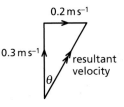

E2 (a) Find the magnitude of the resultant velocity.

(b) Find the angle θ which this velocity makes with the edge of the tray.

K The resultant velocity of an object can be found by adding its separate velocities using a vector triangle.

E3 Suppose the duck walks on the tray at $0.3\,\mathrm{m\,s^{-1}}$ at an angle of 45° to the edges of the tray, while the tray moves at $0.2\,\mathrm{m\,s^{-1}}$ as shown here.

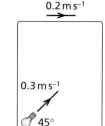

    (a) Sketch a vector triangle for finding the resultant velocity of the duck.

    (b) Draw the vector triangle to scale and use your scale drawing to find the resultant speed and direction of the duck.

Rowing (or driving) a boat on water that is itself moving is essentially the same as moving across a tray that is itself moving. The resultant velocity of the boat (as seen, for example, by someone looking down from above) is the vector sum of the velocity of the boat **relative** to the water and the velocity of the water itself.

Fraser can row his boat at a speed of $2\,\mathrm{m\,s^{-1}}$ in still water.
He is rowing in a river which is flowing parallel to its banks at a constant $1\,\mathrm{m\,s^{-1}}$.
The speed of his boat relative to the water is $2\,\mathrm{m\,s^{-1}}$.

E4 Fraser directs his boat downstream, that is in the direction of the current, as shown in the diagram.
What is his resultant velocity?

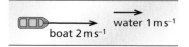

E5 He now directs his boat upstream, that is in the opposite direction to the current.

    (a) Sketch a diagram to show the velocities of the boat and the river.

    (b) What is the resultant velocity?

Fraser now attempts to row his boat across the river, perpendicular to the river bank.

The velocity vectors are as shown.

As Fraser rows across the river, the current moves his boat downstream. He directs the boat across the river, but the resultant velocity is at an angle θ to the bank.

This velocity triangle shows the resultant velocity of the boat.

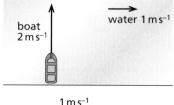

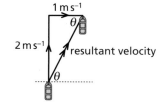

Resultant velocity = velocity of boat relative to the water + velocity of water

E6 **(a)** Find the magnitude of the resultant velocity.

    (b) Find the angle this velocity makes with the bank of the river.

E7 Fraser reduces his velocity to $1\,\mathrm{m\,s^{-1}}$ perpendicular to the river bank. The velocity of the river remains constant at $1\,\mathrm{m\,s^{-1}}$.

    (a) Sketch a velocity triangle showing his resultant velocity.

    (b) Find the magnitude and direction of the resultant velocity.

E8 Fraser rows at $1.5\,\mathrm{m\,s^{-1}}$ across the river flowing at $1\,\mathrm{m\,s^{-1}}$.
Find the magnitude and direction of his resultant velocity.

> **K** When the speed of a boat is given, this is the speed that the boat would
> travel at in still water, or the speed relative to the water.
> The resultant velocity of the boat is the vector sum of the velocity of the boat
> relative to the water and the velocity of the water.

Example 8

A model plane is flying with a constant velocity of $(5\mathbf{i} - \mathbf{j})\,\mathrm{m\,s^{-1}}$ relative to the air.
A wind with velocity $(-\mathbf{i} + 2\mathbf{j})\,\mathrm{m\,s^{-1}}$ is blowing.
Find the magnitude of the resultant velocity and the angle it makes with the vector $\mathbf{i}$.

Solution

Add the velocities to find the resultant. $\mathbf{v} = (5\mathbf{i} - \mathbf{j}) + (-\mathbf{i} + 2\mathbf{j}) = 4\mathbf{i} + \mathbf{j}$

Sketch the resultant velocity.

Use Pythagoras to find the magnitude. $v = \sqrt{4^2 + 1^2}$
$$= \sqrt{17} = 4.1\,\mathrm{m\,s^{-1}} \text{ to 1 d.p.}$$

Use trigonometry to find the angle. $\tan\theta = \frac{1}{4}$

$\theta = 14°$ to the nearest degree

The resultant velocity is $4.1\,\mathrm{m\,s^{-1}}$ at $14°$ to the $\mathbf{i}$-direction.

Exercise E (answers p 144)

1 A plane is flying at a velocity of $50\mathbf{i}\,\mathrm{m\,s^{-1}}$ relative to the air.
The wind is blowing with a velocity of $5\mathbf{j}\,\mathrm{m\,s^{-1}}$.
Find the resultant velocity of the plane.

2 A boat is propelled with velocity $(-3\mathbf{i} + 2\mathbf{j})\,\mathrm{km\,h^{-1}}$ across a river running at
$(2\mathbf{i} - \mathbf{j})\,\mathrm{km\,h^{-1}}$. Find the resultant velocity of the boat.

3 Naomi can swim at a speed of $1\,\mathrm{m\,s^{-1}}$ in still water.
She swims across a river which flows parallel to its banks at $1.5\,\mathrm{m\,s^{-1}}$.
Assume that Naomi's speed relative to the water is $1\,\mathrm{m\,s^{-1}}$ and
the velocity of the water is constant across the width of the river.

(a) Sketch a velocity triangle showing Naomi's resultant velocity if she heads
directly across the river.

(b) Find the magnitude of her resultant velocity.

(c) Find the angle the resultant velocity makes with the bank.

4 A boat has a velocity of $(2\mathbf{i} + 5\mathbf{j})\,\mathrm{m\,s^{-1}}$ relative to the water.
The velocity of the water is $(-\mathbf{i} + \mathbf{j})\,\mathrm{m\,s^{-1}}$.

(a) Find the resultant velocity of the boat.

(b) Find the magnitude of the resultant velocity.

(c) Find the angle the resultant velocity makes with the vector $\mathbf{i}$.

5 Greg can row at a speed of $2.5\,\mathrm{m\,s^{-1}}$ in still water.
He rows across a river perpendicular to the bank.
The river is flowing at a speed of $2\,\mathrm{m\,s^{-1}}$ parallel to its banks.

(a) Find the magnitude and direction of Greg's resultant velocity.

(b) If the speed of the river increased to $3\,\mathrm{m\,s^{-1}}$, what would be the magnitude and direction of his resultant velocity?

*6 Steve rows in a river at a constant speed of $2.4\,\mathrm{m\,s^{-1}}$ relative to the water. He rows 50 m downstream then turns and rows back to his starting point. This takes a total of 75 seconds. Assuming that he can maintain the same speed relative to the water for the whole 75 seconds, find the speed of the water.

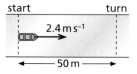

F Acceleration (answers p 144)

Acceleration is a vector quantity, with both magnitude and direction.

For an object moving with constant acceleration,

$$\text{Acceleration} = \frac{\text{change in velocity}}{\text{time taken}}$$

A boat moves from rest with constant acceleration of $(2\mathbf{i} + \mathbf{j})\,\mathrm{m\,s^{-2}}$.

Acceleration is the change in velocity per second, so an acceleration of $(2\mathbf{i} + \mathbf{j})\,\mathrm{m\,s^{-2}}$ means that the velocity of the boat changes by $(2\mathbf{i} + \mathbf{j})\,\mathrm{m\,s^{-1}}$ each second.

F1 (a) Write down the velocity of the boat after

    (i) 1 second   (ii) 2 seconds   (iii) 5 seconds

   (b) Write down an expression for the velocity of the boat at time t seconds.

F2 An object moves with constant acceleration $(-2\mathbf{i} + 5\mathbf{j})\,\mathrm{m\,s^{-2}}$.

(a) Sketch the acceleration vector for the object.

(b) What is the magnitude of the acceleration?

(c) What angle does the acceleration make with the vector $\mathbf{i}$?

An object has an initial velocity of $(\mathbf{i} - 3\mathbf{j})\,\mathrm{m\,s^{-1}}$.
It undergoes a constant acceleration of $(\mathbf{i} + \mathbf{j})\,\mathrm{m\,s^{-2}}$.

Acceleration is the change in velocity per second, so the velocity of the object will change by $(\mathbf{i} + \mathbf{j})\,\mathrm{m\,s^{-1}}$ each second.

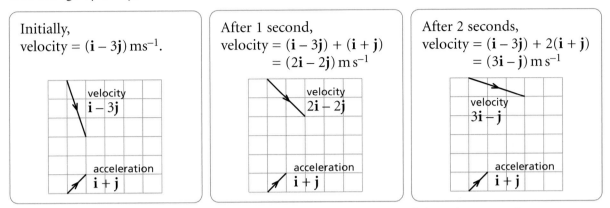

Initially,
velocity $= (\mathbf{i} - 3\mathbf{j})\,\mathrm{ms^{-1}}$.

velocity
$\mathbf{i} - 3\mathbf{j}$

acceleration
$\mathbf{i} + \mathbf{j}$

After 1 second,
velocity $= (\mathbf{i} - 3\mathbf{j}) + (\mathbf{i} + \mathbf{j})$
$= (2\mathbf{i} - 2\mathbf{j})\,\mathrm{m\,s^{-1}}$

velocity
$2\mathbf{i} - 2\mathbf{j}$

acceleration
$\mathbf{i} + \mathbf{j}$

After 2 seconds,
velocity $= (\mathbf{i} - 3\mathbf{j}) + 2(\mathbf{i} + \mathbf{j})$
$= (3\mathbf{i} - \mathbf{j})\,\mathrm{m\,s^{-1}}$

velocity
$3\mathbf{i} - \mathbf{j}$

acceleration
$\mathbf{i} + \mathbf{j}$

The acceleration causes the direction, as well as the magnitude, of the velocity to change.

F3 These are the velocity vectors at one-second intervals for a particle undergoing constant acceleration.

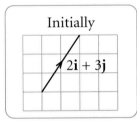

Initially

$2\mathbf{i} + 3\mathbf{j}$

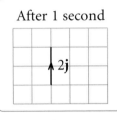

After 1 second

$2\mathbf{j}$

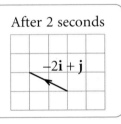

After 2 seconds

$-2\mathbf{i} + \mathbf{j}$

What is the vector for the acceleration?

F4 A plane is moving with constant acceleration.
Its velocity as it flies over a tower is $(70\mathbf{i} - 20\mathbf{j})\,\mathrm{m\,s^{-1}}$.
20 seconds later its velocity has become $(50\mathbf{i} + 10\mathbf{j})\,\mathrm{m\,s^{-1}}$.

(a) Find the change in velocity of the plane.

(b) What is the acceleration of the plane? Sketch the acceleration vector.

Example 9

A particle moves with constant acceleration $(-2\mathbf{i} + 3\mathbf{j})\,\mathrm{m\,s^{-2}}$.
Initially its velocity is $\mathbf{u}\,\mathrm{m\,s^{-1}}$ and after 10 seconds its velocity is $(3\mathbf{i} + 25\mathbf{j})\,\mathrm{m\,s^{-1}}$.
Find its initial velocity.

Solution

Use change in velocity = acceleration × time

$(3\mathbf{i} + 25\mathbf{j}) - \mathbf{u} = (-2\mathbf{i} + 3\mathbf{j}) \times 10$

$\Rightarrow \qquad \mathbf{u} = (3\mathbf{i} + 25\mathbf{j}) - (-20\mathbf{i} + 30\mathbf{j})$

$\Rightarrow \qquad \mathbf{u} = 23\mathbf{i} - 5\mathbf{j}$

Example 10

A ship moves with constant acceleration $(\mathbf{i} - \mathbf{j})\,\mathrm{m\,s^{-2}}$.
Initially the ship is moving with velocity $(5\mathbf{i} + 2\mathbf{j})\,\mathrm{m\,s^{-1}}$.
At what time is the ship moving parallel to the vector $\mathbf{i}$?

Solution

Use change in velocity = acceleration × time to find an expression for the velocity, $\mathbf{v}$, at time t.

$$\mathbf{v} - (5\mathbf{i} + 2\mathbf{j}) = (\mathbf{i} - \mathbf{j})t$$
$$\Rightarrow \qquad \mathbf{v} = (\mathbf{i} - \mathbf{j})t + (5\mathbf{i} + 2\mathbf{j})$$
$$\Rightarrow \qquad \mathbf{v} = (5 + t)\mathbf{i} + (2 - t)\mathbf{j}$$

When the motion is parallel to the vector $\mathbf{i}$, the $\mathbf{j}$ term of the velocity is zero, so $2 - t = 0$.

The ship is moving parallel to the vector $\mathbf{i}$ after 2 seconds .

Exercise F (answers p 144)

1 An object moves from rest with acceleration $(\mathbf{i} - \mathbf{j})\,\mathrm{m\,s^{-2}}$.
   Find the velocity of the object after

   (a) 1 second   **(b)** 5 seconds

2 An object moves with constant acceleration $(2\mathbf{i} - \mathbf{j})\,\mathrm{m\,s^{-2}}$.
   Its initial velocity is $(-\mathbf{i} + \mathbf{j})\,\mathrm{m\,s^{-1}}$.
   What is the velocity of the object after 3 seconds?

3 A model car is initially moving with velocity $(\mathbf{i} - 4\mathbf{j})\,\mathrm{m\,s^{-1}}$.
   After 10 seconds of constant acceleration it is moving with velocity $(3\mathbf{i} + 2\mathbf{j})\,\mathrm{m\,s^{-1}}$.

   (a) Find the change in velocity of the car.

   (b) What is the constant acceleration?

4 An object moves with constant acceleration so that its velocity changes from
   $(16\mathbf{i} + 3\mathbf{j})\,\mathrm{m\,s^{-1}}$ to $(6\mathbf{i} - 2\mathbf{j})\,\mathrm{m\,s^{-1}}$ in 5 seconds.
   Find the acceleration of the object.

5 A ship moves with constant acceleration $(\mathbf{i} - 2\mathbf{j})\,\mathrm{m\,s^{-2}}$, where $\mathbf{i}$ and $\mathbf{j}$
   are unit vectors in the directions east and north respectively.
   Find the magnitude and direction of the acceleration.

6 A particle starts from rest and moves with constant acceleration.
   After 4 seconds its velocity is $(4\mathbf{i} + 2\mathbf{j})\,\mathrm{m\,s^{-1}}$.
   Find the acceleration of the particle.

7 An object moves with constant acceleration of $(4\mathbf{i} - \mathbf{j})\,\mathrm{m\,s^{-2}}$.
   After 3 seconds its velocity is $(12\mathbf{i} + 2\mathbf{j})\,\mathrm{m\,s^{-1}}$.
   Find its initial velocity.

8 A particle P is moving with constant acceleration. Initially its velocity is $(4\mathbf{i} - 18\mathbf{j})\,\mathrm{m\,s^{-1}}$ and 6 seconds later its velocity is $(-14\mathbf{i} + 6\mathbf{j})\,\mathrm{m\,s^{-1}}$. Find the magnitude and direction of the acceleration of P.

9 A model plane starts from rest and moves with constant acceleration $(\mathbf{i} - \mathbf{j})\,\mathrm{m\,s^{-2}}$.

(a) Find an expression for its velocity at time t seconds.

(b) Find the speed of the plane when $t = 8$.

10 A particle is moving with constant acceleration of $(-2\mathbf{i} + \mathbf{j})\,\mathrm{m\,s^{-2}}$. At time $t = 0$ it is moving with velocity $(8\mathbf{i} + 2\mathbf{j})\,\mathrm{m\,s^{-1}}$.

(a) Find an expression for the velocity of the particle at time t.

(b) Find the time when the particle is moving parallel to the vector $\mathbf{j}$.

11 A particle P is moving with constant acceleration. Initially it is moving with velocity $(-4\mathbf{i} + 3\mathbf{j})\,\mathrm{m\,s^{-1}}$ and 5 seconds later it is moving with velocity $(6\mathbf{i} + 8\mathbf{j})\,\mathrm{m\,s^{-1}}$. Find the time at which P is moving parallel to the vector $(\mathbf{i} + \mathbf{j})$.

Key points

- A vector is a quantity that has both magnitude and direction. A vector can be resolved into two components at right angles to each other and represented as a column vector or in terms of the unit vectors $\mathbf{i}$ and $\mathbf{j}$. (pp 31–33)

- Displacement, velocity and acceleration are vector quantities. Distance and speed are scalar quantities. The magnitude of the displacement is the distance. The magnitude of the velocity is the speed. (pp 31, 39, 46)

- The position vector, $\mathbf{r}$, of an object is its displacement from a fixed origin. (p 36)

- Average velocity $= \dfrac{\text{change in position vector}}{\text{time taken}}$
  For an object moving with constant velocity, this is the constant velocity. (p 40)

- The resultant velocity of an object can be found by adding its separate velocities or by using a vector triangle. (p 43)

- For constant acceleration, acceleration $= \dfrac{\text{change in velocity}}{\text{time taken}}$ (p 46)

Mixed questions (answers p 144)

1 Two ships X and Y are modelled as particles moving in straight lines with constant velocities. The velocity of X is $5\,\mathrm{m\,s^{-1}}$ due south and the velocity of Y is $(5\mathbf{i} + 8\mathbf{j})\,\mathrm{m\,s^{-1}}$, where $\mathbf{i}$ and $\mathbf{j}$ are unit vectors directed due east and due north respectively.

Initially X is at the fixed origin O and Y is $200\,\mathrm{m}$ due east of O.
At time t seconds the position vectors of X and Y are $\mathbf{r}\,\mathrm{m}$ and $\mathbf{s}\,\mathrm{m}$ respectively.

(a) Find expressions for $\mathbf{r}$ and $\mathbf{s}$ in terms of t.

(b) Find the distance of Y from the origin when $t = 10$.

(c) Write down an expression for $\overrightarrow{XY}$ in terms of t.

(d) Find the time when the bearing of Y from X is $045°$.

2 A particle, P, moves in a straight line with constant acceleration.
Initially P is moving with velocity $(2\mathbf{i} - 2\mathbf{j})\,\mathrm{m\,s^{-1}}$ and 5 seconds later it is moving with velocity $(17\mathbf{i} - 7\mathbf{j})\,\mathrm{m\,s^{-1}}$.

(a) Find the acceleration of P.

(b) Find the angle between the direction of the acceleration and the vector $\mathbf{i}$.

(c) Find the speed of P after 8 seconds.

3 Ship A is moving with a constant velocity of $6\mathbf{i}\,\mathrm{km\,h^{-1}}$.
Ship B is moving with a constant velocity of $(4\mathbf{i} - \mathbf{j})\,\mathrm{km\,h^{-1}}$.
The unit vectors $\mathbf{i}$ and $\mathbf{j}$ are directed east and north respectively.
Initially, ship A is at the origin O and ship B is $5\,\mathrm{km}$ due north of O.

(a) Find the bearing on which

    (i) A is moving   **(ii)** B is moving

(b) At time t hours after noon, the position vectors of A and B relative to O are $\mathbf{a}\,\mathrm{km}$ and $\mathbf{b}\,\mathrm{km}$ respectively.
Find expressions for $\mathbf{a}$ and $\mathbf{b}$ in terms of t, giving your answers in the form $p\mathbf{i} + q\mathbf{j}$.

(c) Find the time when B is due west of A.

(d) After t hours the distance between A and B is $d\,\mathrm{km}$.
By finding an expression for $\overrightarrow{AB}$, show that $d^2 = 5t^2 - 10t + 25$.

(e) Initially the ships are $5\,\mathrm{km}$ apart.
After how many hours are they again $5\,\mathrm{km}$ apart?

4 A particle moves with constant velocity.
Its position vector relative to a fixed origin O is $\mathbf{r}$ metres at time t seconds.
When $t = 5$, $\mathbf{r} = 12\mathbf{i} + 18\mathbf{j}$ and when $t = 15$, $\mathbf{r} = -6\mathbf{i} + 40\mathbf{j}$.

Find the position vector of the particle when $t = 0$.

Test yourself (answers p 145)

1 A particle P moves with constant acceleration $(3\mathbf{i} - 2\mathbf{j})\,\mathrm{m\,s^{-2}}$.
At time t seconds, its velocity is $\mathbf{v}\,\mathrm{m\,s^{-1}}$.
When $t = 4$, $\mathbf{v} = (16\mathbf{i} + 3\mathbf{j})\,\mathrm{m\,s^{-1}}$.

(a) Find $\mathbf{v}$ when $t = 0$.

(b) Find the value of t when P is moving parallel to the vector $\mathbf{i}$.

(c) Find the speed of P when $t = 10$.

2 Two helicopters P and Q are moving in the same horizontal plane.
They are modelled as particles moving in straight lines with constant speeds.
At noon P is at the point with position vector $(20\mathbf{i} + 35\mathbf{j})\,\mathrm{km}$ with respect to a fixed origin O. At time t hours after noon the position vector of P is $\mathbf{p}\,\mathrm{km}$.
When $t = \frac{1}{2}$ the position vector of P is $(50\mathbf{i} - 25\mathbf{j})\,\mathrm{km}$. Find

(a) the velocity of P in the form $(a\mathbf{i} + b\mathbf{j})\,\mathrm{km\,h^{-1}}$

(b) an expression for $\mathbf{p}$ in terms of t

At noon Q is at O and at time t hours after noon the position vector of Q is $\mathbf{q}\,\mathrm{km}$.
The velocity of Q has magnitude $120\,\mathrm{km\,h^{-1}}$ in the direction of $4\mathbf{i} - 3\mathbf{j}$. Find

(c) an expression for $\mathbf{q}$ in terms of t

(d) the distance, to the nearest km, between P and Q when $t = 2$ Edexcel

3 A model boat moves with constant acceleration.
At time t seconds the velocity of the boat is $\mathbf{v}\,\mathrm{m\,s^{-1}}$.
When $t = 0$, $\mathbf{v} = (2\mathbf{i} - 3\mathbf{j})$ and when $t = 5$, $\mathbf{v} = (12\mathbf{i} - 8\mathbf{j})$.

(a) Find the angle between the direction of motion of the boat when $t = 5$ and the vector $\mathbf{i}$.

(b) Find the acceleration of the boat.

(c) Find an expression for $\mathbf{v}$ in terms of t.

(d) Find the speed of the boat when $t = 3$.

4 A boat B is travelling in a straight line at a constant velocity.
At 1200 B is at the point with position vector $(2\mathbf{i} + 6\mathbf{j})\,\mathrm{km}$ relative to a fixed origin O, where $\mathbf{i}$ and $\mathbf{j}$ are unit vectors in the directions east and north respectively.
At 1230, B is at the point with position vector $(-6\mathbf{i} + 4\mathbf{j})\,\mathrm{km}$.
At time t hours after 1200, B is at the point with position vector $\mathbf{r}\,\mathrm{km}$.

(a) Calculate the bearing on which B is travelling.

(b) Find an expression for $\mathbf{r}$ in terms of t.

(c) Another boat C leaves O at 1200 and travels with constant velocity.
At 1400 C intercepts B. Find the velocity of C.

3 Forces

In this chapter you will learn how to

- combine forces into a single resultant force
- resolve forces into components
- solve problems about forces in equilibrium, including weights, tensions, thrusts and friction forces

A Forces as vectors (answers p 145)

In this picture, Katy is being pulled by a dog.
The dog exerts a **force** on Katy. However, Katy manages to stand still.

Force is measured in **newtons** (N). The way in which a newton is defined will become clear in a later chapter. (To get an idea of what a force of 1 N feels like, hold a medium-sized apple in your hand. The weight of the apple is about 1 N.)

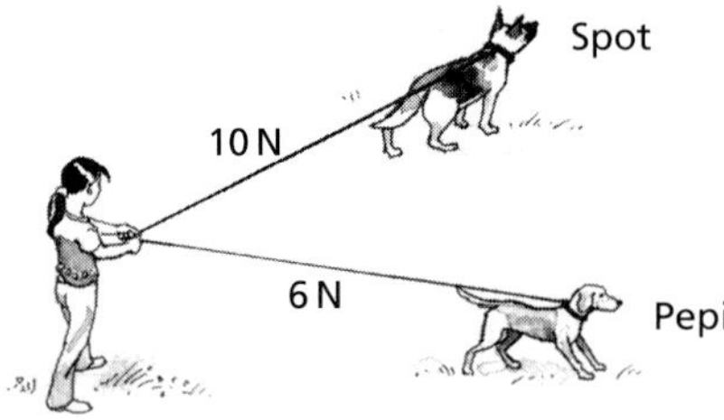

In the next picture, Katy is being pulled by two dogs, Spot and Pepi. Spot is stronger and pulls with a force of 10 N. Pepi pulls with a force of 6 N.

The two forces are in different directions. To specify a force you have to give not only its size, or **magnitude**, but its **direction** as well.

K Force is a vector quantity. A force can be represented by a line in the direction of the force whose length shows the magnitude of the force.

The forces exerted by the two dogs are shown in this vector diagram.
An open arrowhead is used here to denote a force.

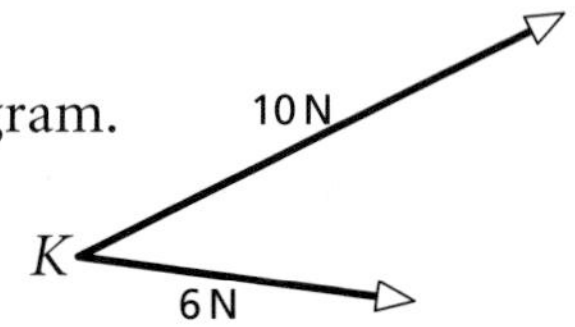

A1 Imagine that Katy weakens and can hold still no longer.
The dogs continue to pull with the same forces in the same directions.

In which of the following directions do you think Katy will start to move?

A The direction in which Spot is pulling

B The direction in which Pepi is pulling

C The direction that exactly bisects the angle between Spot's and Pepi's forces

D A direction between Spot's and Pepi's forces, but nearer to Spot's direction than Pepi's

E A direction between Spot's and Pepi's forces, but nearer to Pepi's direction than Spot's

The two forces exerted by Spot and Pepi can be combined into a single force by the **parallelogram rule**.

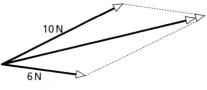

The two forces are represented, in magnitude and direction, by the adjacent sides of a parallelogram. The diagonal from the point where the forces are applied represents the single force equivalent to the two.

This single force (shown by the double arrow) is called the **resultant** of the two forces.

Notice that the direction of the resultant is closer to that of the larger force. (This explains why the correct answer to question A1 is D.)

A2 This diagram shows two forces that are of equal magnitude (10 N) with an angle of 60° between them.

    (a) Copy the diagram, complete the parallelogram and show the resultant of the two forces in your diagram.

    (b) Use trigonometry to work out the magnitude of the resultant force.

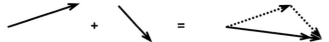

A3 Repeat question A2, but for an angle of 90° between the two forces.

In earlier work on vectors, you added vectors 'tail to head' by a 'triangle rule':

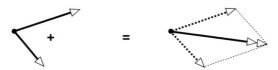

The resultant of two forces can also be found by the triangle rule. However, using a parallelogram rather than a triangle draws attention to the point where the forces are applied, and this can be extremely important in applications.

Two forces that exactly balance each other are said to be **in equilibrium**. One force is then equal and opposite to the other.

Three forces will be in equilibrium if the resultant of any two of them balances the third force.

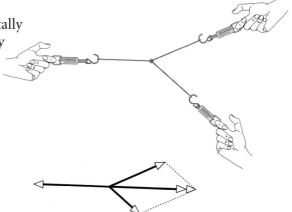

The parallelogram rule can be verified experimentally by using 'newton meters' (which measure forces by stretching a spring).

Three strings, each connected to a newton meter, are knotted at one point (or tied to a small ring). They are pulled tight in different directions.

The readings on the meters are used to draw vectors in the directions of the strings. When two of these vectors are combined by the parallelogram rule, the resultant will be found to be equal and opposite to the third force.

Mechanics is about forces and motion. In chapters 1 and 2 you looked at motion without considering forces. In this chapter you are looking at forces without considering motion. In later work, forces and motion will be brought together and you will learn how a force affects the motion of an object.

Exercise A (answers p 145)

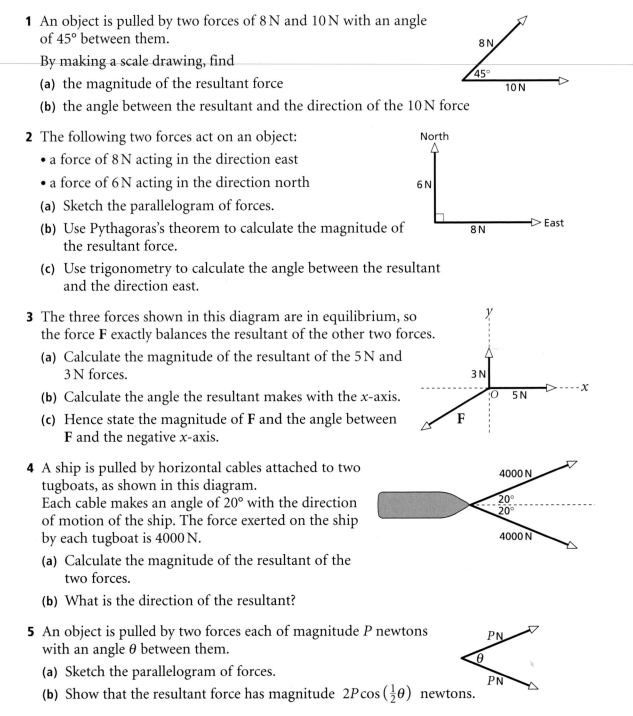

1 An object is pulled by two forces of 8 N and 10 N with an angle of 45° between them.

   By making a scale drawing, find

   (a) the magnitude of the resultant force

   (b) the angle between the resultant and the direction of the 10 N force

2 The following two forces act on an object:

   • a force of 8 N acting in the direction east

   • a force of 6 N acting in the direction north

   (a) Sketch the parallelogram of forces.

   (b) Use Pythagoras's theorem to calculate the magnitude of the resultant force.

   (c) Use trigonometry to calculate the angle between the resultant and the direction east.

3 The three forces shown in this diagram are in equilibrium, so the force **F** exactly balances the resultant of the other two forces.

   (a) Calculate the magnitude of the resultant of the 5 N and 3 N forces.

   (b) Calculate the angle the resultant makes with the x-axis.

   (c) Hence state the magnitude of **F** and the angle between **F** and the negative x-axis.

4 A ship is pulled by horizontal cables attached to two tugboats, as shown in this diagram.
   Each cable makes an angle of 20° with the direction of motion of the ship. The force exerted on the ship by each tugboat is 4000 N.

   (a) Calculate the magnitude of the resultant of the two forces.

   (b) What is the direction of the resultant?

5 An object is pulled by two forces each of magnitude P newtons with an angle θ between them.

   (a) Sketch the parallelogram of forces.

   (b) Show that the resultant force has magnitude $2P\cos\left(\tfrac{1}{2}\theta\right)$ newtons.

B Resolving a force (answers p 146)

You have seen how two forces can be combined into a single force using the parallelogram rule. In the special case where the two forces are at right angles, the parallelogram is a rectangle. In this diagram the two forces $\mathbf{F}_1$ and $\mathbf{F}_2$ combine to give the single force $\mathbf{F}$.

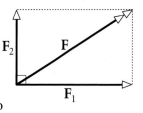

It is often useful to reverse this process and replace a single force by two **components** at right angles to each other.
We say the single force is **resolved** into the two components.

In the diagram above, the force $\mathbf{F}$ has been resolved into the two components $\mathbf{F}_1$ and $\mathbf{F}_2$.

The magnitude of $\mathbf{F}$, in newtons, is denoted by F (not bold).

K In this diagram, the force with magnitude F is resolved into components in the two perpendicular directions a and b.

Let θ be the angle between the force F and direction a.
From the shaded right-angled triangle, the components are

$$F \cos\theta \quad \text{in direction } a$$

and $\quad F \sin\theta \quad$ in direction b

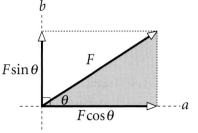

A force can be resolved in **any** two perpendicular directions.
In the diagram on the right, the force of magnitude 8 N has been resolved into two components in the directions p and q.

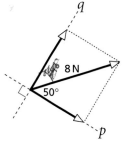

B1 Calculate the component of this force in each of the two directions p and q.

B2 A force of 20 N acts at an angle of 18° to a line l.
Calculate the component of the force

(a) in the direction l

(b) perpendicular to the direction l

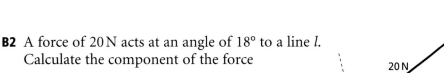

B3 The components of a force in two perpendicular directions are 9 N and 4 N, as shown in this diagram.

Calculate

(a) the magnitude of the force

(b) the angle θ

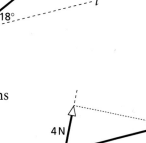

Components can be used to find a resultant of two or more forces.

B4 This diagram shows two forces acting at a point O.

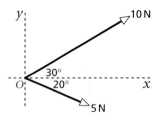

(a) Find the component of the 10 N force in the direction Ox.

(b) Find the component of the 5 N force in the direction Ox.

(c) Verify that the total of these two components is 13.359 N (to 3 d.p.).
This is the total component in the direction Ox, in other words the component of the resultant force in the direction Ox.

(d) Find the component of the 10 N force in the direction Oy.

(e) Find the component of the 5 N force in the direction Oy.

(f) Explain why the total of these two components is 3.290 N (to 3 d.p.).

(g) The resultant of the two forces has a component 13.359 N in the direction Ox, and a component 3.290 N in the direction Oy.

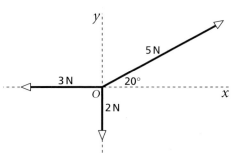

Calculate, to 3 s.f.,

(i) the magnitude R of the resultant force

(ii) the angle θ between the resultant and the direction Ox.

Example 1

Forces of 5 N, 3 N and 2 N act in the directions shown in the diagram.

Find the magnitude of the resultant force and the direction the resultant makes with Ox.

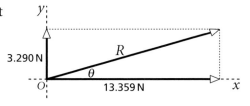

Solution

Resolve each force in the direction Ox.

The 5 N force has a component $5\cos 20°$ in the direction Ox.
The 3 N force has a component -3 in the direction Ox.
The 2 N force has no component in the direction Ox.

Total component in direction $Ox = (5\cos 20° - 3)\,\text{N} = 1.698\,\text{N}$ (to 3 d.p.)

Resolve each force in the direction Oy.

The 5 N force has a component $5\sin 20°$ in the direction Oy.
The 3 N force has no component in the direction Oy.
The 2 N force has a component -2 in the direction Oy.

Total component in direction $Oy = (5\sin 20° - 2)\,\text{N} = -0.290\,\text{N}$ (to 3 d.p.)

Sketch a diagram showing the components of the resultant force **R**.
The component –0.290 N *acts in the downward direction.*

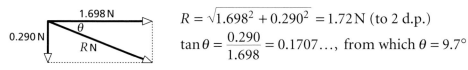

$R = \sqrt{1.698^2 + 0.290^2} = 1.72\,\text{N}$ (to 2 d.p.)

$\tan\theta = \dfrac{0.290}{1.698} = 0.1707\ldots$, from which $\theta = 9.7°$

So the resultant has magnitude 1.72 N and makes an angle 9.7° below *Ox*.

To avoid rounding errors, use more decimal places than are finally needed.

Exercise B (answers p 146)

1 A force of 20 N acts at angle of 60° to the direction *Ox*.
   Find the component of the force

   (a) in the direction *Ox*

   (b) in the direction *Oy*

2 A force of 15 N acts at an angle of 40° to the direction *Oy*.
   Find the component of the force

   (a) in the direction *Ox*

   (b) in the direction *Oy*

3 Forces **P** and **Q**, of magnitudes 6 N and 4 N, act in the
   directions shown in the diagram.

   (a) Calculate the component of **P** in the direction *Ox*.

   (b) Calculate the component of **P** in the direction *Oy*.

   (c) Calculate the total of the components of **P** and **Q**
   in the direction *Ox*.

   (d) Calculate the magnitude of the resultant of **P** and **Q**.

   (e) Calculate the angle the resultant makes with *Ox*.

4 The vectors **i** and **j** shown here are perpendicular unit vectors.
   The forces **P** and **Q**, in newtons, can be written as
   P = 2**i** + 3**j**, **Q** = 2**i** – 2**j**.

   (a) Find, in terms of **i** and **j**, the resultant force **P** + **Q**.

   (b) Find the magnitude of the resultant force and the angle
   between the resultant and the vector **i**.

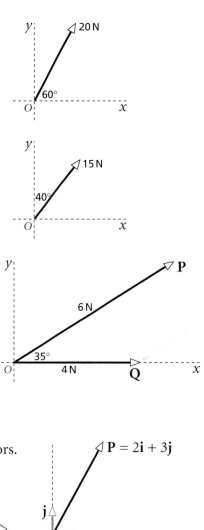

5 Two forces act at a point O as shown in the diagram. Find the magnitude of the resultant force and the angle the resultant makes with Ox.

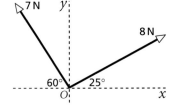

6 Find the magnitude of the resultant of the three forces shown in this diagram, and the angle the resultant makes with Ox.

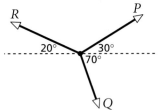

C Resolving coplanar forces in equilibrium (answers p 146)

Three or more forces that act in the same plane (for example, a horizontal plane or a vertical plane) are called **coplanar**. All sets of forces in this book will be coplanar.

The three forces P, Q and R in this diagram are acting on a stationary small object.
The object remains stationary, so the forces are in equilibrium.
The resultant of P, Q and R is zero.

Because the resultant is zero, the components of P, Q and R, in any direction, add up to zero.

For example, resolving to the right along the dotted line, we get

$$P\cos 30° + Q\cos 70° - R\cos 20° = 0$$

Problems about forces in equilibrium can be tackled by resolving the forces and using the fact that the total component will always be zero.

C1 The three forces in this diagram are in equilibrium.

(a) Write down an expression, in terms of P, for

   (i) the component of force P in the direction Ox (call this the x-component of force P)

   (ii) the y-component of force P

(b) Explain why $P\cos 35° = 10\cos 75°$.

(c) Explain why $P\sin 35° + 10\sin 75° = Q$.

(d) From the equation in (b), find the value of P.

(e) From the equation in (c), find the value of Q.

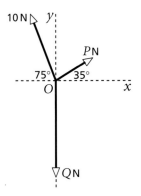

C2 The three forces in this diagram are in equilibrium.

(a) Explain why $U\cos 40° = V\cos 70°$.

(b) Write down expressions for the y-components of U and V.

(c) Explain why the total of the y-components of U and V must be 5 N.

(d) From parts (a) and (c) you will have two simultaneous equations for U and V. Solve the equations to find the values of U and V, correct to 3 s.f.

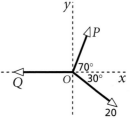

In future, all forces will be assumed to be in newtons. So a force labelled '8' in a diagram is a force of 8 newtons.

Example 2

The three forces shown here are in equilibrium.
Find the values of P and Q.

Solution

Resolve in the x-direction: $P\cos 70° + 20\cos 30° = Q$ (1)

Resolve in the y-direction: $P\sin 70° = 20\sin 30°$ (2)

From (2), $P = \dfrac{20\sin 30°}{\sin 70°} = 10.642$ (to 3 d.p.)

Substitute for P in (1): $10.642\cos 70° + 20\cos 30° = Q$

$\Rightarrow \quad Q = 20.960$

$P = 10.6$, $Q = 21.0$ (to 3 s.f.)

Exercise C (answers p 146)

1 The three forces shown in this diagram are in equilibrium.

(a) By resolving in the direction Ox, show that $P = Q$.

(b) Explain why $2P\sin 25° = 5$, and hence find the value of P, to 3 s.f.

2 These three forces are in equilibrium.

(a) By resolving in the direction Oy, show that $P = 12.2$, to 3 s.f.

(b) Find the value of Q.

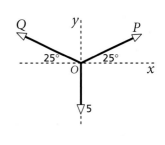

3 These three forces are in equilibrium.

(a) By resolving in the x-direction, find the value of θ.

(b) Find the value of P.

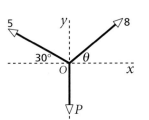

4 Three forces, of magnitudes 15, 12 and P newtons, act at a point in the directions shown in the diagram. The forces are in equilibrium. Find

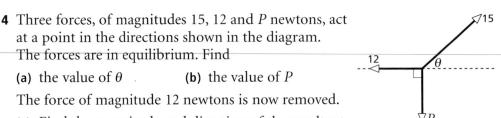

(a) the value of θ (b) the value of P

The force of magnitude 12 newtons is now removed.

(c) Find the magnitude and direction of the resultant of the two remaining forces.

5 The three forces shown here are in equilibrium.

(a) Show that $P\cos\theta = 7$.

(b) Show that $P\sin\theta = 6\sin 60°$

(c) Use the fact that $\tan\theta = \dfrac{\sin\theta}{\cos\theta}$ to show that

$\tan\theta = \dfrac{6\sin 60°}{7}$, and hence find the value of θ.

(d) Find the value of P.

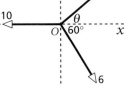

6 The three forces $p\mathbf{i} + 3\mathbf{j}$, $2\mathbf{i} - 4\mathbf{j}$ and $-7\mathbf{i} + q\mathbf{j}$ are in equilibrium. Find the values of p and q.

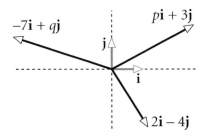

7 These three forces are in equilibrium. Find the values of P and Q, to 3 s.f.

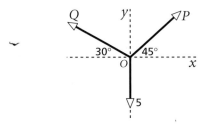

D Weight, tension and thrust (answers p 146)

These are some of the most common types of force occurring in mechanics.

Weight	**Tension**	**Thrust**
Objects are pulled vertically downwards by the force of gravity. This force acting on an object is its weight. 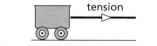	A tension is a pulling force, for example in a rope pulling on an object.	A thrust is a pushing force.

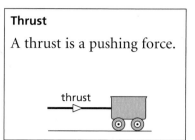

In all the questions that follow, the object on which the forces act will be small in size (though not necessarily in weight). Such an object is called a **particle**.

The reason for working only with particles at this stage is that forces on a large object have different effects depending on exactly where they act.

For example, if a stationary box is pulled by two equal forces in line with each other, the forces will be in equilibrium and the box will not move.

But if the forces are still equal but not in line, the box will twist.

A particle can be treated as a point, so all forces acting on a particle act at the same point and the issue of twisting does not arise.

In practice, even a large object can be treated as a particle provided it can be assumed that all the forces on it act at the same point.

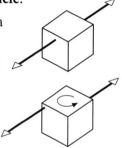

Force diagrams

The first step in solving a problem about forces on an object is to draw a diagram showing **all** the forces acting on the object.

This picture shows a stationary particle held in position by two light strings. Each string is attached to a ceiling.

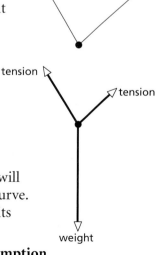

This force diagram shows the three forces acting on the particle: the tensions in the two strings and the particle's weight.
The ceiling is not shown, because the purpose of this diagram is to show the forces acting on the particle.

The particle is stationary, so the three forces are in equilibrium.

There is a reason for describing the strings as 'light'. A heavy string will not hang in a straight line – its own weight will cause it to form a curve. Of course, no real string can be weightless, but if it is light enough its weight can be ignored.

Treating the strings as weightless is an example of a **modelling assumption**. A model simplifies a real situation by leaving out things whose effects are so small they can be ignored.

D1 Sketch a diagram showing the forces acting on the particle in each case below. Label each force 'weight', 'tension', and so on.

    (a) A particle hanging from a vertical string

    (b) A particle supported by a vertical rod

D2 Two particles A and B are connected to each other by a light horizontal string.

    Each particle is attached to a light string inclined at an angle to the horizontal. The other end of each string is attached to a ceiling.

    (a) Sketch a force diagram showing the forces acting on particle A.

    (b) Sketch a force diagram showing the forces acting on particle B.

D3 A smooth bead is threaded on to a light string.

    (a) What happens to the bead if both ends of the string are held at the same height? Draw a diagram of the forces acting on the bead.

    (b) What happens to the bead if the ends of the string are held at different heights? (You could see if you are right by trying this out with a real bead and a length of nylon thread.) Draw a diagram of the forces acting on the bead.

When a smooth bead is threaded on to a string the magnitude of the tension will be the same throughout the string.
If the bead is fixed to the string, the bead is in effect a particle attached to two separate strings so the tensions in the two parts of the string may be different.

Example 3

A particle of weight 3 newtons is attached to the lower end of a light string, whose upper end is attached to a fixed point.
The string makes an angle of $25°$ to the vertical.
The particle is held in position by a light horizontal string.
Find the tension in each string.

Solution

Always start by drawing a diagram showing all the forces acting on the object. There are three forces in this case, the weight and the two tensions. The diagram will explain the meaning of any new letters you introduce (in this case the two tensions T and S).

Choose directions in which to resolve the forces. Here the obvious directions are horizontal and vertical.

*Notice that the angle of S with the **vertical** is given, so the horizontal component of S is $S\sin 25°$.*

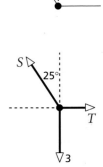

Resolve horizontally: $T = S \sin 25°$ (1)

Resolve vertically: $3 = S \cos 25°$ (2)

From equation (2), $S = \dfrac{3}{\cos 25°} = 3.310$ (to 3 d.p.)

So from equation (1), $T = 3.310 \times \sin 25° = 1.399$

To 3 s.f. the tensions are 1.40 N in the horizontal string and 3.31 N in the inclined string.

Exercise D (answers p 147)

1 A particle is is held in equilibrium by two light strings.
One string is horizontal and the other is inclined at 25°
to the horizontal. The tension in the inclined string is 15 N.

(a) Draw a diagram showing the forces acting on the particle.

(b) **(i)** Find the weight of the particle.

  (ii) Find the tension in the horizontal string.

2 A particle of weight 6 N is attached to one end of a light string.
The other end of the string is attached to a fixed point O.
The particle is held in equilibrium by a horizontal force P applied to it,
with the string making an angle of 20° with the vertical.

Find

(a) the tension in the string

(b) the value of P

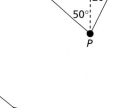

3 A particle P is attached to two points A and B by two light strings,
as shown here. The particle hangs in equilibrium.
The tension in string PA is 10 N.

Find

(a) the tension in string PB

(b) the weight of the particle

4 A particle of weight 20 N is held in equilibrium by two
light strings. One is horizontal and the other is inclined
at an angle α to the horizontal. The tension in the horizontal
string is 12 N. Find

(a) the angle α **(b)** the tension in the inclined string

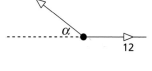

5 A bead of weight 5 N is threaded on to a light string,
the ends of which are attached to a ceiling.
Given that the tension in the string is 8 N, find the angle α.

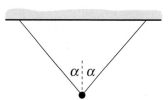

6 A particle of weight W newtons is held in equilibrium by
two light strings, each inclined at an angle α to the vertical.

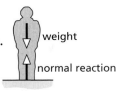

(a) Show that the tension in each string is $\dfrac{W}{2\cos\alpha}$ newtons.

(b) Does the tension in each string increase or decrease if
the angle α is increased? Justify your answer.

(c) What happens as α approaches 90°?

7 A lantern of weight 10 N is attached to two fixed points A and
B by two light ropes, as shown in the diagram.

Find the tension in each rope.

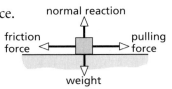

E Friction (answers p 147)

Imagine a horizontal sheet of ice on which objects can slide without any
resistance at all. This kind of 'perfectly smooth' surface does not exist in
reality, but is a useful idea.

If the ice is strong enough, then an object standing on it will not fall through.
This is because the ice surface exerts an upward force on the object,
and this upward force counteracts the object's weight.

The force exerted on the object by the surface is called a **normal reaction**.
(The word 'normal' means 'at right angles to the surface' – it doesn't mean
normal in the sense of ordinary.)

If the ice is perfectly smooth, it can provide a normal reaction but can offer
no resistance to a force pulling or pushing the object sideways.

Now imagine a rough horizontal surface with an object standing on it.
As before, the surface exerts a normal reaction on the object counteracting
the object's weight.

Imagine that the object is pulled sideways by a horizontal force.

E1 Suppose the pulling force is very small at first and is then gradually increased.
What do you think will happen? Check by pulling a real object on a rough surface.

A rough surface is able to resist a horizontal pulling (or pushing) force.
It does this by means of a force acting in the opposite direction
to the pulling force. This force is called the **friction** force.
As the pulling force increases, so does the friction force, and the
object remains in equilibrium.

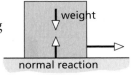

But the surface is able to resist only up to a certain limit. If the pulling force
exceeds this limit, the object will move. When the force has just reached the limit,
so that the object is just about to move, the object is in **limiting equilibrium**.

Experiments have shown that the maximum friction force F_{max} is proportional to the normal reaction R. The constant of proportionality is denoted by μ ('mu'), so $F_{max} = \mu R$.

μ is a measure of the roughness of the interface between the object and what it is in contact with: the larger the value of μ, the rougher the interface. Some approximate values of μ are given in this table.

Steel/steel	$\mu = 0.75$
Teflon/Teflon	$\mu = 0.04$
Wood/brick	$\mu = 0.6$

K If an object on a rough surface is kept in equilibrium by a friction force of magnitude F, then $F \le \mu R$, where R is the magnitude of the normal reaction and μ is the coefficient of friction.
In limiting equilibrium, when the object is about to move, $F = \mu R$.

E2 A small box of weight $20\,\text{N}$ is on a rough horizontal floor.
It is pulled by a horizontal force of $8\,\text{N}$ and is in limiting equilibrium.

(a) Draw a diagram showing all the forces acting on the box.

(b) What is the magnitude of

   (i) the friction force acting on the box

   (ii) the normal reaction of the floor on the box

(c) Find the coefficient of friction between the box and the floor.

E3 An object of weight $12\,\text{N}$ is on a rough horizontal floor.
The coefficient of friction between the object and the floor is 0.35.
The object is pulled by a light horizontal rope and is in limiting equilibrium.
Find the tension in the rope.

E4 An object of weight $W\,\text{N}$ is on a rough horizontal surface.
The coefficient of friction between the object and the surface is 0.3.
The object is pulled by a horizontal force of $7.5\,\text{N}$ and is in equilibrium (but not necessarily limiting equilibrium).

(a) The normal reaction of the surface on the object is $R\,\text{N}$.
   Explain why $R = W$.

(b) State the magnitude of the friction force F on the object.

(c) Use the inequality $F \le \mu R$ to show that $W \ge 25$.

D **E5** A small object rests on a rough surface. It is pulled by a light rope inclined at an angle to the horizontal and is in equilibrium.
Sketch a force diagram for the object, labelling each force.

E6 These two diagrams show the same object on the same horizontal surface. In the first, the object rests on the surface. In the second, it is pulled by an inclined force and is in equilibrium.

For each situation, sketch a diagram showing all the forces acting on the object.
Explain why the normal reaction of the surface on the object is less in the second case than in the first.

E7 A sledge of weight 40 N is on rough horizontal ground.
It is pulled by a force of 20 N inclined at 25° to the horizontal.
The sledge is in equilibrium.

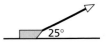

(a) Modelling the sledge as a particle, draw a diagram showing all the forces acting on it.

(b) By resolving forces in a suitable direction, show that the normal reaction R of the ground on the sledge is 31.5 N (to 3 s.f.).

(c) Show that the frictional force F on the sledge is 18.1 N (to 3 s.f.).

(d) The coefficient of friction between the sledge and the ground is μ.
By using the inequality $F \leq \mu R$, show that $\mu \geq 0.57$ (to 2 d.p.).

Example 4

A small object of weight 10 N is standing on a rough horizontal surface.
The object is pulled by a force of 6 N acting at an angle of 30°
to the horizontal. The object is in limiting equilibrium.

Find

(a) the friction force

(b) the normal reaction of the surface on the object

(c) the coefficient of friction

Solution

*As usual, start by drawing a diagram showing **all** the forces acting
on the object. To make the diagram clearer, leave out the surface
itself (but of course include the forces it provides).*

The friction force is labelled F.

Choose directions for resolving the forces.
Here the obvious directions are horizontal and vertical.

(It may help to draw a second diagram showing each component separately.)

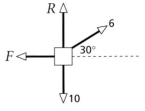

(a) Resolve horizontally: $F = 6\cos 30° = 5.196$ (to 4 s.f.)

(b) Resolve vertically: $R + 6\sin 30° = 10$

So $R = 10 - 6\sin 30° = 7$

(c) The object is in limiting equilibrium, so $F = \mu R$.

$$5.196 = \mu \times 7$$

$$\Rightarrow \quad \mu = \frac{5.196}{7} = 0.742 \text{ (to 3 s.f.)}$$

In the previous example you were told that the object is in **limiting** equilibrium.
If you were told only that it is in equilibrium, then you could use the
inequality $F \leq \mu R$ to find a range of possible values of μ, like this:

$$F \leq \mu R$$
$$5.196 \leq \mu \times 7$$
$$\Rightarrow \qquad \mu \geq \frac{5.196}{7} = 0.742 \text{ (to 3 s.f.). So } \mu \geq 0.742$$

Example 5

A particle of weight 20 N rests in equilibrium on a horizontal surface.
The coefficient of friction between the particle and the surface is 0.3.
A thrust of P N acts on the particle at an angle of 20° to the horizontal.
Show that $P \leq 7.17$ (to 3 s.f.).

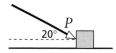

Solution

For clarity, the thrust P is shown as a 'pull'.

Resolve vertically:	$R = 20 + P\sin 20° = 20 + 0.3420P$
Resolve horizontally:	$F = P\cos 20° = 0.9397P$
Use $F \leq \mu R$:	$0.9397P \leq 0.3(20 + 0.3420P)$
$\Rightarrow$	$0.8371P \leq 6$
$\Rightarrow$	$P \leq \dfrac{6}{0.8371} = 7.17$ (to 3 s.f.)

___

Exercise E (answers p 147)

1 A small object of weight 15 N is on a rough horizontal surface.
It is pulled by a horizontal force of 12 N and is in limiting equilibrium.

(a) Sketch a diagram showing the forces acting on the object.

(b) Find the coefficient of friction.

2 An object of weight 8 N is on a rough horizontal surface.
The coefficient of friction between the object and the surface is 0.45.
The object is pulled by a horizontal force P N and is in limiting equilibrium.
Find the value of P.

3 An object of weight 10 N on a rough horizontal surface is in equilibrium
when pulled by a force of 4 N inclined at 30° to the horizontal.
The coefficient of friction between the object and the surface is μ.

(a) Find the normal reaction of the surface on the object.

(b) Show that $\mu \geq 0.433$.

4 A particle of weight 9 N is on a rough horizontal table.
A thrust of 6 N acts on the particle at an angle of 50° to the horizontal.
The particle is in limiting equilibrium.
Find the coefficient of friction.

5 A particle on a rough horizontal surface is pulled by a force of 1.5 N inclined at an angle of 40° the horizontal and is in limiting equilibrium. The coefficient of friction between the particle and the surface is 0.4.

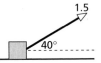

(a) Show that the friction force on the particle is 1.15 N.

(b) Find the normal reaction of the surface on the particle.

(c) Find the weight of the particle.

6 A particle of weight 7 N rests in equilibrium on a horizontal surface. The coefficient of friction between the particle and the surface is 0.25. The particle is pulled by a force of P newtons inclined at 45° to the horizontal.

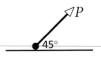

(a) Show that the normal reaction R is equal to $(7 - 0.707P)$ N.

(b) Show that $P \leq 1.98$ (to 3 s.f.).

7 A particle of weight 6 N lies on a horizontal surface. The coefficient of friction between the particle and the surface is μ. The particle is pulled by a force of 3 N acting at 60° to the horizontal and is in equilibrium.

(a) Find the magnitude of the normal reaction between the surface and the particle.

(b) Show that $\mu \geq 0.44$.

8 A particle of weight 10 N is in equilibrium on a horizontal plane. The coefficient of friction between the particle and the plane is 0.2.

The particle is acted on by a horizontal force PN and a force of 6 N inclined at 45° to the horizontal, as shown in the diagram.

By considering separately the cases in which the friction force acts to the left or to the right, show that $3.09 \leq P \leq 5.39$ (to 2 d.p.).

F Friction: inclined surfaces (answers p 148)

D

F1 Imagine an object resting on a rough plane. The plane is horizontal to start with, but is gradually tilted so that its angle to the horizontal increases.

What do you think will happen?

Explain, with the help of a force diagram, why it happens.

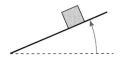

A particle of weight 5 newtons rests on a rough plane inclined at 35° to the horizontal. The particle is in limiting equilibrium, about to slide down.

F2 Explain why the angle between the direction at right angles to the plane and the vertical is also 35°.

The normal reaction is perpendicular to the plane, as always.
So in this case it is not vertical, but inclined at 35° to the vertical.

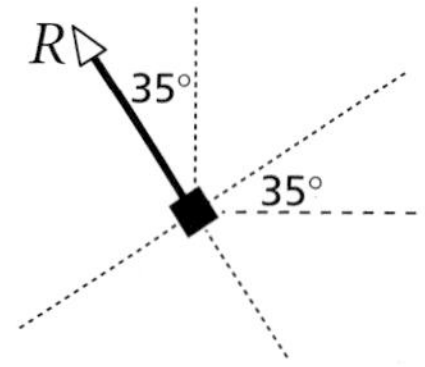

F3 The normal reaction R is shown in the diagram on the right.
Copy the diagram and complete it to show all the forces acting
on the particle.

K In problems involving inclined planes, it is usually best to resolve forces in
directions parallel to the plane and perpendicular to the plane, rather than
horizontally and vertically.

F4 Because the particle is about to slide down the plane, the friction force acts
up the plane. It is in limiting equilibrium so $F = \mu R$. This force balances the
component of the weight in the direction down the plane.
Write down an equation which says this.

F5 Write down the equation you get from resolving the forces into components
perpendicular to the plane.

F6 (a) Eliminate R from the two equations you got in F4 and F5 and hence
find the value of μ to 3 s.f.

(b) Use one of the equations to find the value of R.

Example 6

A particle of weight 8 newtons rests on a rough plane inclined
at 30° to the horizontal. The coefficient of friction is 0.2.
The particle is pushed by a horizontal force P and is in limiting
equilibrium, about to move up the plane. Find the value of P.

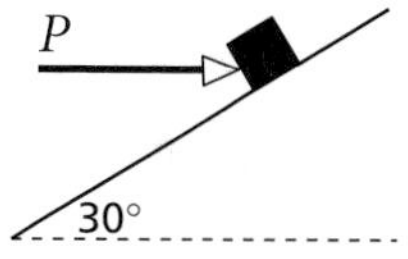

Solution

The horizontal force P is shown as a pull in the diagram.
This is just to make the diagram clearer. It makes no difference.

The particle is about to move up the plane, so the friction force acts
down the plane.

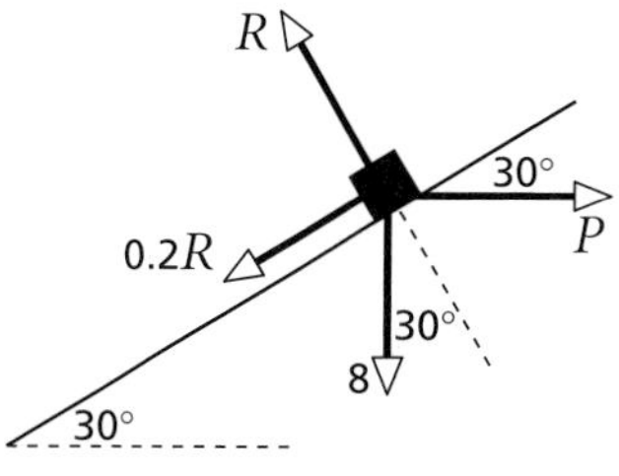

Friction force $F = 0.2R$

Resolve up the plane: $\qquad P\cos 30° = 8\sin 30° + 0.2R \qquad$ (1)

Resolve perpendicular to the plane: $\quad R = 8\cos 30° + P\sin 30° \quad$ (2)

Substitute for R in (1): $\qquad P\cos 30° = 8\sin 30° + 1.6\cos 30° + 0.2P\sin 30°$

$\Rightarrow \qquad P(\cos 30° - 0.2\sin 30°) = 8\sin 30° + 1.6\cos 30°$

$\Rightarrow \qquad P = \dfrac{8\sin 30° + 1.6\cos 30°}{\cos 30° - 0.2\sin 30°} = 7.03$

Example 7

A particle of weight 20 newtons rests in equilibrium on a rough surface inclined at an angle α to the horizontal. The coefficient of friction between the particle and the surface is 0.4. A force of P newtons acts on the particle in a direction parallel to the plane and downwards.

Show that $P \le 8\cos\alpha - 20\sin\alpha$.

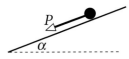

Solution

The friction force, which must act up the plane, is shown as F.
As the friction may not be limiting this cannot be replaced by μR.

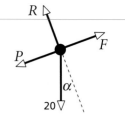

Resolve perpendicular to the plane:	$R = 20\cos\alpha$
Resolve parallel to the plane:	$F = 20\sin\alpha + P$
Use $F \le \mu R$:	$20\sin\alpha + P \le 0.4 \times 20\cos\alpha$
$\Rightarrow$	$P \le 8\cos\alpha - 20\sin\alpha$

Exercise F (answers p 148)

1 A particle of weight 5 newtons is at rest on a rough plane which is inclined at 30° to the horizontal. The particle is in limiting equilibrium.

  (a) Sketch a diagram showing all the forces acting on the particle.

  (b) Find the normal reaction between the plane and the particle.

  (c) Find the coefficient of friction.

2 A particle of weight 8 newtons is on a rough plane which is inclined at 40° to the horizontal. The coefficicient of friction is 0.25. The particle is attached to a string which is parallel to the plane. The particle is in limiting equilibrium, about to move down the plane.

  (a) Apart from the weight and the tension in the string, there are two other forces acting on the particle. Show all four forces in a sketch.

  (b) By resolving parallel and perpendicular to the plane, find

    (i) the normal reaction of the plane on the particle

    (ii) the tension in the string

  (c) Suppose instead that the particle is in limiting equilibrium but about to move **up** the plane. Find in this case

    (i) the normal reaction   (ii) the tension in the string

3 A particle of weight 10 newtons is on rough plane inclined at 30° to the horizontal. The particle is pushed by a force P acting parallel to the plane as shown. The particle is in limiting equilibrium, about to move up the plane. The coefficient of friction is 0.1.

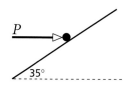

Find the value of P.

4 A particle of weight 5 newtons rests on a rough plane inclined at 35° to the horizontal. The coefficient of friction is 0.2.
A horizontal force P acts on the particle as shown in the diagram.

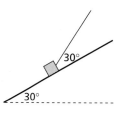

The particle is in limiting equilibrium, on the point of moving down the plane.

(a) Find the value of P.

(b) Suppose instead that the particle is in limiting equilibrium but on the point of moving **up** the plane. Find the value of P in this case.

5 A box of weight 15 newtons is on a rough plane inclined at 30° to the horizontal. The coefficient of friction between the box and the plane is 0.3. A light string is attached to the box and is inclined at 30° to the plane, as shown in the diagram.
The box is in limiting equilibrium, about to move up the plane.

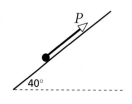

Find the tension in the string.

6 A particle of weight 10 newtons is placed on a plane inclined at 40° to the horizontal. The coefficient of friction between the particle and the plane is 0.2.

(a) Show that the particle cannot remain in equilibrium in this position.

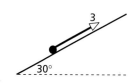

In order to keep the particle in equilibrium a force P newtons is applied parallel to and up the plane.

(b) Given that the friction force acts up the plane, show that $P \geq 10 \sin 40° - 2 \cos 40°$.

(c) Given that the friction force acts down the plane, show that $P \leq 10 \sin 40° + 2 \cos 40°$.

(d) Hence show that, to 3 s.f., $4.90 \leq P \leq 7.96$.

7 A particle of weight 8 newtons is on a plane inclined at 30° to the horizontal. A force of 3 newtons acts on the particle in a direction parallel to and up the plane. The particle is in equilibrium.

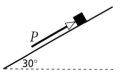

(a) Explain why the friction force F on the particle acts up the plane.

(b) Show that $\mu \geq 0.144$ (to 3 s.f.).

Key points

- Force is a vector quantity.
  The resultant of two forces is found by the parallelogram rule. (pp 52–53)

- A force **F** of magnitude F can be resolved into
  components $F \cos \theta$ and $F \sin \theta$ in two directions
  at right angles to each other.

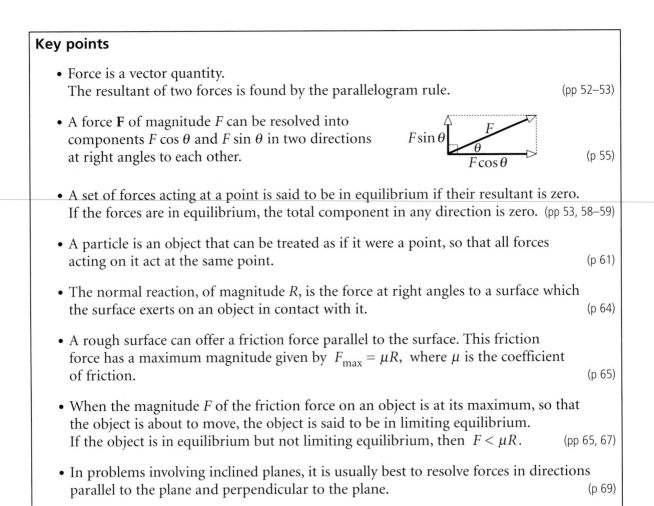

  (p 55)

- A set of forces acting at a point is said to be in equilibrium if their resultant is zero.
  If the forces are in equilibrium, the total component in any direction is zero. (pp 53, 58–59)

- A particle is an object that can be treated as if it were a point, so that all forces
  acting on it act at the same point. (p 61)

- The normal reaction, of magnitude R, is the force at right angles to a surface which
  the surface exerts on an object in contact with it. (p 64)

- A rough surface can offer a friction force parallel to the surface. This friction
  force has a maximum magnitude given by $F_{max} = \mu R$, where μ is the coefficient
  of friction. (p 65)

- When the magnitude F of the friction force on an object is at its maximum, so that
  the object is about to move, the object is said to be in limiting equilibrium.
  If the object is in equilibrium but not limiting equilibrium, then $F < \mu R$. (pp 65, 67)

- In problems involving inclined planes, it is usually best to resolve forces in directions
  parallel to the plane and perpendicular to the plane. (p 69)

Mixed questions (answers p 149)

1 The forces **P** and **Q** shown here can be written, in newtons, as
   P = 5**i** + 4**j**, **Q** = 3**i** − 2**j**.

   (a) Find, in terms of **i** and **j**, the resultant force **P** + **Q**.

   (b) Find the magnitude of the resultant and the angle between
   it and the vector **i**.

2 Two forces, of magnitude 6 N and 3 N, act on a particle.
   The angle between the two forces is 120°. Find

   (a) the magnitude of the resultant of the two forces

   (b) the angle the resultant makes with the direction of
   the 6 N force

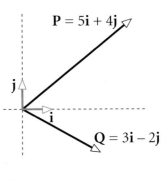

3 The three forces shown in this diagram are in equilibrium.

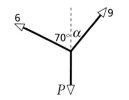

Find

(a) the size of angle α

(b) the value of P

4 A particle of weight 8 N is attached to two light strings inclined at angles of 30° and 50° to the vertical, as shown here. The particle is in equilibrium. Find the tension in each string.

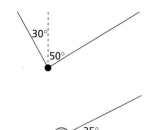

5 A bead of weight 2 N is threaded on to a rough horizontal pole. The coefficient of friction between the bead and the pole is 0.3. The bead is attached to a light string which is at an angle of 25° to the pole.
The bead is in limiting equilibrium.

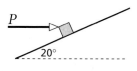

(a) Find the tension in the string.

(b) Find the normal reaction on the bead.

6 A box of weight 20 N rests on a rough plane inclined at an angle of 20° to the horizontal. A horizontal thrust of magnitude P N acts on the box.
The box is in limiting equilibrium, about to slide down the plane.
The coefficient of friction between the box and the plane is 0.3.

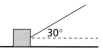

(a) Draw a diagram showing all the forces acting on the box.

(b) Find the value of P.

(c) Find the normal reaction on the box.

7 A small object of weight 5 N is on a rough horizontal surface. The coefficient of friction between the object and the surface is 0.5. The object is pulled by a string inclined at 30° to the horizontal and is in equilibrium. The tension in the string is of magnitude T N.

(a) Show that the normal reaction is of magnitude $(5 - 0.5T)$ N.

(b) Show that $T \leq 2.24$.

8 A box of weight 25 N is on a rough plane inclined at 40° to the horizontal. A light string is attached to the box and is inclined at an angle of 15° to the plane as shown in the diagram. The tension in the string is 20 N.
The box is in limiting equilibrium, about to move up the plane.

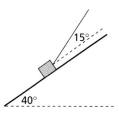

Find the coefficient of friction.

Test yourself (answers p 149)

1 Two constant forces, $(5\mathbf{i} - 3\mathbf{j})\,$N and $(2\mathbf{i} + 7\mathbf{j})\,$N, act on a particle, where $\mathbf{i}$ and $\mathbf{j}$ are perpendicular unit vectors.

(a) Find, in the form $(a\mathbf{i} + b\mathbf{j})$, the resultant force $\mathbf{F}$ acting on the particle.

(b) Find the magnitude of $\mathbf{F}$.

(c) Find the angle between $\mathbf{F}$ and the unit vector $\mathbf{j}$.

2 Two forces, $\mathbf{P}$ and $\mathbf{Q}$, act on a particle. The force $\mathbf{P}$ has magnitude 5 N and the force $\mathbf{Q}$ has magnitude 3 N. The angle between the directions of $\mathbf{P}$ and $\mathbf{Q}$ is 40°, as shown. The resultant of $\mathbf{P}$ and $\mathbf{Q}$ is $\mathbf{F}$.

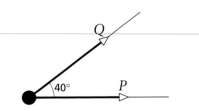

(a) Find, to three significant figures, the magnitude of $\mathbf{F}$.

(b) Find, in degrees to one decimal place, the angle between the directions of $\mathbf{F}$ and $\mathbf{P}$.

Edexcel

3 The three forces shown in this diagram are in equilibrium. Find the values of P and Q.

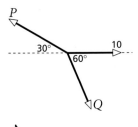

4 A particle of weight 3 N is attached to one end of a light inextensible string. The other end of the string is attached to a fixed point O. A horizontal force of magnitude 2 N is applied to the particle as shown. The particle is in equilibrium.

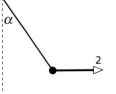

(a) Find the angle, α, the string makes with the vertical.

(b) Find the tension in the string.

5 A sledge of weight 15 N rests on horizontal ground. The coefficient of friction between the sledge and the ground is 0.3. The sledge is pulled by a force of 4 N acting at an angle of 30° to the horizontal. It is also pushed by a horizontal force of P N. The sledge is in equilibrium and can be modelled as a particle.

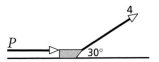

(a) Find the magnitude of the normal reaction of the ground on the sledge.

(b) Show that $P \leq 0.436$ (to 3 s.f.).

6 A box of weight 20 N lies on a rough plane inclined at 25° to the horizontal. A horizontal force of magnitude 30 N acts on the box as shown in the diagram.

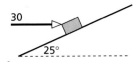

The box is in limiting equilibrium, on the point of moving up the plane. Find the coefficient of friction between the box and the plane.

4 Newton's laws of motion 1

In this chapter you will learn how to
- solve problems involving impulse and the conservation of momentum
- use Newton's first and second laws of motion

A Mass and momentum (answers p 150)

The **mass** of an object is measured in kilograms. It is the 'quantity of matter' in the object.

Mass is not the same as weight. Weight is the force of gravity acting downwards on an object and is measured in newtons. If the object is moved to the surface of the Moon, the force of gravity there is less than that of the Earth, so the object weighs less on the Moon. But the mass stays the same, wherever the object is.

A1 Imagine a light plastic ball and a heavy metal ball.
You kick the light ball and then give a kick of the same strength to the heavy ball.
Which ball will move faster?

The fundamental principles of mechanics were formulated by Isaac Newton (1642–1727). When Newton considered the situation just described, he started with the idea that the same 'amount of kick' should give the same 'amount of motion' to the two objects. He may have thought something like this:

> Imagine that I have a 1 kg object. I give it a kick and it moves away at $10\,\text{m s}^{-1}$.
> Now imagine that I have a 2 kg object and I give it the same amount of kick.
> The 2 kg object can be thought of as two 1 kg objects and the kick is shared
> equally between the two. Each 1 kg object gets half the amount of kick, and
> so moves at $5\,\text{m s}^{-1}$. In other words, the whole 2 kg object moves at $5\,\text{m s}^{-1}$.

Notice that the product mass × velocity is the same in both cases. Newton called this quantity **momentum**. The kick, when given to a 1 kg object, gives it a momentum of $1 \times 10 = 10\,\text{kg m s}^{-1}$. (Notice the units.) The same kick given to a 2 kg object gives it the same momentum of $2 \times 5 = 10\,\text{kg m s}^{-1}$.

Because velocity is a vector quantity, so is momentum. If objects are all moving along a straight line, momentum is positive in one direction and negative in the other.

$\overset{2\,\text{m s}^{-1}}{\longrightarrow}$ $\overset{3\,\text{m s}^{-1}}{\longleftarrow}$
(7 kg)   (5 kg)
Momentum: $14\,\text{kg m s}^{-1}$ $-15\,\text{kg m s}^{-1}$

> **K**
> The momentum of a moving object is the product mass × velocity.
> Momentum is a vector quantity.

A2 A footballer gives the same kick to two balls, one of mass 0.5 kg and the other of mass 1.5 kg. The first ball moves at $6\,\text{m s}^{-1}$.
What is the velocity of the second?

A3 An object of mass 2.4 kg is kicked and moves with a velocity of $5\,\text{m s}^{-1}$.
The same kick given to a second object causes it to move with a velocity of $3\,\text{m s}^{-1}$.
What is the mass of the second object?

Conservation of momentum

Imagine two objects A and B moving towards each other on a straight line.

> A has a mass of 2 kg and a velocity of 8 m s⁻¹.
> B has a mass of 3 kg and a velocity of -4 m s⁻¹
> (that is, 4 m s⁻¹ in the opposite direction).

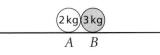

The objects collide with each other.

When they collide, it is as if each object 'kicks' the other. Newton assumed that the two kicks are equal and opposite.

If the two objects are considered together, the total amount of kick on the pair is zero, because the two kicks are equal and opposite.

From this it follows that the total momentum of the two objects will be the same before and after the collision.

> Suppose that, after the collision, A moves with velocity v_A and B with velocity v_B.
>
> Before the collision, the momentum of A (in kg m s⁻¹) was $2 \times 8 = 16$, and the momentum of B was $3 \times -4 = -12$.
>
> So the total momentum before the collision was $16 - 12 = 4$.
>
> The total momentum afterwards is $2v_A + 3v_B$.
>
> It follows that $2v_A + 3v_B = 4$.

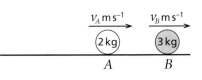

This equation is not enough to find the values of v_A and v_B. But if one of the values is given, the other can be calculated.

> **K** If two objects moving on a straight line collide, the total momentum before the collision is equal to the total momentum after the collision.
>
> Suppose that an object with mass m_1 and velocity u_1 collides with an object with mass m_2 and velocity u_2. Afterwards m_1 moves with velocity v_1 and m_2 with velocity v_2. Then
>
> $$m_1u_1 + m_2u_2 = m_1v_1 + m_2v_2$$
>
> This is called the **principle of conservation of linear momentum**.

Here are some of the things that might happen when two objects, moving on a straight line, collide.

Before

Collision

After

| Both moving forwards before and after | 1st moving backwards after | 2nd stationary before; moving forwards after | 2nd stationary before; 1st stationary after | 2nd moving backwards before; forwards after |

There is one case that sometimes arises in problems. This is where the two objects stick together, or **coalesce**, after the collision. They become one combined object.

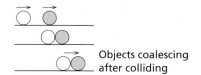

Objects coalescing after colliding

The mass of the combined object is, of course, the sum of the masses of the individual objects.

Whenever the velocity of an object, before or after the collision, is **backwards**, it must be entered as **negative** in the conservation of momentum equation.

Example 1

An object of mass 0.5 kg moving on a straight line with a speed of $6 \, \text{m s}^{-1}$ collides with an object of mass 2.5 kg moving in the same direction with a speed of $2 \, \text{m s}^{-1}$.

After the collision, the 0.5 kg object moves backwards at $0.4 \, \text{m s}^{-1}$. What are the speed and direction of the other object after the collision?

Solution

Sketch the situation before and after the collision.

Substitute the known values into $m_1 u_1 + m_2 u_2 = m_1 v_1 + m_2 v_2$.

Notice that v_1 is negative (backwards), so $v_1 = -0.4$.

From conservation of momentum: $0.5 \times 6 + 2.5 \times 2 = 0.5 \times -0.4 + 2.5 v_2$

$$\Rightarrow \qquad 8.2 = 2.5 v_2$$

$$\Rightarrow \qquad v_2 = 3.28$$

The 2.5 kg object moves at $3.28 \, \text{m s}^{-1}$ forwards.

Example 2

An object of mass 3 kg moving on a straight line with a speed of $8 \, \text{m s}^{-1}$ collides with a stationary object of mass 2 kg.

After the collision the two objects coalesce. Find the speed of the combined object after the collision.

Solution

Sketch the situation before and after the collision.
Notice that the speed of the second object before the collision is 0.
The final speed of the combined object has been called $v \, \text{m s}^{-1}$.

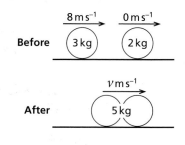

From conservation of momentum: $3 \times 8 + 2 \times 0 = 5v$

$$\Rightarrow \qquad 24 = 5v$$

$$\Rightarrow \qquad v = 4.8$$

The combined object moves at $4.8 \, \text{m s}^{-1}$ after the collision.

Exercise A (answers p 150)

1 Two objects A and B are moving on a straight line.
   A has mass 7 kg and is moving forwards at 2.5 m s^{-1}.
   B has mass 5 kg and is moving backwards at 1.5 m s^{-1}.

   (a) Find the momentum of A.

   (b) Explain why the momentum of B is not 7.5 kg m s^{-1} and write
   down the correct value.

2 An object of mass 5 kg moving on a straight line with a speed of 4 m s^{-1} collides
   with an object of mass 2 kg moving in the same direction with a speed of 3 m s^{-1}.

   Immediately after the collision, the 5 kg object moves forwards at 3.6 m s^{-1}.
   What are the speed and direction of the other object after the collision?

3 An object of mass 3.5 kg moving on a straight line with a speed of 6 m s^{-1} collides with
   an object of mass 1.5 kg moving in the opposite direction with a speed of 2 m s^{-1}.

   Immediately after the collision, the 3.5 kg object moves forwards at 3 m s^{-1}.
   What are the speed and direction of the other object after the collision?

4 A model railway truck of mass 0.6 kg is moving along a straight horizontal track
   with a speed of 0.5 m s^{-1} when it collides with a stationary truck of mass 0.9 kg.

   On colliding, the two trucks are coupled and move together at the same speed.
   Find the speed of the trucks immediately after the collision.

5 Three trucks A, B, C, of masses 5 kg, 3 kg and 2 kg respectively, are on a
   straight horizontal track as shown in the diagram below.
   A is moving towards B with a speed of 0.8 m s^{-1}. B and C are stationary.

   0.8 m s^{-1}

   | A | 5 kg | | B | 3 kg | | C | 2 kg |

   A collides with B and attaches itself to B. Then the pair collides with C and all
   three trucks are attached together and move with the same speed. Find this speed.

6 A particle of mass m kg is moving in a straight line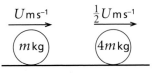
   with a velocity of U m s^{-1}.
   A second particle of mass $4m$ kg is moving in the
   same straight line, ahead of the first particle, with
   a velocity of $\frac{1}{2}U$ m s^{-1}.

   The particles collide and coalesce. Show that the velocity of the combined
   particle immediately after the collision is $\frac{3}{5}U$ m s^{-1}.

7 An object A of mass 3 kg, moving in a straight line with a speed of 0.2 m s^{-1}, collides
   with an object B, of mass m kg, moving in the opposite direction with the same speed as A.

   Immediately after the collision A is stationary and B moves with a speed of 0.3 m s^{-1}.
   Find the value of m.

B Force, momentum and impulse (answers p 150)

The most significant advances in mechanics were made by Isaac Newton. From the time of the ancient Greeks it had been assumed that if an object is moving, then there has to be an explanation – a cause of the motion. It was thought that if this cause was removed, the object would stop moving.

Newton said, however, that if an object has a certain momentum, then it will continue to have this momentum, unless a force acts on the object and changes its momentum.

Imagine, for example, an object of mass 3 kg sliding in a straight line on perfectly smooth horizontal ice with a velocity of $2\,\mathrm{m\,s^{-1}}$ (so that its momentum is $6\,\mathrm{kg\,m\,s^{-1}}$). There is no horizontal force acting on the object, so it will continue to move with the same velocity for ever unless a force acts on it to change its momentum.

In reality, of course, a horizontal force does act on the object, even on the smoothest ice – the force of friction. It is this force that causes the object to lose momentum and thus slow down. If there were no friction, the momentum, and so the velocity, of the object would not change.

An object at rest is simply an object whose velocity is zero. If an object is at rest and the resultant force acting on it is zero, then its momentum will not change – in other words it stays at rest.

Newton's first law of motion

K   An object at rest or moving in a straight line with constant velocity will continue like that unless acted upon by a force.

In this section and sections C and D we shall assume that all motion is in a horizontal straight line. Vertical forces (weight and normal reaction) balance out and so do not need to be considered.

D **B1** Imagine an object that can slide on a perfectly smooth horizontal surface. It is initially at rest.

(a) You blow on the object for a few seconds. What do you think will happen to the object

    (i) while you are blowing   (ii) after you have stopped blowing

(b) What do you think will be the effect of

    (i) blowing on the object (with the same force) but for twice the time

    (ii) blowing twice as hard but for the same time as originally

B2 Now imagine that you have two objects, one heavier than the other, both on a smooth horizontal surface. You blow, with the same force and for the same time, on each of them.

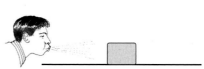

What do you think will happen?

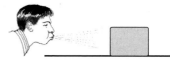

Newton said that the effect of a force on an object is to change its momentum. The change in momentum is related to the magnitude of the force and the time for which it acts.

In fact, the general rule is

change in momentum = force × time

In metric units (which had not been invented in Newton's time), the unit of force is called a **newton**. A force of 1 newton is defined as a force that produces $1\,\mathrm{kg\,m\,s^{-1}}$ of momentum when acting for 1 second.

The quantity force × time is called the **impulse**.
The impulse exerted by a force is equal to the change in momentum produced.
The units of impulse are newton seconds (N s).
Momentum can be measured either in kilogram metres per second ($\mathrm{kg\,m\,s^{-1}}$) or in newton seconds.

So, for example, a force of 3 newtons acting for 8 seconds will produce an impulse of $24\,\mathrm{N\,s}$. This could cause a 2 kg object to move at $12\,\mathrm{m\,s^{-1}}$, or a 4 kg object to move at $6\,\mathrm{m\,s^{-1}}$, and so on.

B3 Find the impulse exerted by a force of 6 newtons acting for 10 seconds.

B4 Jess blows with a force of 4 newtons on an object that is initially at rest. She blows for 10 seconds.

  (a) What is the impulse exerted on the object?

  (b) What is the change in momentum of the object?

  (c) If the mass of the object is 5 kg, what will its velocity be when Jess has stopped blowing?

If a force acts on an object that is already moving, then what happens depends on the direction of the force.

B5 An object of mass 4 kg is moving initially at $5\,\mathrm{m\,s^{-1}}$. Jess blows on the object with a force of 2 newtons for 3 seconds, in the same direction as the object is moving.

  (a) What was the object's momentum before Jess started blowing?

  (b) What is the magnitude of the impulse exerted on the object?

  (c) What is the object's momentum when Jess stops blowing?

  (d) Find the object's velocity when Jess stops blowing.

B6 Imagine that an object is sliding towards you on a smooth surface. You blow on the object for a time.

  (a) What will happen at first?

  (b) What will happen if you continue to blow on the object?

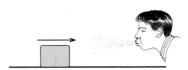

Force, impulse and momentum are all vector quantities, so direction is important. A force acting in the opposite direction to an object's motion will exert a negative impulse, so the object's momentum will be reduced.

Example 3

An object of mass 5 kg is moving with a velocity of $3\,\text{m}\,\text{s}^{-1}$.
A force of 4 newtons acts on the object for 2 seconds.
Find the final velocity of the object

(a) if the force acts in the same direction as the object's motion

(b) if the force acts in the opposite direction to the object's motion

Solution

(a) To start with, the object's momentum is $5 \times 3 = 15\,\text{N}\,\text{s}$.

The impulse exerted by a force of 4 N acting for 2 s $= 4 \times 2 = 8\,\text{N}\,\text{s}$.

So the object's final momentum $= 15 + 8 = 23\,\text{N}\,\text{s}$.

So its final velocity = momentum $\div$ mass $= 23 \div 5 = 4.6\,\text{m}\,\text{s}^{-1}$.

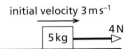

(b) In this case the force is $-4\,\text{N}$.

So the impulse exerted $= -4 \times 2 = -8\,\text{N}\,\text{s}$.

So the final momentum $= 15 - 8 = 7\,\text{N}\,\text{s}$.

So final velocity $= 7 \div 5 = 1.4\,\text{m}\,\text{s}^{-1}$.

Example 4

A ball of mass 0.5 kg is kicked towards a wall.
The motion of the ball is perpendicular to the wall.
Immediately before the ball hits the wall its speed is $5\,\text{m}\,\text{s}^{-1}$ and it rebounds with a speed of $3\,\text{m}\,\text{s}^{-1}$.
Find the magnitude of the impulse exerted by the wall on the ball during the impact.

Solution

Sketch the situation before and after the impact.
Notice that the velocity of the ball after the collision is negative.

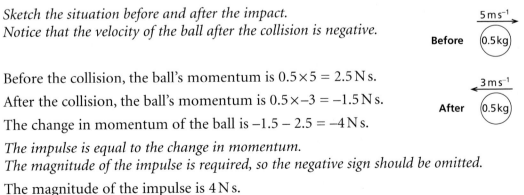

Before the collision, the ball's momentum is $0.5 \times 5 = 2.5\,\text{N}\,\text{s}$.

After the collision, the ball's momentum is $0.5 \times -3 = -1.5\,\text{N}\,\text{s}$.

The change in momentum of the ball is $-1.5 - 2.5 = -4\,\text{N}\,\text{s}$.

The impulse is equal to the change in momentum.
The magnitude of the impulse is required, so the negative sign should be omitted.

The magnitude of the impulse is $4\,\text{N}\,\text{s}$.

Exercise B (answers p 150)

1 A force of 2 newtons acts for 6 seconds on an object that is initially at rest.

   (a) Find the impulse, in N s, exerted by the force.

   (b) Given that the mass of the object is 3 kg, find its final velocity.

2 An object of mass 6 kg is initially moving with a velocity of $5 \, \text{m s}^{-1}$.
A force of 4 newtons acts on the object in the direction of motion for 3 seconds.

   (a) What is the initial momentum of the object?

   (b) Find the impulse exerted by the force on the object.

   (c) What is the final momentum of the object?

   (d) What is the final velocity of the object?

3 An object of mass 1.4 kg is moving with a velocity of $6.5 \, \text{m s}^{-1}$.
A force of 3.5 newtons acts on the object for 2 seconds in the direction
opposite to the object's motion. Find the final velocity of the object.

4 An object of mass 6 kg is moving on a straight line at $10 \, \text{m s}^{-1}$.
It is given an impulse and it continues to move on the straight line at $14 \, \text{m s}^{-1}$.
What is the magnitude of the impulse?

5 A ball of mass 0.25 kg is travelling on a straight line at $5 \, \text{m s}^{-1}$.
It is kicked and moves in the opposite direction on the same straight line at $7 \, \text{m s}^{-1}$.
What is the magnitude of the impulse exerted on the ball?

6 An object of mass 4 kg is moving on a straight line at $8 \, \text{m s}^{-1}$.
It is given an impulse in its direction of motion of 10 N s.
Find its velocity after receiving the impulse.

7 An object of mass 2 kg moving on a straight line with a speed of $6 \, \text{m s}^{-1}$ collides
with an object of mass 3 kg moving in the same direction with a speed of $2 \, \text{m s}^{-1}$.

   Immediately after the collision the 2 kg object moves forward at $3 \, \text{m s}^{-1}$.

   (a) Find the impulse exerted on the 2 kg object during the collision.

   (b) Use the principle of conservation of linear momentum to find the speed
       of the 3 kg object after the collision.

   (c) Find the impulse exerted on the 3 kg object during the collision.
       Comment on your answer.

8 A truck of mass 4 kg is moving along a straight horizontal track with a speed of $2.5 \, \text{m s}^{-1}$
when it collides with a truck of mass 1 kg moving towards it with a speed of $1.5 \, \text{m s}^{-1}$.

   The trucks are coupled during the collision and move together at the same speed.

   (a) Find the speed of the trucks immediately after the collision.

   (b) Find the magnitude of the impulse exerted by the 4 kg truck on the 1 kg truck
       during the collision.

9 A particle P, of mass $0.1\,\text{kg}$, is moving in a straight line with speed $3\,\text{m}\,\text{s}^{-1}$ when it collides with a stationary particle Q, of mass $0.5\,\text{kg}$. After the collision, P and Q move directly away from each other, each with speed $v\,\text{m}\,\text{s}^{-1}$.

(a) Find the value of v.

(b) Find the magnitude of the impulse exerted by P on Q during the collision.

C Force, mass and acceleration (answers p 150)

Suppose an object of mass $m\,\text{kg}$ is initially moving with velocity $u\,\text{m}\,\text{s}^{-1}$.
A force of F newtons acts on the object for a time t seconds.
As a result, the object's final velocity is $v\,\text{m}\,\text{s}^{-1}$.

We can use the relationship 'force × time = change in momentum' to find an equation linking F, t, m, u and v.

$$\text{It is} \quad Ft = mv - mu$$

From this it follows that $\quad Ft = m(v - u)$

$$\Rightarrow \quad F = m\left(\frac{v-u}{t}\right)$$

The expression $\dfrac{v-u}{t}$ represents $\dfrac{\text{change in velocity}}{\text{time}}$, which is the acceleration, a.

$$\text{So} \quad F = ma$$

This result is

Newton's second law of motion

K If a force of F newtons, acting on an object of mass $m\,\text{kg}$, causes an acceleration $a\,\text{m}\,\text{s}^{-2}$, then $F = ma$. The acceleration continues for as long as the force is acting, and if the force is constant, so is the acceleration.

This is one of the most frequently used equations in mechanics. When referring to it, you can shorten 'Newton's second law' to 'N2L'.

In diagrams, a double-headed arrow is usually used to show an acceleration.

C1 A force acting on an object of mass $2.5\,\text{kg}$ causes the object to accelerate at $6\,\text{m}\,\text{s}^{-2}$.
Find the magnitude of the force.

$6\,\text{m}\,\text{s}^{-2}$
$\boxed{2.5\,\text{kg}}$ —▷ $F\,\text{N}$

C2 A force of $24\,\text{N}$ acts on an object of mass $3\,\text{kg}$.
Find the object's acceleration.

$a\,\text{m}\,\text{s}^{-2}$
$\boxed{3\,\text{kg}}$ —▷ $24\,\text{N}$

C3 A force of $4.5\,\text{N}$ acts on an object and causes it to accelerate at $0.9\,\text{m}\,\text{s}^{-2}$.
Find the mass of the object.

A common situation to which Newton's second law can be applied is that of a vehicle moving on a horizontal road or track.

The force causing the vehicle's acceleration could be the tension in a cable or rope pulling the vehicle, or the thrust of a person pushing the vehicle.

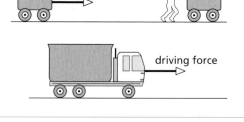

In a vehicle such as a car, lorry or train, the vehicle's engine exerts a **driving force** (or **propulsive force**). Although the engine is part of the vehicle, the driving force can be treated as if it were an external force. (The reason for this is given in chapter 6.)

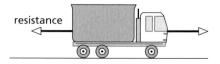

There may also be forces acting in the opposite direction resisting the motion of the vehicle. Such forces of resistance include friction (dealt with in more detail in chapter 5), air resistance, and the force of the vehicle's brakes.

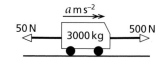

The force F that appears in the equation $F = ma$ is the resultant force on the vehicle, that is: driving force − resistance.

Forces of resistance stop acting as soon as the vehicle comes to rest. (For example, putting on a car's brakes will bring the car to rest, but keeping them on will not propel the car backwards!)

C4 A van of mass 3000 kg is being driven on a horizontal road. The van's engine exerts a driving force of 500 N. Resistances to motion amount to 50 N.

(a) What is the resultant horizontal force on the van?

(b) Use the equation $F = ma$ to calculate the acceleration of the van.

K If an object is moving with constant velocity, then its acceleration is zero. So the resultant force on the object is zero (propulsive force and resistance cancel out).

Example 5

A car of mass 1200 kg, travelling on a straight horizontal road, is accelerating at $0.4 \, \text{m s}^{-2}$. The driving force of the car's engine is 1520 N. Find the force of resistance.

Solution

Start by drawing a sketch. The sketch shows that R N stands for the unknown force of resistance. Vertical forces (which cancel out) are not shown here.

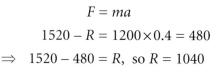

The resultant force acting on the car is $(1520 − R)$ N.

Use N2L ('Newton's second law'):

$$F = ma$$
$$1520 − R = 1200 \times 0.4 = 480$$
$$\Rightarrow \quad 1520 − 480 = R, \text{ so } R = 1040$$

The force of resistance is 1040 N.

---

1 A lorry of mass 7500 kg is being driven along a straight horizontal road. The driving force of the lorry's engine is 8000 N. The force of resistance is 2000 N. Find the acceleration of the lorry.

2 A truck of mass 320 kg is pulled along a horizontal track by a horizontal cable. The truck is accelerating at $0.2\,\mathrm{m\,s^{-2}}$. Forces of resistance amount to 60 N. Find the tension in the cable.

3 The driving force of a railway locomotive is 24 000 N. The mass of the locomotive is 20 000 kg. Given that the locomotive is accelerating at $1.1\,\mathrm{m\,s^{-2}}$ along a straight horizontal track, find the force of resistance.

4 A car is travelling at a constant speed of $3\,\mathrm{m\,s^{-1}}$ along a straight horizontal road.

(a) What is the acceleration of the car?

(b) The driving force of the car's engine is 180 N. What is the force of resistance?

5 A van of mass 640 kg is being driven along a straight horizontal road. The engine is switched off and the brakes applied. The braking force is 200 N and other resistances to motion amount to 40 N.

(a) The equation $F = ma$ is applied to this situation. If the direction of motion is taken as positive, explain why F is negative.

(b) Find the value of the acceleration a, and explain what it means.

6 A motor boat is of mass 800 kg. The propulsive force of its engine can be varied. When the propulsive force is P N, the boat's acceleration is $1.5\,\mathrm{m\,s^{-2}}$. When the propulsive force is $2P$ N, the acceleration is $3.2\,\mathrm{m\,s^{-2}}$.

Assuming that the force of resistance, R N, is the same in both cases, find the values of P and R.

D Solving problems in one dimension (answers p 151)

The equation $F = ma$ can be used together with the constant acceleration equations ($v = u + at$ and so on) to solve problems. The problems are generally of two types.

- Given F and m, use $F = ma$ to find a.
  Then use the constant acceleration equations to find other quantities.

- Given some of the values of u, v, s, t, use the constant acceleration equations to find a.
  Then use $F = ma$ to find F.

D1 A car of mass 1200 kg is travelling on a straight horizontal road. The driving force of the engine is 760 N. Resistance to motion is 40 N.

(a) Find the acceleration of the car.

(b) Find the time taken for the car to increase its velocity from $1.5\,\mathrm{m\,s^{-1}}$ to $4.5\,\mathrm{m\,s^{-1}}$.

(c) Show that the distance travelled by the car during this time is 15 m.

D2 A van of mass 500 kg travelling on a straight horizontal road increases its velocity from $3\,\text{m\,s}^{-1}$ to $6\,\text{m\,s}^{-1}$ over a distance of 27 m.
Given that the resultant force on the van is of constant magnitude, find

(a) the acceleration of the van **(b)** the resultant force on the van

Example 6

A boat of mass 400 kg has an outboard motor with a propulsive force of 350 N.
The boat is initially at rest. The motor is started and run for 6 seconds.
During this time a constant force of resistance acts on the boat.
At the end of the 6 seconds the velocity of the boat is $4.2\,\text{m\,s}^{-1}$.

(a) Find the acceleration of the boat.

(b) Find the force of resistance on the boat.

The motor is switched off. The force of resistance remains the same.

(c) Find the deceleration of the boat.

(d) Find the time taken for the boat to come to rest.

(e) Find the distance travelled by the boat in this time.

Solution

(a) *Find a by using the constant acceleration equations.*
$u = 0$, $v = 4.2$, $t = 6$, $a = ?$

Use $v = u + at$: $4.2 = 0 + 6a$

$\Rightarrow \quad a = 0.7$

The acceleration is $0.7\,\text{m\,s}^{-2}$.

(b) *Sketch a force diagram.*

Apply N2L: $350 - R = 400 \times 0.7 = 280$

$\Rightarrow \quad R = 70$

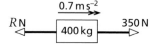

The force of resistance is 70 N.

(c) *With the motor switched off, the only force on the boat is the resistance.*
As this acts in the opposite direction to the motion, its value is $-70\,\text{N}$.

Apply N2L: $-70 = 400a$

$\Rightarrow \quad a = -0.175$

The deceleration is $0.175\,\text{m\,s}^{-2}$.

(d) For this part of the motion, $u = 4.2$, $v = 0$, $a = -0.175$, $t = ?$

Use $v = u + at$: $0 = 4.2 - 0.175t$

$\Rightarrow \quad t = \dfrac{4.2}{0.175} = 24$

The time taken is 24 s.

(e) Use $s = \frac{1}{2}(u + v)t$: $s = \frac{1}{2}(4.2 + 0) \times 24 = 50.4$ (*Or you could use $v^2 = u^2 + 2as$.*)

The distance travelled is 50.4 m.

Exercise D (answers p 151)

1 A lorry of mass 4500 kg has an engine with a driving force of 1800 N.
Given that there are no resistances to motion, find

  (a) the acceleration of the lorry

  (b) the time taken for the lorry to reach a speed of $5\,\text{m s}^{-1}$ from rest on level ground

  (c) the distance travelled by the lorry in this time

2 A boat of mass 250 kg has an engine with a propulsive force of 230 N.
As the boat moves through water it experiences a constant force of resistance $R\,\text{N}$.
The boat accelerates from rest and moves in a straight line.
After travelling for 10 seconds it is 40 m from its starting point.

  (a) Find the acceleration of the boat.

  (b) Find the value of R.

3 A car of mass 800 kg, whose engine has a driving force of 3600 N, is travelling
along a horizontal straight road with a constant velocity of $15\,\text{m s}^{-1}$.

  (a) Find the force of resistance.

The car's engine is disengaged. The force of resistance stays the same.

  (b) Find the deceleration of the car.

  (c) Find the distance the car travels before coming to rest.

4 A boat of mass 400 kg is at rest on a calm sea when a wind starts blowing with a
constant force on the boat. As a result the boat reaches a velocity of $1.5\,\text{m s}^{-1}$
after travelling a distance of 50 m. Find the resultant force acting on the boat
during this motion.

5 A van of mass 7500 kg has an engine whose driving force is 4000 N.
When it travels on a straight horizontal road it is subject to a resistance $R\,\text{N}$,
which is always the same.
When the van carries no load it will accelerate from rest to $5\,\text{m s}^{-1}$ in 10 s.

  (a) Find the value of R.

  (b) Find the time taken for the van to reach a speed of $5\,\text{m s}^{-1}$ from rest
    when it carries a load of mass 1500 kg.

6 A lorry accelerates uniformly along a straight horizontal road.
Its speed increases from $10\,\text{m s}^{-1}$ to $20\,\text{m s}^{-1}$ in 25 seconds.

  (a) Find the acceleration of the lorry.

  (b) Find the distance travelled in this time.

  (c) The mass of the lorry is 12 tonnes and the driving force of its engine is 6000 N.
    Find the force of resistance acting on the lorry.

E Vertical motion (answers p 151)

From the time of the ancient Greeks, people believed that heavy objects fall to the ground faster than light objects. The Italian scientist Galileo Galilei (1564–1642) showed that not only was this untrue, but that all objects, whatever their mass, fall with the same constant acceleration (provided air resistance is ignored).

Galileo used an interesting argument to show that the earlier belief was incorrect.

Suppose a heavy object falls faster than a light object. What should happen if you connect a light object to a heavy one? Because the light object falls more slowly it should drag the heavy one back and cause it to fall more slowly.

On the other hand, the combined object is heavier than the heavy object alone and so should fall faster. The only way to resolve this dilemma is for the light and heavy objects to fall together.

Later measurements have shown the following to be true.

> In the absence of air resistance, all objects fall to the Earth with the same constant acceleration, whose value is approximately $9.8 \, \text{m s}^{-2}$.
> This acceleration due to gravity is denoted by g. (In fact, there is a small variation in the value of g over the Earth's surface: it is larger at the equator than at the poles.)

From Newton's second law ($F = ma$) it follows that the force of gravity acting on an object of mass m kg is mg N. This downward force is, of course, the object's weight.

> An object of mass m kg has a weight of mg newtons.

Although g is an acceleration, in most problems it appears as a multiplier from mass m (kg) to weight mg (newtons).

E1 What is the weight, in newtons, of a ball of mass 1.5 kg?

E2 An object of mass 5 kg falls towards the ground. Air resistance acting on the object is 2.5 N.

    (a) Copy the sketch and complete it by adding the weight of the object in newtons.

    (b) Use Newton's second law to find the object's acceleration.

Example 7

A bucket of mass 2.5 kg is pulled upwards by a rope.
The bucket is accelerating at $2.2 \, \text{m s}^{-2}$. Find the tension in the rope.

Solution

The weight of the bucket $= mg = 2.5 \times 9.8 = 24.5 \, \text{N}$.

The sketch shows the two forces acting on the bucket.

Apply N2L: $T - 24.5 = 2.5 \times 2.2 = 5.5$

        $\Rightarrow$ $T = 30$

The tension in the rope is 30 N.

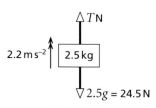

1 A load of mass 4 kg is pulled upwards by a rope.
   The tension in the rope is 45 N.

   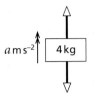

   (a) Copy the sketch and label each force with its
       magnitude in newtons.

   (b) What is the resultant upward force on the load?

   (c) Find the acceleration of the load.

2 An object of mass 3.5 kg is pulled upwards by a cable.

   (a) Suppose that the object is moving with constant speed.
       Explain why the tension in the cable must be 3.5g newtons.

   (b) Now suppose the object moves with an upward acceleration of $1.2\,\text{m s}^{-2}$.
       Find the tension in the cable.

   (c) The maximum tension that the cable can withstand is 50 newtons.
       Find the maximum upward acceleration of the object, to 3 s.f.

3 A lift of mass 600 kg is attached to a cable which pulls it upwards.
   The tension in the cable has a maximum possible value.

   (a) When the lift is empty, its maximum possible upward acceleration is $2.5\,\text{m s}^{-2}$.
       Find the maximum possible tension in the cable.

   (b) Find the maximum possible upward acceleration of the lift when it carries
       a load of mass 100 kg.

4 A ball of mass 0.4 kg is dropped from the top of a cliff of height 35 m.
   As it falls, the ball is subject to a constant force of air resistance of magnitude 1.5 N.

   (a) Find the magnitude of the resultant downward force on the ball as it falls.

   (b) Find the acceleration of the ball as it falls.

   (c) Find the time it takes the ball to reach the foot of the cliff.

5 A stone of mass 0.5 kg is thrown upwards from the ground.
   Air resistance on the stone has a constant magnitude of 0.7 N.

   (a) Show that the deceleration of the stone as it travels upwards is $11.2\,\text{m s}^{-2}$.

   (b) Find the acceleration of the stone as it travels downwards.

   (c) Given that the stone was thrown with an initial speed of $14\,\text{m s}^{-1}$,
       find the maximum height reached by the stone.

6 A ball of mass 0.5 kg is dropped from the surface of a swimming pool.
   As it falls through the water the ball is subject to a constant force of resistance
   of 2.5 N. The depth of the pool is 3.5 m.

   (a) Show that the acceleration of the ball is $4.8\,\text{m s}^{-2}$.

   (b) Find the time taken for the ball to reach the bottom of the pool.

   (c) Find the speed of the ball when it hits the bottom.

F Motion in two dimensions

K

Force and acceleration are both vector quantities.
In vector form, Newton's second law is $\mathbf{F} = m\mathbf{a}$.

Problems in two dimensions can be solved using the equations $\mathbf{F} = m\mathbf{a}$ and

$$\text{acceleration} = \frac{\text{change in velocity}}{\text{time taken}}.$$

Example 8

A particle of mass 3 kg is moving with a velocity of $(2\mathbf{i} + 3\mathbf{j})\,\text{m s}^{-1}$.
A constant force $\mathbf{F}$ newtons acts on the particle.
After 10 seconds the particle is moving with velocity $(5\mathbf{i} - 2\mathbf{j})\,\text{m s}^{-1}$. Find

(a) the acceleration of the particle   **(b)** the magnitude of $\mathbf{F}$

Solution

(a) *Use* $\text{acceleration} = \dfrac{\text{change in velocity}}{\text{time taken}}.$ $\mathbf{a} = \dfrac{(5\mathbf{i} - 2\mathbf{j}) - (2\mathbf{i} + 3\mathbf{j})}{10}$

$$= \frac{3\mathbf{i} - 5\mathbf{j}}{10} = 0.3\mathbf{i} - 0.5\mathbf{j}$$

The acceleration of the particle is $(0.3\mathbf{i} - 0.5\mathbf{j})\,\text{m s}^{-2}$.

(b) Use N2L $(\mathbf{F} = m\mathbf{a})$: $\mathbf{F} = 3(0.3\mathbf{i} - 0.5\mathbf{j}) = 0.9\mathbf{i} - 1.5\mathbf{j}$

So $F = \sqrt{0.9^2 + 1.5^2} = 1.75$ (to 3 s.f.)

The magnitude of $\mathbf{F}$ is 1.75 N (to 3 s.f.).

Exercise F (answers p 151)

1 A particle of mass 5 kg is initially at the origin and moving with velocity $(\mathbf{i} + \mathbf{j})\,\text{m s}^{-1}$.
It accelerates uniformly at $(4\mathbf{i} - 3\mathbf{j})\,\text{m s}^{-2}$. Find

(a) the resultant force on the particle   **(b)** the velocity of the particle after 20 seconds

2 A particle of mass 0.2 kg is moving with velocity $(5\mathbf{i} - 2\mathbf{j})\,\text{m s}^{-1}$ when it is
acted on by a constant force of $(3\mathbf{i} + 4\mathbf{j})$ newtons. Find

(a) the acceleration of the particle   **(b)** the velocity of the particle after 4 seconds

3 A particle of mass 2.5 kg acted on by a constant force passes through a point A
with velocity $(2\mathbf{i} + 3\mathbf{j})\,\text{m s}^{-1}$ and a point B with velocity $(10\mathbf{i} - \mathbf{j})\,\text{m s}^{-1}$.
The time taken to travel from A to B is 5 seconds. Find

(a) the acceleration of the particle

(b) the magnitude of the force acting on the particle

(c) the velocity of the particle when it passes through point C, 10 seconds
after passing through A.

4 A particle of mass 0.5 kg is moving under the action of a constant force. The initial velocity of the particle is $(-2\mathbf{i} + 3\mathbf{j})\,\text{m s}^{-1}$. After 10 seconds the velocity of the particle is $(6\mathbf{i} - 3\mathbf{j})\,\text{m s}^{-1}$.

(a) Find the magnitude of the force acting on the particle.

(b) Find the angle the direction of the force makes with the vector $\mathbf{i}$.

5 A particle of mass 2 kg is acted on by forces of $(2\mathbf{i} + 3\mathbf{j})\,\text{N}$ and $(4\mathbf{i} - 5\mathbf{j})\,\text{N}$.

(a) Find the resultant force acting on the particle.

(b) Given that the particle was initially at rest, find its velocity after 6 seconds.

6 A particle P, of mass 0.5 kg, moves under the action of two constant forces $(-\mathbf{i} + 4\mathbf{j})\,\text{N}$ and $(3\mathbf{i} + 2\mathbf{j})\,\text{N}$.

(a) Find the resultant force $\mathbf{F}$ acting on P.

(b) Find the magnitude of the acceleration of P.

(c) Given that the initial velocity of P is $(2\mathbf{i} - \mathbf{j})\,\text{m s}^{-1}$, find its velocity after 5 seconds.

Key points

- The momentum of an object is defined as mass $\times$ velocity.
  Momentum is a vector quantity.
  Its units are kilogram metres per second (kg m s^{-1}) or newton seconds (N s). (pp 75, 80)

- If an object of mass m_1 travelling with velocity u_1 collides with an object of mass m_2 travelling with velocity u_2, and if v_1 and v_2 are the velocities of the objects immediately after the collision, then

$$m_1 u_1 + m_2 u_2 = m_1 v_1 + m_2 v_2$$

  This is called the principle of conservation of linear momentum. (p 76)

- The quantity force $\times$ time is called impulse.
  The impulse exerted by a force is equal to the change in momentum produced.
  The units of impulse are newton seconds. (p 80)

- An object at rest or moving in a straight line with constant velocity will continue like that unless acted upon by a force. (Newton's first law) (p 79)

- If a force of F newtons, acting on an object of mass m kg, causes an acceleration $a\,\text{m s}^{-2}$, then $F = ma$. (Newton's second law) (p 83)

- If an object is moving with constant velocity, then its acceleration is zero. So the resultant force on the object is zero. (p 84)

- An object of mass m kg has a weight of mg newtons ($g = 9.8$). (p 88)

- In vector form, Newton's second law is $\mathbf{F} = m\mathbf{a}$. (p 90)

Mixed questions (answers p 151)

1 A particle A of mass m kg, moving in a straight line with speed u m s^{-1}, collides with a second particle B, of mass $4m$ kg, moving in the opposite direction with speed u m s^{-1}. As a result of the collision, the direction of A is reversed and A moves with speed $\frac{1}{2}u$ m s^{-1}.

Show that the speed of B after the collision is $\frac{5}{8}u$ m s^{-1}.

2 A van of mass 2500 kg drives along a straight horizontal road at a constant speed of 14 m s^{-1} for 30 seconds. As it approaches a junction its brakes are applied for 10 seconds, reducing its speed to 5 m s^{-1}.

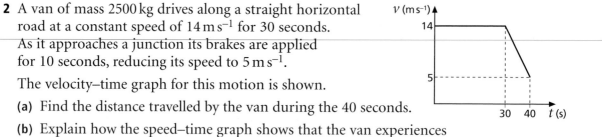

The velocity–time graph for this motion is shown.

(a) Find the distance travelled by the van during the 40 seconds.

(b) Explain how the speed–time graph shows that the van experiences a constant retarding force when the brakes are applied.

(c) Find the magnitude of the retarding force.

3 A truck A, of mass 2 kg, is moving on a smooth horizontal track at 6 m s^{-1}. A truck B, of mass 3 kg, is moving on the same track in the same direction as A at 4 m s^{-1}. The trucks collide directly. During the collision A and B are coupled and move off together.

(a) Find the speed of the trucks immediately after the collision.

(b) Find the magnitude of the impulse exerted on B during the collision.

(c) After the collision, the trucks experience a constant force of resistance R N. The trucks come to rest 15 seconds after the collision. Find the value of R.

4 A particle of mass 5 kg, initially moving at $2\mathbf{j}$ m s^{-1}, is acted upon by a constant force of $(6\mathbf{i} - 4\mathbf{j})$ N.

Find an expression for the velocity of the particle at time t seconds.

5 A ball is projected vertically upwards with speed u m s^{-1} from a point A which is 1.5 m above the ground. The ball moves freely under gravity until it reaches the ground. The greatest height attained by the ball is 25.6 m above A.

(a) Show that $u = 22.4$.

The ball reaches the ground T seconds after it has been projected from A.

(b) Find, to two decimal places, the value of T.

The ground is soft and the ball sinks 2.5 cm into the ground before coming to rest. The mass of the ball is 0.6 kg. The ground is assumed to exert a constant resistive force of magnitude F newtons.

(c) Find, to three significant figures, the value of F.

(d) State one physical factor which could be taken into account to make the model used in this question more realistic.

Edexcel

Test yourself (answers p 152)

1 Two particles A and B have mass $0.12\,\text{kg}$ and $0.08\,\text{kg}$ respectively.
They are initially at rest on a smooth horizontal table.
Particle A is then given an impulse in the direction AB so that it moves
with speed $3\,\text{m s}^{-1}$ directly towards B.

(a) Find the magnitude of this impulse, stating clearly the units in which
your answer is given.

Immediately after the particles collide, the speed of A is $1.2\,\text{m s}^{-1}$, its direction
of motion being unchanged.

(b) Find the speed of B immediately after the collision.

(c) Find the magnitude of the impulse exerted on A during the collision.   Edexcel

2 A particle A of mass $0.4\,\text{kg}$ is moving along a straight line with speed $3\,\text{m s}^{-1}$.
Another particle B of mass $0.8\,\text{kg}$ is moving on the same straight line towards A
with a speed of $4\,\text{m s}^{-1}$. The particles collide directly.

Immediately after the collision A and B move in the same direction and
the speed of A is twice the speed of B.

(a) Find the speed of A immediately after the collision.

(b) Find the magnitude of the impulse exerted on A in the collision.

3 A go-kart of mass $500\,\text{kg}$ is travelling in a horizontal straight line with constant
acceleration. The go-kart's speed increases from $3.5\,\text{m s}^{-1}$ to $11\,\text{m s}^{-1}$ in 5 seconds.

(a) Calculate the acceleration of the go-kart.

(b) Calculate the distance the go-kart travels in the 5 seconds.

(c) The resistance to the motion of the go-kart is $95\,\text{N}$.
Find the driving force of the go-kart's engine.

4 A lift of mass $700\,\text{kg}$ is attached to a single vertical cable.
The lift accelerates upwards from rest at $0.4\,\text{m s}^{-2}$ for 5 seconds, travels at
constant speed for 20 seconds and then decelerates at $0.2\,\text{m s}^{-2}$ before coming to rest.

(a) Sketch a speed–time graph for the motion of the lift.

(b) Find the distance travelled by the lift.

(c) Find the tension in the cable while the lift is accelerating.

5 A particle of mass $3\,\text{kg}$ moves under the action of a constant force.
The initial velocity of the particle is $(-2\mathbf{i} + 3\mathbf{j})\,\text{m s}^{-1}$.
After 5 seconds the velocity of the particle is $(8\mathbf{i} + 18\mathbf{j})\,\text{m s}^{-1}$.

(a) Find the acceleration of the particle.

(b) Find the angle between the direction of the acceleration and the vector $\mathbf{j}$.

(c) Find the magnitude of the force acting on the particle.

(d) Find the speed of the particle after 10 seconds.

5 Newton's laws of motion 2

In this chapter you will
- learn about the friction force when an object is moving
- solve problems involving inclined surfaces

A Resolving forces (answers p 152)

In chapter 3 (page 55) you saw that a force can be resolved into two components at right angles to one another.

The force F, acting at an angle θ to Ox, is resolved into components

$F\cos\theta$ in direction Ox $\qquad$ $F\sin\theta$ in direction Oy

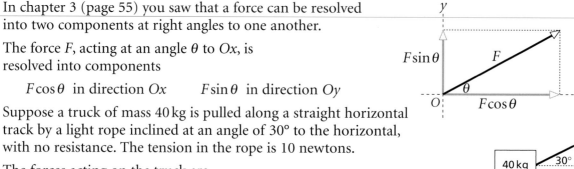

Suppose a truck of mass 40 kg is pulled along a straight horizontal track by a light rope inclined at an angle of 30° to the horizontal, with no resistance. The tension in the rope is 10 newtons.

The forces acting on the truck are

- the weight, $40g$ newtons (there is no need to replace g by 9.8 at this stage)
- the normal reaction, R newtons, of the track on the truck
- the tension, 10 newtons, in the rope

These three forces are shown in the force diagram, in which the truck is treated as a particle.

The truck has an acceleration, $a\,\text{m s}^{-2}$, which is shown by the double-headed arrow.

A1 The tension in the rope can be resolved into a horizontal component and a vertical component. Find the horizontal component.

A2 The acceleration of the truck is horizontal. The only force acting in this direction is the horizontal component of the tension. Use Newton's second law ($F = ma$) to find the acceleration of the truck.

A3 There is no vertical acceleration, so the resultant force in the vertical direction is zero. In other words, upward and downward forces balance each other.

The total upward force consists of R newtons and the vertical component of the tension. Use this fact, and the fact that $g = 9.8$, to find the value of R.

> **K** In situations involving horizontal motion, resolve vertically and horizontally.
>
> The acceleration is horizontal, so use Newton's second law horizontally.
> There is no vertical motion, so forces are in equilibrium vertically.

Example 1

A truck of mass 90 kg is pulled along a horizontal track by a rope inclined at 20° to the horizontal. The tension in the rope is 48 N. A horizontal force of resistance F N acts on the truck, which is moving with constant velocity. Find the value of F.

Solution

Sketch a force diagram.

The resultant horizontal force is $(48\cos 20° - F)$ N.

The velocity of the truck is constant, so its acceleration is 0.

Apply N2L: $48\cos 20° - F = 90 \times 0$. So $F = 48\cos 20° = 45.1$ (to 3 s.f.)

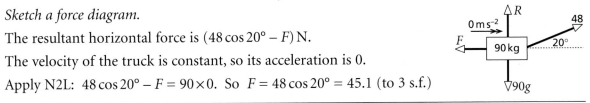

Example 2

A truck of mass 500 kg is pulled along a horizontal track by a rope inclined at 40° to the horizontal. A horizontal force of resistance, of magnitude 30 newtons, acts on the truck. The truck is accelerating at $0.2 \, \text{m s}^{-2}$. Find

(a) the tension in the rope   **(b)** the normal reaction of the track on the truck

Solution

Sketch a force diagram and show the acceleration on it.

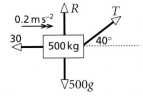

(a) The resultant horizontal force is $(T\cos 40° - 30)$ N.

Apply $F = ma$: $T\cos 40° - 30 = 500 \times 0.2$

$\Rightarrow \qquad T = \dfrac{130}{\cos 40°} = 169.7$

(b) Resolve vertically. (*There is no acceleration in this direction so upward and downward components balance.*)

$$T\sin 40° + R = 500g$$

$\Rightarrow \qquad 169.7\sin 40° + R = 500 \times 9.8$

$\Rightarrow \qquad R = 4900 - 109.1 = 4790$ (to 3 s.f.)

The tension is 170 N and the normal reaction is 4790 N (to 3 s.f.).

Exercise A (answers p 152)

1 A boat of mass 400 kg is pulled by a light cable inclined at 20° to the horizontal. The tension in the cable is 220 N. A horizontal resisting force of 50 newtons acts on the boat.

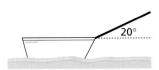

   (a) Draw a force diagram.

   (b) Show that the horizontal force on the boat is 157 N.

   (c) Find the acceleration of the boat.

2 A truck of mass 90 kg is pulled along a straight horizontal track by a light rope inclined at 30° to the horizontal. The truck experiences a horizontal force of resistance of 25 newtons.

(a) Given that the truck moves with a constant velocity, find

    (i) the tension in the rope

    (ii) the normal reaction of the track

(b) Redo part (a) given that the truck accelerates at $0.5 \, \text{m s}^{-2}$.

3 A truck of mass 800 kg is pulled along a straight horizontal track by a light cable inclined at 25° to the horizontal. A horizontal force of resistance, F newtons, acts on the truck. The tension in the cable is 320 newtons and the truck is accelerating at $0.3 \, \text{m s}^{-2}$. Find

(a) the value of F

(b) the normal reaction of the track on the truck

4 A ship of mass 50 000 kg is being pulled by two horizontal cables each making an angle of 20° with the direction of motion of the ship. The tension in each cable is 4000 newtons. The ship experiences a horizontal force of resistance of 1500 newtons. Find the acceleration of the ship.

5 The diagram shows a design for a fairground ride. A trolley moves along a raised horizontal track. Hanging from the trolley is a light cable attached to a seat, in which a person sits. Trolley, cable and person move with an acceleration in the direction of the arrow, with the cable making a constant angle of 60° with the horizontal. Air resistance can be ignored.

The mass of the seat plus person is 80 kg. The tension in the cable is T newtons.

(a) Explain why $T\sin 60° = 80g$ and hence find the value of T.

(b) Find the acceleration.

B Friction (answers p 152)

In chapter 3 (page 64), you saw that an object on a rough surface is able to resist a pulling force, but only up to a certain limit.

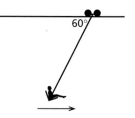

If the friction force is F, then $F \leq \mu R$, where R is the normal reaction of the surface on the object and μ is the coefficient of friction.

Once the object is moving, the magnitude of the friction force stays constant at μR.

(In reality the coefficient of friction is often smaller for a moving object than for a stationary one. This difference will be ignored.)

K   If an object is moving on a rough surface, the friction force F is equal to μR.

B1 A block of mass 60 kg is being pulled across a rough horizontal surface by a horizontal force P. The block is accelerating at $0.5\,\mathrm{m\,s^{-2}}$. The coefficient of friction between the block and the surface is 0.4.

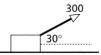

(a) Sketch a diagram showing all the forces acting on the block.

(b) Explain why the normal reaction R of the surface on the block is $60g$ newtons.

(c) Find the friction force on the block.

(d) Find the value of P.

B2 The same block is pulled across the same surface, but this time the pulling force is 300 N inclined at $30°$ to the horizontal.

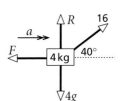

(a) Sketch a force diagram.

(b) By resolving vertically, find the normal reaction.

(c) Find the friction force on the block.

(d) By resolving horizontally and applying Newton's second law, find the acceleration of the block.

Example 3

A particle of mass 4 kg is pulled across a rough horizontal surface by a light rope inclined at $40°$ to the horizontal. The coefficient of friction between the surface and the particle is 0.2. The tension in the rope is 16 newtons. Find

(a) the normal reaction   (b) the friction force   (c) the acceleration of the particle

Solution

(a) Resolve vertically: $R + 16\sin 40° = 4g = 4 \times 9.8 = 39.2$

           So $R = 39.2 - 16\sin 40° = 28.92\,\mathrm{N}$

(b) $F = 0.2R = 5.784\,\mathrm{N}$

(c) Resolve horizontally and apply N2L: $16\cos 40° - 5.784 = 4a$

       So $a = \dfrac{6.473}{4} = 1.62$ (to 3 s.f.)

The acceleration is $1.62\,\mathrm{m\,s^{-2}}$ (to 3 s.f.).

Exercise B (answers p 152)

1 A sledge of mass 15 kg is pulled by a horizontal force of 78 newtons across a rough horizontal surface whose coefficient of friction is 0.5. Find the acceleration of the sledge.

2 A box of mass 50 kg is pushed across a rough horizontal floor by a horizontal force P newtons. The coefficient of friction between the floor and the box is 0.3. The box accelerates at $0.2\,\mathrm{m\,s^{-2}}$. Find the value of P.

3 A block of mass 25 kg is at rest on a rough horizontal floor.
The block is pushed by a horizontal force of 80 N.
The coefficient of friction between the floor and the block is 0.35.
Will the block start to move? Explain your answer.

4 A particle of mass 3 kg is sliding in a straight line across a smooth horizontal surface at a speed of $30\,\mathrm{m\,s^{-1}}$. It encounters a rough patch of length 50 m, where the coefficient of friction between the surface and the particle is 0.4.

$30\,\mathrm{m\,s^{-1}}$

—50 m—

(a) Calculate the deceleration of the particle as it moves over the rough patch.

(b) Calculate the speed with which it leaves the rough patch.

5 A sledge of mass 10 kg is pulled across a horizontal snow field by a light rope inclined at 30° to the horizontal.
The coefficient of friction between the sledge and the snow is 0.1.
The tension in the rope is 20 newtons.

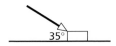

(a) Show that the normal reaction of the surface on the sledge is 88 newtons.

(b) Find the friction force on the sledge.

(c) Find the acceleration of the sledge.

6 A block of mass 20 kg is pushed across a rough floor by a force of 70 newtons inclined downwards at an angle of 35° to the horizontal.
The coefficient of friction between the block and the floor is 0.2.

(a) Show that the normal reaction of the floor on the block is approximately 236 N.

(b) Find the magnitude of the friction force on the block.

(c) Find the acceleration of the block.

7 A box of mass 30 kg is at rest on a horizontal floor.
It is pushed by a force P inclined at 20° to the horizontal.
The coefficient of friction between the box and the floor is 0.25.

(a) Find the maximum value of P for the box to remain in equilibrium.

(b) The force P is increased to 100 N. Find the acceleration of the box.

8 A sledge of mass 18 kg is pulled from rest across rough horizontal ground by a rope inclined at 25° to the horizontal.
The tension in the rope is 30 newtons.
After 10 seconds the sledge is moving at a speed of $4\,\mathrm{m\,s^{-1}}$.

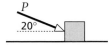

(a) Find the acceleration of the sledge.

(b) Find the coefficient of friction between the sledge and the ground.

(c) How long does it take for the sledge to travel 50 m?

C Smooth inclined surfaces (answers p 153)

C1 Imagine an object resting on a perfectly smooth plane.
The plane is horizontal to start with, but is gradually tilted
so that its angle to the horizontal increases.

What will happen? Explain why.

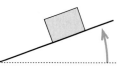

This diagram shows the forces acting on a particle of mass 5 kg placed on a
smooth plane inclined at 35° to the horizontal. These forces are the weight
(vertically downwards) and the normal reaction (at right angles to the plane).

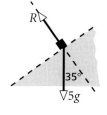

In chapter 3 we saw that in problems involving inclined planes it is usually
best to resolve forces in directions parallel to the plane and perpendicular to
the plane.

These two directions are shown in the diagram above as dotted lines.

The next diagram shows how the weight, 5g, is resolved into

a component $5g \cos 35°$ perpendicular to the plane

a component $5g \sin 35°$ down the plane

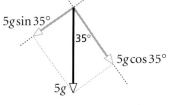

C2 Here again is the force diagram for a particle of mass 5 kg on
a smooth plane inclined at 35° to the horizontal.

The particle accelerates down the plane.

(a) Explain why $R = 5g \cos 35°$, and hence find the value of R.

(b) By resolving forces down the plane and using Newton's second law,
show that the acceleration of the particle is approximately $5.6 \, \text{m s}^{-2}$.

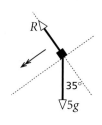

C3 A particle of mass 1.5 kg slides down a smooth plane inclined at 25°
to the horizontal.

(a) Sketch a diagram showing the forces acting on the particle.

(b) By resolving forces perpendicular to and parallel to the plane, find

   (i) the magnitude of the normal reaction of the plane on the particle

   (ii) the acceleration of the particle

In situations involving inclined planes, resolve parallel to the plane and
perpendicular to the plane.

The acceleration is in the direction of the plane so use Newton's second law
parallel to the plane.

There is no motion perpendicular to the plane so forces are in equilibrium
perpendicular to the plane.

Example 4

An object of mass 2.8 kg is pulled up a smooth plane inclined at 40°
to the horizontal by a light string parallel to the plane. Given that the
object is accelerating at 0.5 m s^{-2} up the plane, find

(a) the tension in the string

(b) the normal reaction between the plane and the object

Solution

Sketch the force diagram.

(a) Resolve up the plane.
The resultant component up the plane is $(T - 2.8g\sin 40°)$ N.

Apply N2L in this direction: $T - 2.8g\sin 40° = 2.8 \times 0.5$

$$\Rightarrow \quad T = 2.8 \times 9.8 \times \sin 40° + 1.4$$
$$= 19.0 \text{ (to 3 s.f.)}$$

(b) Resolve perpendicular to the plane.
There is no acceleration perpendicular to the plane, so $R = 2.8g\cos 40°$
$$= 21.0 \text{ (to 3 s.f.)}$$

The tension is 19.0 N and the normal reaction 21.0 N.

Exercise C (answers p 153)

1 A particle of mass 4 kg slides down a smooth plane inclined at 30° to the horizontal.

(a) Sketch a diagram showing the forces acting on the particle.

(b) Find the acceleration of the particle.

(c) Find the magnitude of the normal reaction of the plane on the particle.

2 A sledge of mass 15 kg is pulled up a smooth slope inclined at 25° to the horizontal
by a light rope parallel to the slope. The tension in the rope is 80 N. Find

(a) the acceleration of the sledge

(b) the normal reaction of the slope on the sledge

3 A box of mass 8 kg is pulled up a smooth slope inclined at 15° to the horizontal
by a light cable parallel to the slope.
Given that the box moves with a constant velocity, find the tension in the cable.

4 A child of mass 12 kg slides down a smooth slope inclined at 33° to the horizontal.
The slope is 15 metres long and the child starts from rest at the top.
Modelling the child as a particle, find

(a) the acceleration of the child

(b) the time taken to reach the foot of the slope

(c) the magnitude of the normal reaction on the child during the motion

5 A particle of mass 20 kg lies on a smooth slope inclined at 15°
to the horizontal.
The particle is held in position by a horizontal force P N as shown.
Find the value of P.

D Rough inclined surfaces (answers p 153)

A rough plane is able to provide not only a normal reaction R but a friction
force F on an object in contact with it. If the plane is inclined, the friction
force may be either down or up the slope, depending on whether the object
is moving (or is about to move) up or down the slope.

If the object is stationary, then $F \leq \mu R$. If it is moving, then $F = \mu R$.

D1 The diagram on the right shows the forces acting on a sledge of
mass 3 kg (modelled as a particle) which is sliding down a rough plane
inclined at 30° to the horizontal. The coefficient of friction is 0.2.

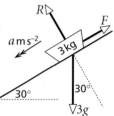

(a) Explain why the normal reaction of the plane on the sledge is
$3g \cos 30°$ newtons.

(b) Find the value of F.

(c) Find the acceleration of the sledge down the plane.

D2 A load of mass 10 kg is hauled up a rough plane inclined at 20° to
the horizontal, by a force P newtons parallel to the plane.
The coefficient of friction between the load and the plane is 0.3.

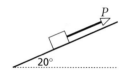

(a) Sketch a diagram showing the forces acting on the load.

(b) Show that the normal reaction of the plane on the load is 92.1 N.

(c) Find the friction force on the load.

(d) Find the value of P

(i) when the load is moving with constant speed up the slope

(ii) when the load is accelerating at $2 \, \text{m s}^{-2}$ up the slope

If an object is in equilibrium, the friction force F satisfies the inequality $F \leq \mu R$.
This can be used to find an inequality involving μ.

D3 An object of mass 5 kg rests in equilibrium on a rough plane
inclined at 25° to the horizontal.
The diagram shows the forces acting on the particle.

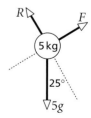

(a) Show that $R = 44.4$ (to 3 s.f.).

(b) Show that $F = 20.7$ (to 3 s.f.).

(c) Hence show that $\mu \geq 0.466$.

Example 5

A sledge of mass 15 kg is pulled up a slope inclined at 30° to the horizontal by a rope parallel to the slope. The coefficient of friction between the sledge and the slope is 0.3.

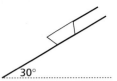

(a) Find the normal reaction of the slope on the sledge.

(b) Find the tension in the rope

　　(i) when the sledge moves up the slope with a constant speed

　　(ii) when the sledge accelerates up the slope at 2.5 m s^{-2}

(c) State two modelling assumptions you have made in your solutions.

Solution

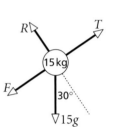

(a) Resolve perpendicular to the slope:　$R = 15g\cos 30°$

$$= 15 \times 9.8 \times \cos 30° = 127$$

　　The normal reaction is 127 newtons (to 3 s.f.).

(b) (i) When the speed is constant, acceleration $= 0$.
　　　Friction force $F = 0.3R$
　　　Resolve up the slope and use N2L:

$$T - 0.3R - 15g\sin 30° = 15 \times 0$$

$$\Rightarrow \quad T = 0.3 \times 127 + 15 \times 9.8 \times \sin 30° = 112$$

　　The tension in the rope is 112 newtons (to 3 s.f.).

　(ii) Resolve up the slope and use N2L:

$$T - 0.3R - 15g\sin 30° = 15 \times 2.5$$

$$\Rightarrow \quad T = 0.3 \times 127 + 15 \times 9.8 \times \sin 30° + 15 \times 2.5 = 149$$

　　The tension in the rope is 149 newtons (to 3 s.f.).

(c) The sledge has been treated as a particle.
　　The rope has been treated as light (of negligible mass or weight).

Exercise D (answers p 153)

1 A particle of mass 10 kg slides down a rough plane inclined at 30° to the horizontal. The coefficient of friction is 0.25.

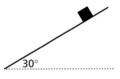

　(a) Draw a diagram showing the forces acting on the particle.

　(b) Show that the acceleration of the particle is 2.8 m s^{-2} (to 2 s.f.).

2 A sledge of mass 30 kg slides down a plane inclined at 20° to the horizontal. The coefficient of friction between the sledge and the plane is 0.15.

　(a) Find the normal reaction of the plane on the sledge.

　(b) Show that the friction force on the sledge is 41.4 newtons (to 3 s.f.).

　(c) Find the acceleration of the sledge.

3 A box of mass 20 kg rests in limiting equilibrium on a rough plane inclined at 30° to the horizontal.

   (a) Show that the normal reaction of the plane on the box is approximately 170 N.

   (b) Show that the coefficient of friction between the box and the plane is 0.58 (to 2 s.f.).

4 A box of mass 50 kg is pulled up a plane inclined at 15° to the horizontal by a rope parallel to the plane. The coefficient of friction between the box and the plane is 0.5. The box accelerates at 0.1 m s^{-2}.

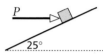

   (a) Find the tension in the rope.

   (b) State any modelling assumptions you have made.

5 A box of mass 40 kg lies on a rough plane inclined at 25° to the horizontal. It is held in equilibrium by a horizontal force P N.
   The box is in limiting equilibrium about to move down the slope.
   The coefficient of friction between the box and the plane is 0.3.
   Find the value of P.

6 **(a)** A particle of mass 4 kg slides with constant speed down a plane inclined at 30° to the horizontal. Find the coefficient of friction between the particle and the plane.

   (b) The same particle slides down a different plane, also inclined at 30° to the horizontal. Given that the particle accelerates at 2 m s^{-2} down this plane, find the coefficient of friction between the particle and the plane.

7 A small block of mass 2 kg is placed on a plane inclined at 40° to the horizontal.

   (a) Find the normal reaction of the plane on the block.

   (b) Show that if the coefficient of friction μ is greater than or equal to a certain value, then the block will remain at rest on the plane. Find this value.

   (c) Given that $\mu = 0.4$, find the acceleration of the block down the plane.

8 A block of mass 5 kg is pulled from rest up a plane inclined at 30° to the horizontal by a rope parallel to the plane. The coefficient of friction between the block and the plane is 0.25. The tension in the rope is 40 N.

   (a) Find the acceleration of the block.

   (b) Find the speed of the block when it has travelled 1.5 m up the plane.

Key points

- In problems involving motion in a straight line, resolve forces parallel to and perpendicular to the direction of motion.
  Use Newton's second law parallel to the direction of motion.
  Forces are in equilibrium perpendicular to the direction of motion. (pp 94, 99)

- If an object is moving on a rough surface, the friction force F is equal to μR. (pp 96, 101)

Mixed questions (answers p 154)

1 A box of mass 20 kg is pulled across a rough floor by a rope inclined at 25° to the horizontal. The coefficient of friction between the box and the ground is 0.3. The box is modelled as a particle. The diagram shows the forces acting on the box.

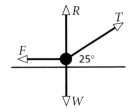

(a) Show that the weight of the box in newtons, W, is 196.

(b) Given that $T = 70$, show that $R = 166.4$, to 1 d.p.

(c) Find the value of F, the friction force acting on the box.

(d) Find the acceleration of the box.

(e) The box is initially at rest. Find the distance travelled by the box in 5 seconds.

2 A ring of mass 0.3 kg is threaded on a fixed, rough horizontal curtain pole. A light inextensible string is attached to the ring. The string and the pole lie in the same vertical plane. The ring is pulled downwards by the string which makes an angle α to the horizontal, where $\tan \alpha = \frac{3}{4}$, as shown. The tension in the string is 2.5 N. Given that, in this position, the ring is in limiting equilibrium,

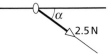

(a) find the coefficient of friction between the ring and the pole.

The direction of the string is now altered so that the ring is pulled upwards. The string lies in the same vertical plane as before and again makes an angle α with the horizontal, as shown. The tension in the string is again 2.5 N.

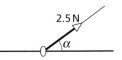

(b) Find the normal reaction exerted by the pole on the ring.

(c) State whether the ring is in equilibrium in the position shown, giving a brief justification for your answer. You need make no further detailed calculation of the forces acting.   Edexcel

3 A ball A of mass 0.4 kg is moving on a horizontal table with speed 3 m s⁻¹. Another ball B of mass 0.8 kg is moving in the same direction as A at 2 m s⁻¹. The balls collide directly.
Immediately after the collision A and B move in opposite directions and their speeds are the same.

(a) Find the speed of A immediately after the collision.

(b) Find the magnitude of the impulse exerted by B on A during the collision.

(c) The table is rough. After the collision A moves a distance of 5 m on the table before coming to rest.
Find the coefficient of friction between A and the table.

Test yourself (answers p 154)

1 A box of mass 10 kg is at rest on a rough horizontal floor.
  A rope is attached to the box at 25° to the horizontal.
  The coefficient of friction between the box and the floor is 0.3.

  (a) Draw a diagram showing all the forces acting on the box.

  (b) Given that the box is in limiting equilibrium, find the magnitude of

     (i) the tension in the rope   (ii) the normal reaction on the box

  (c) The tension in the rope is increased to 35 N.
      Find the acceleration of the box.

2 A sledge of mass 20 kg slides down a smooth slope inclined at an angle of 28°
  to the horizontal.

  (a) Find the acceleration of the sledge.

  (b) Find the normal reaction of the slope on the sledge.

3 The diagram shows a boat B of mass 400 kg held at rest
  on a slipway by a rope.
  The boat is modelled as a particle and the slipway as
  a rough plane inclined at 15° to the horizontal.
  The coefficient of friction between B and the slipway is 0.2.
  The rope is modelled as a light, inextensible string, parallel to a line
  of greatest slope of the plane. The boat is in equilibrium and on the
  point of sliding down the slipway.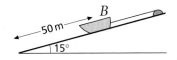

  (a) Calculate the tension in the rope.

  The boat is 50 m from the bottom of the slipway. The rope is detached from
  the boat and the boat slides down the slipway.

  (b) Calculate the time taken for the boat to slide to the bottom of the slipway.   Edexcel

4 A boy of mass 28 kg slides from rest down a slope inclined at an angle of 35° to
  the horizontal. The boy is modelled as a particle and the slope as a rough plane.
  The acceleration of the boy is $0.15\,\text{m s}^{-2}$.

  (a) Find the frictional force acting on the boy.

  (b) Find the coefficient of friction between the boy and the slope.

  (c) The boy takes 20 seconds to reach the bottom of the slope.
      Find his speed at the bottom of the slope and the length of the slope.

5 A particle of mass 2 kg is projected up a rough plane inclined at 15° to the
  horizontal. The coefficient of friction between the particle and the plane is 0.3.

  (a) Find the deceleration of the particle as it travels up the plane.

  (b) Given that the initial speed of the particle is $8\,\text{m s}^{-1}$, find the time taken before
      it comes to instantaneous rest.

6 Newton's laws of motion 3

In this chapter you will
* learn about the process of modelling
* use Newton's third law of motion to solve problems

A Modelling (answers p 154)

Many of the situations studied in mechanics are quite complicated. The first step is usually to simplify the situation. In this section we shall look at a particular mechanical system, the Lynton and Lynmouth Cliff Railway in Devon.

The railway is shown in this picture
It connects Lynton, at the top of the cliff, with Lynmouth at the bottom.

There are two parallel tracks inclined at an angle of 35° to the horizontal.

A single car runs on each track. The two cars are connected by a cable that runs round a pulley wheel at the top.

(There is also a similar cable running round a pulley at the bottom, but the function of this cable is secondary.)

Each car is fitted with a water tank.
These tanks can be filled from a stream at the top and emptied into the sea at the bottom.

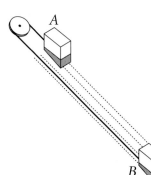

To understand how the railway works, suppose that one car (*A*) is at the top and the other (*B*) at the bottom and that both tanks are full.

People get into each car.

If *A* is heavier than *B*, it will start to descend and *B* will ascend.

If *A* is not heavier than *B*, water is let out of *B*'s tank until *A* is heavier than *B*.

When *B* gets to the top, its tank is filled and the whole process starts again.

D **A1** If the system consisted only of the things mentioned so far – cars, tracks, cable, water tanks – what do you think would happen to the cars once they had started to move?

What other things does the system need to be operated safely?

Imagine that the railway is being designed. The design of the track and the cars has been settled. Some of the questions that need to be considered are:

- How strong should the cable be?
- How fast will the cars travel?
- What will be the force on the cars' axles?

The first step in answering questions like these, or at least getting reasonable estimates, is to simplify the mechanism to its essentials, as shown in the diagram on the right.

The simplified version of the mechanism is called a **model**.

A model does not have to be a physical model. Most models in mechanics are descriptions in words, diagrams or symbols.

In the very simple model shown here, each car, including the people in it and the water in its tank, is modelled as a particle sliding on an inclined surface.

Having modelled the cars as particles, what about the cable? The cable (it is in fact about 370 m long) is itself quite heavy, but nowhere near as heavy as the cars. So in this simple model its mass could be ignored. In modelling language, the cable could be treated as 'light' (that is, of negligible mass).

Of course in practice such a 'light' cable could not do its job of pulling the heavy cars. But models often contain imaginary or 'ideal' elements, in this case a cable that is of negligible mass but strong.

It is also common to assume in a model like this that the cable is **inextensible**. This means that it will not stretch.

You may begin to wonder whether the simplified model is so unlike the real mechanism as to be useless. A model will be inadequate if an important factor is left out. For example, the model described so far would be inadequate if the mass of the cable is comparable with the mass of the cars, or if the cable is known to be highly elastic.

The process of modelling often starts with a highly simplified model. This model would include only the most important factors but would be good enough to answer some basic questions about the real mechanism or get good estimates of quantities. Then the model could be gradually improved to take account of other factors.

For example, in the model above the cars are modelled as particles. A particle is simple to deal with because all the forces on it act at the same point.

However, this is not true for the real car and a more detailed model would be needed in order to study the forces acting on the cars.

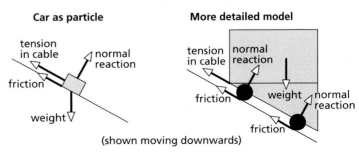

(shown moving downwards)

The **modelling process** is shown in the diagram below.

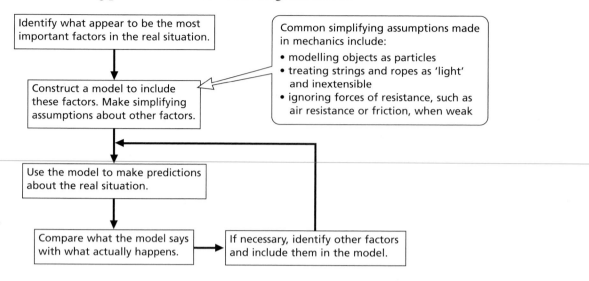

D **A2** Jack is studying the motion of an ice skater as she makes a complicated movement.
Would it be appropriate to model the skater as a particle?
Give reasons for your answer.

A3 There is an old joke about a mechanics exam question that starts
'An elephant of negligible mass …'.

Can you imagine circumstances in which an elephant could be said
to have negligible mass?

A4 A railway engineer is studying the motion of a tube train.
She is considering what might happen if both of these happen together:

• the brakes fail on a train as it is moving forward

• there is another train stopped ahead in the tunnel

Would it be realistic to ignore air resistance in this case?

What other factors do you think the model may need to include?

A5 A diver jumps from a diving board situated 5 metres above the surface
of the water in a swimming pool.
Why might it be inappropriate to model the diver as a particle?

In this book you have already met a number of examples where simplifying
assumptions have been made. More will occur in this chapter.

B Newton's third law of motion (answers p 154)

These diagrams show some situations where objects exert forces on one another.
(Other forces that may be acting on the objects are not shown.)

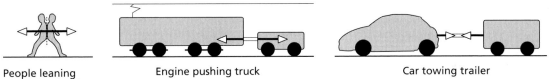

People leaning against each other

Engine pushing truck

Car towing trailer

Newton's third law of motion says

K   If an object A exerts a force on an object B, then B exerts an equal and opposite force on A.

(Newton's own wording was 'Action and reaction are equal and opposite.')

For example, if you hit an object like a punch bag, you exert a force on the bag;
the bag exerts an equal force on your fist that you probably feel with some pain.

The three situations shown above frequently arise in mechanics.
Newton's third law applies whether the objects are stationary (as in the leaning people)
or moving with constant speed or acceleration (as in the pushing and towing).

In the case of the leaning people, the objects are in direct contact.
In the other cases, the forces are 'transmitted' between the objects by a bar
(where the force is a thrust) or a rope or bar (where the force is a tension).

B1 A car of mass 1200 kg is pulling a trailer
of mass 400 kg on a horizontal road.

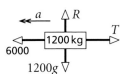

The car and trailer are connected by a
light horizontal rope.

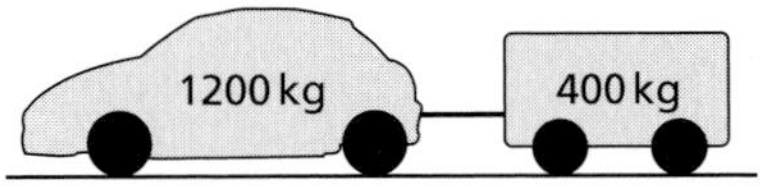

The driving force of the car is 6000 N. The acceleration of the car and trailer is $a\,\mathrm{m\,s^{-2}}$.
Ignore friction and air resistance.

(a) Model the car as a particle.
Here is a diagram showing the forces acting on the car.
The tension in the rope is T N.
(The normal reaction R balances the weight.)

Use Newton's second law to write down an equation
involving T and a.

(b) Draw a diagram showing the forces acting on the trailer.
Why is the magnitude of the horizontal force equal to T N?

(c) By applying Newton's second law to the trailer, write down another equation
involving T and a.

(d) You now have two simultaneous equations. Solve them to find the values of T and a.

D   (e) The rope is described as 'light' so its mass can be ignored. What else has to be
true about the rope if the acceleration of the car and the trailer are to be equal?

In question B1 it is also possible to treat 'car + trailer' as a single particle of mass 1600 kg.

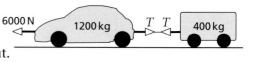

When this is done, the two forces of T and $-T$ cancel out. As far as the combined object is concerned, they are 'internal' forces. The only external force acting on the combined object is the driving force of the car.

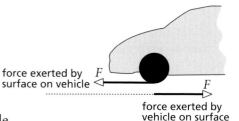

B2 (a) Write down the equation you get by applying Newton's second law to the combined particle 'car + trailer'.

(b) Solve the equation for a and check that the result is the same as before.

Note that if you use this 'combined object' method to find the acceleration, you still need to use Newton's second law on one of the separate objects to find the tension.

Driving force

Newton's third law explains how an engine inside a vehicle can provide an external driving force on the vehicle. The key to the explanation is the friction between the vehicle's wheels and the surface (road or rail).

The engine causes the wheels to push backwards on the surface with a force F. So, by Newton's third law, the surface provides an equal and opposite forward force F on the vehicle.

force exerted by
surface on vehicle

force exerted by
vehicle on surface

This works only if the surface is rough enough. For example, on an icy surface the wheels will spin and the vehicle will not move forwards.

Example 1

A car of mass 2000 kg tows a trailer of mass 500 kg on a straight horizontal road. The driving force of the car's engine is of magnitude 9000 N. Forces of resistance are 150 N on the car and 50 N on the trailer. Find

(a) the acceleration of the car and trailer

(b) the tension in the coupling between the car and the trailer

Solution

Draw separate force diagrams for car and trailer. (Vertical forces balance out and are not shown.)

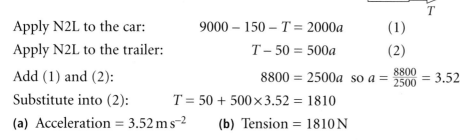

Apply N2L to the car: $\qquad$ $9000 - 150 - T = 2000a$ $\qquad$ (1)

Apply N2L to the trailer: $\qquad$ $T - 50 = 500a$ $\qquad$ (2)

Add (1) and (2): $\qquad$ $8800 = 2500a$ so $a = \frac{8800}{2500} = 3.52$

Substitute into (2): $\qquad$ $T = 50 + 500 \times 3.52 = 1810$

(a) Acceleration $= 3.52 \, \mathrm{m \, s^{-2}}$ $\qquad$ **(b)** Tension $= 1810 \, \mathrm{N}$

Example 2

A car of mass 2500 kg pulls a trailer of mass 500 kg on a straight horizontal road. The driving force of the car's engine is of magnitude 8000 N. Horizontal resisting forces of 800 N and 300 N act on the car and the trailer respectively.

(a) Find the acceleration of the car and trailer.

(b) The coupling between the car and trailer becomes disconnected when they are moving at 18 m s⁻¹. Find the distance travelled by the trailer between becoming disconnected and coming to rest.

Solution

(a) *As the tension in the coupling is not required, the car and trailer can be treated as a single particle.*
Draw a force diagram for 'car + trailer'.
The resisting force is the sum of the individual resisting forces.

Apply N2L to the car and trailer: $8000 - 1100 = 3000a$

$$\text{so } a = \frac{6900}{3000} = 2.3$$

The acceleration is 2.3 m s⁻².

(b) *Draw a force diagram for the trailer when disconnected.*
The only force acting on the trailer is the resisting force.

Apply N2L to the trailer: $-300 = 500a$

$$\text{so } a = \frac{-300}{500} = -0.6$$

Use the constant acceleration equations. $u = 18, v = 0, a = -0.6, s = ?$

$v^2 = u^2 + 2as$ gives $0^2 = 18^2 + 2 \times -0.6 \times s \Rightarrow s = \dfrac{18^2}{2 \times 0.6} = 270$

The distance travelled is 270 m.

Exercise B (answers p 154)

1 A car of mass 3600 kg pulls a trailer of mass 400 kg on a straight horizontal road.
The driving force of the car's engine is 3200 N.
Resistance to motion may be ignored. Find

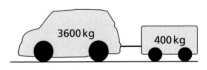

(a) the acceleration of the car and trailer

(b) the tension in the coupling between the car and the trailer

2 A van of mass 5200 kg pulls a trailer of mass 1200 kg on a straight horizontal road. The driving force of the van's engine is 4800 N. Horizontal resisting forces of 600 N and 200 N act on the van and the trailer respectively. Find

(a) the acceleration of the van and trailer

(b) the tension in the coupling between the van and the trailer

3 A railway engine pushes a carriage along a straight horizontal track. The mass of the engine is 10 500 kg. The mass of the carriage is 1500 kg. The engine and carriage are accelerating at $0.2\,\mathrm{m\,s^{-2}}$. Resistance to motion may be ignored. Find

(a) the propulsive force of the engine

(b) the magnitude of the force exerted by the engine on the carriage

4 A car pulls a trailer on a straight horizontal road. The mass of the car is 4200 kg; the mass of the trailer is 600 kg. There are no resistances to motion. The maximum tension in the coupling between the car and trailer is 480 N. Find

(a) the maximum acceleration of the car and trailer

(b) the driving force of the car's engine when the acceleration has its maximum value

5 A car of mass 1500 kg pulls a trailer of mass 500 kg on a straight horizontal road. Resistances to motion are constant at 200 N on the car and 100 N on the trailer.

(a) Find the magnitude of the force in the towbar between the car and the trailer when the car and trailer travel with constant speed.

(b) During the journey a braking force is applied to the car, with the result that the car and trailer decelerate at a constant rate of $0.2\,\mathrm{m\,s^{-2}}$.

   (i) By applying Newton's second law to the trailer, find the magnitude of the force in the towbar.

   (ii) Find the braking force applied to the car.

6 A crate of mass 120 kg is pulled vertically upwards by a cable attached to it. A box of mass 30 kg is attached to the underside of the crate by a light inextensible rope. The crate and box are accelerating upwards at $0.1\,\mathrm{m\,s^{-2}}$. Air resistance may be ignored.

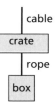

(a) Draw separate force diagrams for the crate and the box.

(b) Find the tension in the cable.

(c) Find the tension in the rope connecting the crate and the box.

(d) The rope connecting the crate and the box snaps when they are travelling at $1\,\mathrm{m\,s^{-1}}$ and the box is 5 m above ground level.

   (i) What is the acceleration of the box after the rope has snapped?

   (ii) At what speed will the box hit the ground?

7 A car of mass 1600 kg pulls a trailer of mass 400 kg on a straight horizontal road. The driving force of the car's engine is 5000 N. Resistances to motion are constant at 400 N on the car and 100 N on the trailer.

(a) Find the acceleration of the car and trailer.

(b) Find the tension in the coupling between the car and the trailer.

(c) The coupling becomes disconnected when the car and trailer are moving at $20\,\mathrm{m\,s^{-1}}$. Find the time taken for the trailer to come to rest.

C Pulleys and pegs (answers p 155)

This diagram shows two particles A and B connected by a light inextensible string that passes over a fixed pulley or peg.

Particle A slides on a horizontal surface and particle B hangs vertically. Between the pulley and particle A the string is horizontal.

The force exerted by each particle on the other is transmitted by the string. Although the string changes direction as it goes round the pulley, the magnitude of the tension will be the same throughout, provided that the pulley (or peg) is frictionless, or 'smooth'. This will be assumed in all the work that follows.

D **C1** Imagine that particle A is held in position and then released.
Describe what happens

    (a) if the horizontal surface is perfectly smooth

    (b) if the surface is rough

C2 In the diagram above, the mass of A is 3 kg and the mass of B is 2 kg.
The horizontal surface is smooth.

    (a) Draw a diagram showing all the forces acting on A.

    (b) Let $a\,\mathrm{m\,s^{-2}}$ be the acceleration of particle A.
    Use Newton's second law to write down an equation connecting T and a.

    (c) Draw a diagram showing all the forces acting on B.

    (d) What fact about the string means that the magnitude of the acceleration of B is the same as that of A?

    (e) Use Newton's second law for B to write down another equation connecting T and a.

    (f) Solve the two equations to find the values of a and T.

C3 The masses of A and B are as before, but the surface is rough, with coefficient of friction 0.2.

    (a) Draw a diagram showing all the forces acting on A.

    (b) Explain why the normal reaction of the surface on A must be $3g$ newtons.

    (c) Assuming that A moves, explain why the friction force on A is 5.88 newtons.

    (d) Use Newton's second law for A to write down an equation connecting T and a.

    (e) Draw a force diagram for B and find a second equation connecting T and a.

    (f) Find the values of a and T.

C4 A particle of mass 4 kg situated on a horizontal surface is connected to a hanging particle of mass 3 kg by a string that passes over a smooth peg. Find the acceleration of the system and the tension in the string

    (a) when the surface is smooth

    (b) when the surface is rough with $\mu = 0.5$

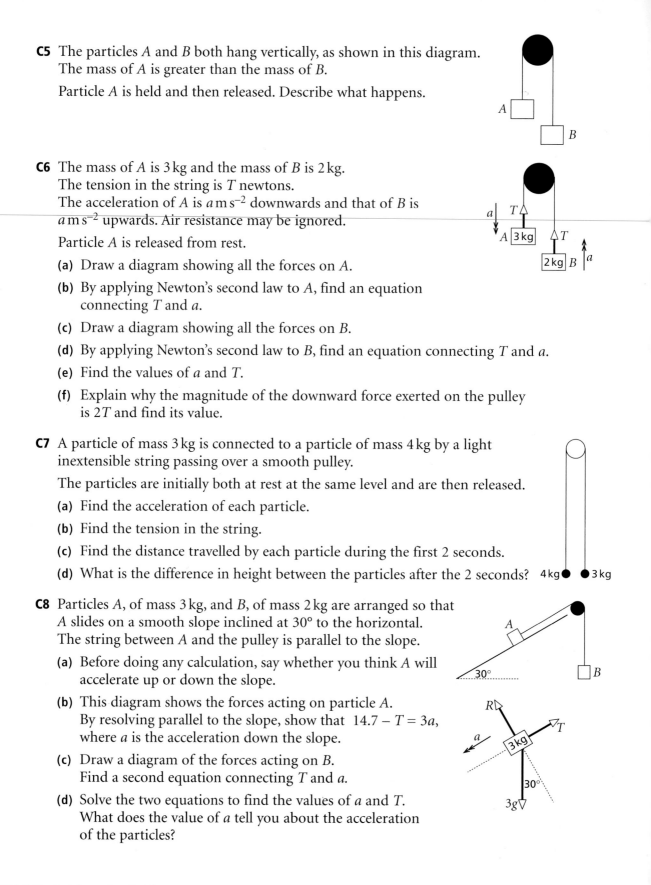

C5 The particles A and B both hang vertically, as shown in this diagram. The mass of A is greater than the mass of B.

Particle A is held and then released. Describe what happens.

C6 The mass of A is 3 kg and the mass of B is 2 kg.
The tension in the string is T newtons.
The acceleration of A is a m s^{-2} downwards and that of B is a m s^{-2} upwards. Air resistance may be ignored.

Particle A is released from rest.

(a) Draw a diagram showing all the forces on A.

(b) By applying Newton's second law to A, find an equation connecting T and a.

(c) Draw a diagram showing all the forces on B.

(d) By applying Newton's second law to B, find an equation connecting T and a.

(e) Find the values of a and T.

(f) Explain why the magnitude of the downward force exerted on the pulley is $2T$ and find its value.

C7 A particle of mass 3 kg is connected to a particle of mass 4 kg by a light inextensible string passing over a smooth pulley.

The particles are initially both at rest at the same level and are then released.

(a) Find the acceleration of each particle.

(b) Find the tension in the string.

(c) Find the distance travelled by each particle during the first 2 seconds.

(d) What is the difference in height between the particles after the 2 seconds?

C8 Particles A, of mass 3 kg, and B, of mass 2 kg are arranged so that A slides on a smooth slope inclined at 30° to the horizontal. The string between A and the pulley is parallel to the slope.

(a) Before doing any calculation, say whether you think A will accelerate up or down the slope.

(b) This diagram shows the forces acting on particle A.
By resolving parallel to the slope, show that $14.7 - T = 3a$, where a is the acceleration down the slope.

(c) Draw a diagram of the forces acting on B.
Find a second equation connecting T and a.

(d) Solve the two equations to find the values of a and T.
What does the value of a tell you about the acceleration of the particles?

Example 3

Two particles, of mass 5 kg and 2 kg respectively, are connected by a light inextensible string passing over a smooth peg. Both particles hang vertically with one particle held at rest. The particle is released. Find

(a) the acceleration of the system   **(b)** the tension in the string

(c) the downward force on the peg

Solution

(a), (b) Apply N2L to the 5 kg particle: $5g - T = 5a$ (1)

Apply N2L to the 2 kg particle: $T - 2g = 2a$ (2)

Add (1) and (2): $3g = 7a$, so $a = 3 \times \dfrac{9.8}{7} = 4.2$

Substitute in (2): $T = 2g + 2a = 28$

Acceleration $= 4.2 \, \text{m s}^{-2}$; tension $= 28 \, \text{N}$

(c) The downward force on the peg is $2T \, \text{N}$ (see diagram) $= 56 \, \text{N}$.

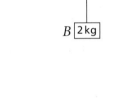

Example 4

A particle A of mass 5 kg on a rough horizontal plane is connected by a light inextensible string passing over a smooth pulley to a second particle B of mass 2 kg that hangs freely.

The coefficient of friction between particle A and the plane is 0.1.

Particle A is held at rest and then released. Find

(a) the acceleration of the system

(b) the tension in the string

(c) the time taken, to the nearest 0.1 s, for B to fall 10 metres

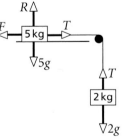

Solution

(a) Resolve vertically the forces on A: $R = 5g = 49$

Friction force on particle A: $F = \mu R = 0.1 \times 49 = 4.9$

Apply N2L to A: $T - 4.9 = 5a$ (1)

Apply N2L to B: $2g - T = 2a$ (2)

Add (1) and (2): $2g - 4.9 = 7a$

$\Rightarrow \quad 7a = 19.6 - 4.9 = 14.7$, so $a = 2.1$

The acceleration is $2.1 \, \text{m s}^{-2}$.

(b) From (1), $T = 5 \times 2.1 + 4.9 = 15.4$ The tension is $15.4 \, \text{N}$.

(c) *Use the constant acceleration equations.* $u = 0$, $a = 2.1$, $s = 10$, $t = ?$

$s = ut + \frac{1}{2}at^2$ gives $10 = 1.05t^2 \Rightarrow t = \sqrt{\dfrac{10}{1.05}} = 3.1$ (to 1 d.p.)

The time taken is $3.1 \, \text{s}$.

Example 5

A particle A of mass $2\,$kg slides on a smooth plane inclined at $30°$ to the horizontal. Particle A is connected to a particle B of mass $5\,$kg by a light inextensible string passing over a smooth peg.

The system is released from rest with B at a height of $0.5\,$m above horizontal ground.

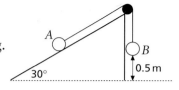

(a) Find the acceleration of each particle.

(b) Find the tension in the string.

(c) The particle B hits the ground.
Given that A does not reach the peg, find the time between the instant B hits the ground and the instant when A reaches its highest point.

Solution

(a) The only motion of A is along the plane.
So resolve forces in this direction and apply N2L:

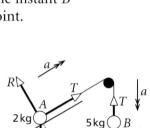

$$T - 2g\sin 30° = 2a$$
$$\text{so } T - 9.8 = 2a \quad (1)$$

Apply N2L to B:
$$5g - T = 5a$$
$$\text{so } 49 - T = 5a \quad (2)$$

Add (1) and (2):
$$49 - 9.8 = 7a$$
$$\Rightarrow \qquad a = 5.6$$

The acceleration is $5.6\,\mathrm{m\,s^{-2}}$.

(b) From (1), $T = 9.8 + 2a = 9.8 + 11.2 = 21$

The tension is $21\,$N.

(c) *Use the constant acceleration equations to find the speed of the particles when B hits the ground.* $\quad u = 0,\ a = 5.6,\ s = 0.5,\ v = ?$

Use $v^2 = u^2 + 2as.$ $\quad v^2 = 0 + 2 \times 5.6 \times 0.5 = 5.6,$ *from which* $v = \sqrt{5.6}$

When B hits the ground, the string becomes slack, so $T = 0$.

Resolve forces on A along the plane and apply N2L:
$$-2g\sin 30° = 2a \text{ so } a = -4.9$$

When A reaches its highest point, its speed is zero.
Use the constant acceleration equations for the motion after B has hit the ground.
$$u = \sqrt{5.6},\ v = 0,\ a = -4.9,\ t = ?$$

Use $v = u + at.$ $\quad 0 = \sqrt{5.6} + -4.9 \times t \ \Rightarrow\ t = \dfrac{\sqrt{5.6}}{4.9} = 0.483 \text{ (to 3 s.f.)}$

A reaches its highest point $0.483\,$s (to 3 s.f.) after B hits the ground.

1 A particle of mass m_1 kg slides on a smooth horizontal surface. It is connected to a particle of mass m_2 kg by a light inextensible string passing over a smooth peg. The second particle hangs vertically as shown.

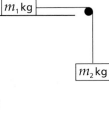

The system is released from rest. In each case below, find

    (i) the acceleration of the system   **(ii)** the tension in the string

(a) $m_1 = 4$, $m_2 = 2$ **(b)** $m_1 = 2$, $m_2 = 4$ **(c)** $m_1 = 5$, $m_2 = 3$

2 Two particles of masses m_1 kg and mass m_2 kg are connected by a light inextensible string passing over a fixed smooth pulley. Both particles hang vertically. The system is released from rest. In each case below, find

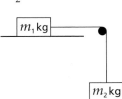

    (i) the acceleration of the system   **(ii)** the tension in the string

    (iii) the downward force on the pulley

(a) $m_1 = 4$, $m_2 = 2$ **(b)** $m_1 = 5$, $m_2 = 3$ **(c)** $m_1 = 3.5$, $m_2 = 1.5$

3 A particle of mass m_1 kg slides on a rough horizontal surface with coefficient of friction μ. The particle is connected to a second particle of mass m_2 kg by a light inextensible string passing over a smooth peg. The second particle hangs vertically.

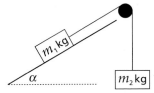

The system is released from rest. In each of the cases below, find

    (i) the acceleration of the system   **(ii)** the tension in the string

(a) $m_1 = 4$, $m_2 = 2$, $\mu = 0.1$ **(b)** $m_1 = .2$, $m_2 = 4$, $\mu = 0.2$

(c) $m_1 = 5$, $m_2 = 3$, $\mu = 0.5$ **(d)** $m_1 = 4$, $m_2 = 3$, $\mu = 0.5$

4 A particle of mass m_1 kg slides on a smooth plane inclined at angle α to the horizontal. It is connected to a particle of mass m_2 kg by a light inextensible string passing over a smooth peg. The second particle hangs vertically as shown.

The system is released from rest. In each of the cases below, find

    (i) the acceleration and direction of motion of m_1 **(ii)** the tension in the string

(a) $m_1 = 4$, $m_2 = 3$, $\alpha = 30$ **(b)** $m_1 = 2$, $m_2 = 4$, $\alpha = 45$

(c) $m_1 = 5$, $m_2 = 3$, $\alpha = 45$ **(d)** $m_1 = 2$, $m_2 = 4$, $\alpha = 60$

5 A particle A of mass 5 kg is on a rough horizontal surface. The coefficient of friction between A and the surface is μ. A is connected to a particle B, of mass 2 kg, by a light inextensible string that passes over a fixed smooth peg.

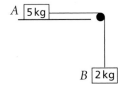

(a) Given that B hangs at rest, find the range of possible values of μ.

(b) When B is replaced by a particle C of mass 3 kg, the system accelerates at $0.49 \, \text{m s}^{-2}$. Find the value of μ.

6 Two small objects A and B, each of mass 0.3 kg, are connected by a light inextensible string passing over a smooth pulley and hang vertically. Initially the system is at rest.

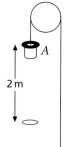

A 'collar' of mass 0.1 kg is placed on A. As a result the system accelerates. After A has fallen a distance of 2 metres, it passes through a ring which removes the collar. Find

2 m

(a) the acceleration of A while the collar is in place

(b) the time during which the collar is in place, to the nearest 0.1 s

(c) the distance travelled by A in the first 3 seconds after the collar is removed

B

7 A particle A of mass 2 kg slides on a smooth plane inclined at an angle α to the horizontal, where $\tan \alpha = \frac{3}{4}$. It is connected to a particle B, of mass 6 kg, by a light inextensible string passing over a smooth pulley. The system is released from rest with B hanging freely at a height of 0.25 m above the ground.

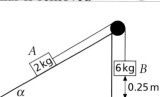

(a) Find the acceleration of the system.

(b) Find the speed of the particles at the instant when B hits the ground.

(c) Given that A does not reach the pulley, find the time between the instant when B hits the ground and the instant when A reaches its highest point.

8 A particle A of mass 4 kg is on a rough horizontal surface. The coefficient of friction between A and the surface is 0.3. A is connected by a light inextensible string that passes over a smooth pulley to a particle B of mass 3 kg that hangs freely. The system is released from rest with B 1 m above the ground.

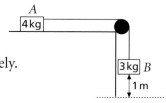

(a) Find the acceleration of the system.

(b) Find the time taken for B to reach the ground.

(c) Assuming that A does not reach the pulley, find the distance travelled by A after B hits the ground before A comes to rest.

9 The Lynton and Lynmouth Cliff Railway is modelled as a pair of particles sliding on a smooth slope inclined at 35° to the horizontal. The particles are connected by a light inextensible cable passing round a smooth pulley at the top of the plane. Air resistance is ignored.

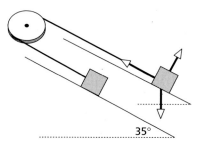

(a) Given that the masses of the particles are 8000 kg and 4000 kg, find the acceleration of the system and the tension in the cable.

Diagram showing the forces acting on one of the particles

(b) The railway is 360 m long. Imagine that the brakes fail when the heavier particle is at the top. Find the speed with which this particle reaches the bottom of the slope.

(c) State two features of the real railway that are left out of the model.

Key points

- Modelling assumptions are made in order to simplify a situation by including only the most important factors. If a model is inadequate it may be improved by including further factors. (p 108)

- If an object A exerts a force on an object B, then B exerts an equal and opposite force on A. (Newton's third law of motion) (p 109)

- If two objects are connected by a light string that passes round a frictionless peg or pulley, the magnitude of the tension in the string is the same throughout. (p 113)

Mixed questions (answers p 156)

1 Two particles A and B, of mass 2 kg and 3 kg respectively, are joined by a light inextensible string.
   Initially the particles are at rest on a rough horizontal surface with the string taut.
   The coefficient of friction between each particle and the surface is 0.2.
   A constant force of magnitude 25 N is then applied to B as shown.

   (a) Find the acceleration of the particles.

   (b) Find the tension in the string when the system is moving.

   (c) After the particles have been moving for 5 seconds the string breaks.
   Find the distance travelled by A after the string has broken.

2 A van of mass 2800 kg pulls a trailer of mass 1200 kg on a straight horizontal road.
   The driving force of the van's engine is 6500 N. Resisting forces of 500 N and 200 N act on the van and the trailer respectively.

   (a) Find the acceleration of the van and trailer.

   (b) The two vehicles come to a hill inclined at 5° to the horizontal.
   The driving force and the resistances are unchanged.
   Find the acceleration of the van and trailer as they move up the hill.

3 Two particles A and B of masses m and km respectively, where $k > 1$, are connected by a light inextensible string passing over a smooth fixed peg.
   The particles hang vertically and the system is released from rest.
   The particles move with an acceleration of magnitude $\frac{1}{2}g$.

   (a) Find, in terms of m and g, the tension in the string.

   (b) Find the value of k.

4 Two particles A and B, of masses 6 kg and 8 kg, are connected by a light inextensible string which passes over a smooth pulley. Particle A is held on a smooth slope inclined at 30° to the horizontal and particle B hangs with the string vertical.

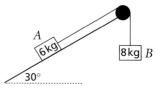

The system is released from rest with the string taut.

(a) Show that the magnitude of the acceleration of the particles is 3.5 m s^{-2}.

(b) Find the tension in the string.

5 A particle A, of mass $3m$, rests on a rough horizontal plane. The particle is connected to a particle B, of mass $4m$, by a light inextensible string passing over a smooth peg. The system is released from rest with the string taut and B hanging vertically.

The particles move with an acceleration of magnitude $\frac{2}{5}g$.

(a) Find the tension in the string.

(b) Find the coefficient of friction between A and the plane.

6 Two particles A and B, of mass 3 kg and 5 kg respectively, are connected by a light inextensible string passing over a smooth fixed peg. Particle A is held resting on a rough plane inclined at an angle α to the horizontal, where $\tan \alpha = \frac{4}{3}$. The coefficient of friction between A and the plane is $\frac{1}{3}$.

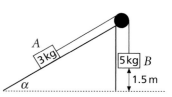

The system is released from rest with particle B hanging freely at a height of 1.5 m above horizontal ground.

(a) Find the acceleration of the system.

(b) Find the tension in the string.

(c) B hits the ground. Given that A does not reach the pulley, find the total time taken between the system being released and A reaching its highest point on the plane.

Test yourself (answers p 156)

1 A van of mass 1600 kg pulls a trailer of mass 900 kg on a straight horizontal road. The driving force of the van's engine is 4500 N. Resistances to motion are constant at 500 N on the van and 250 N on the trailer.

(a) Find the acceleration of the van and trailer.

(b) Find the tension in the coupling between the van and the trailer.

(c) When the van and trailer are travelling at 15 m s^{-1} the coupling becomes disconnected. The resistances to motion remain unchanged. Find the time taken for the trailer to come to rest.

2 Two particles A and B are connected by a light inextensible string which passes over a smooth fixed peg. The mass of A is 2 kg and the mass of B is m kg, where $m > 2$.
The system is released from rest with the particles hanging vertically. The particles move with constant acceleration of magnitude 4.2 m s^{-2}.

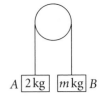

A $\boxed{2\,\text{kg}}$ $\boxed{m\,\text{kg}}$ B

(a) Show that the magnitude of the tension in the string is 28 N.

(b) Find the value of m.

(c) Find the magnitude of the force exerted by the string on the peg.

3 Two particles A and B have masses m and $2m$ respectively. Particle A lies on a rough horizontal table and is connected to particle B by a light inextensible string which passes over a smooth peg fixed at the edge of the table.
The coefficient of friction between A and the table is 0.5.
The system is released from rest with the string taut and B hanging freely 0.75 m above the ground.

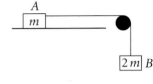

(a) Find, in terms of g, the acceleration of B.

(b) Find, in terms of m and g, the tension in the string.

(c) Find the time taken for B to hit the ground.

4 Particles A and B, of mass $2m$ and m respectively, are attached to the ends of a light inextensible string.
The string passes over a small smooth pulley fixed at the edge of a rough horizontal table.
Particle A is held on the table, while B rests on a smooth plane inclined at 30° to the horizontal, as shown in the diagram.
The string is in the same vertical plane as a line of greatest slope of the inclined plane. The coefficient of friction between A and the table is μ.
The particle A is released from rest and begins to move.

By writing down an equation of motion for each particle,

(a) show that, while both particles move with the string taut, each particle has an acceleration of magnitude $\frac{1}{6}(1 - 4\mu)g$.

When each particle has moved a distance h, the string breaks.
The particle A comes to rest before reaching the pulley. Given that $\mu = 0.2$,

(b) find, in terms of h, the total distance moved by A.

For the model described above,

(c) state two physical factors, **apart** from air resistance, which could be taken into account to make the model more realistic.

Edexcel

7 Moments

In this chapter you will learn
• what is meant by the moment of a force
• the conditions for equilibrium of a rigid body

A Moment of a force (answers p 156)

In the situations studied so far in this book, we have looked at forces acting on a particle. In this case all the forces act at the same point.

If the object is not a particle, it is possible for the forces acting on it to be applied at different points.

For example, imagine a ruler is placed on a smooth horizontal table and you are looking down on it.
In the first diagram below, two forces that are equal and opposite act on the ruler at the same point.
In the second diagram, the same two forces act at different points.

D **A1** Describe what happens to the ruler in each case.

In the second case the two forces are equal and opposite but are not in equilibrium. Because their **lines of action** are different (in fact parallel), the effect on the ruler is different – it will turn.

The ruler is an example of a **rigid body**: this means an object that is not distorted by the forces acting on it – it stays the same shape and size.

D **A2** A spanner is used to loosen a nut. A force is applied to the spanner as shown. Describe the effect of the force in each case shown.

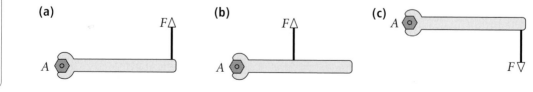

The turning effect of a force depends not only on the magnitude of the force but also on its point of application. If the magnitude stays the same but the line of action is moved further away from the point A about which the spanner turns, the turning effect is increased. The turning effect will be either clockwise or anticlockwise, depending on the direction of the force.

The turning effect about A is measured by the product of the magnitude of the force and the distance of the line of action from A.
This quantity is called the **moment** of the force about A.

Moment of force F about point A = magnitude of $F\times$ distance of line of action from A

K The moment of a force about a point is the product of the magnitude of the force and the perpendicular distance from the point to the line of action of the force.

Moment of F about $O = Fd$

The **sense** of a moment is either clockwise or anticlockwise. Anticlockwise moments are taken as positive and clockwise moments as negative.

The units of a moment are newton metres (N m).

A3 Find the moment of each force about point O.

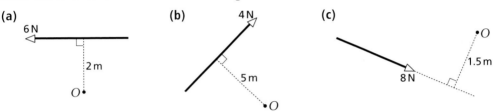

(a)   (b)   (c)

A **lamina** is an object which can be modelled as a plane area with mass but negligible thickness.

$ABCD$ is a square lamina of side 2 m.
A force of 10 N acts at vertex A as shown.
If the lamina were fixed at vertex B, the force would cause a turning effect about B. This is the moment of the force about B.
The moment of the force about B is $10\times2 = 20$ N m clockwise, or -20 N m.

A4 Calculate the moment of the 10 N force about

(a) C (b) D (c) A

A5 The force is moved so that it acts as shown.
Calculate the moment of the 10 N force about

(a) A (b) B

(c) C (d) D

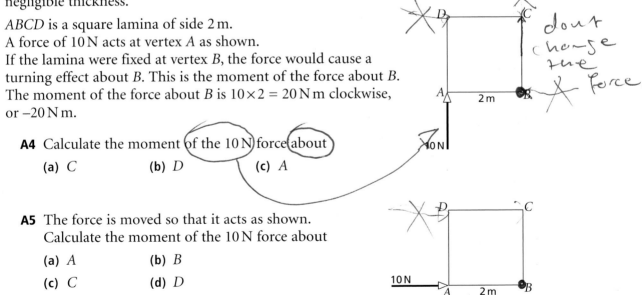

dout change the force.

K If the line of action of a force acts through a point, then the moment of the force about that point is zero.

Example 1

Forces of 4 N and 6 N act on the lamina *ABCD* as shown.

Find the total moment of these forces about *O*.

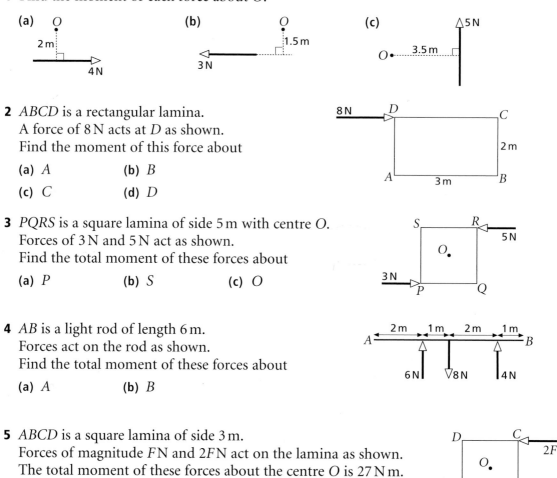

Solution

If O were fixed, the 4 N force would cause the lamina to move clockwise and the 6 N force would cause it to move anticlockwise.

Moment of 4 N force about $O = 4 \times 1.5 = 6$ N m clockwise

Moment of 6 N force about $O = 6 \times 1.5 = 9$ N m anticlockwise

The total moment is the sum of the moments of the individual forces.
Remember anticlockwise moments are positive and clockwise moments are negative.

Total moment $= 9 - 6 = 3$ N m anticlockwise

Exercise A (answers p 156)

1 Find the moment of each force about *O*.

(a) **(b)** **(c)**

2 *ABCD* is a rectangular lamina.
A force of 8 N acts at *D* as shown.
Find the moment of this force about

(a) *A* (b) *B*

(c) *C* (d) *D*

3 *PQRS* is a square lamina of side 5 m with centre *O*.
Forces of 3 N and 5 N act as shown.
Find the total moment of these forces about

(a) *P* (b) *S* (c) *O*

4 *AB* is a light rod of length 6 m.
Forces act on the rod as shown.
Find the total moment of these forces about

(a) *A* (b) *B*

5 *ABCD* is a square lamina of side 3 m.
Forces of magnitude *F* N and 2*F* N act on the lamina as shown.
The total moment of these forces about the centre *O* is 27 N m.
Find the value of *F*.

B Equilibrium of a rigid body (answers p 156)

Imagine these two children playing on a seesaw
of length 4 m and mass 30 kg, pivoted at its mid-point.
They want to get the seesaw to balance.

Sasha 25 kg

Kieran 20 kg

D **B1 (a)** Describe what happens to the seesaw if they sit at equal distances
on either side of the central pivot.

(b) Who do you think should move to try to get the seesaw to balance?

The seesaw can be modelled as a **uniform rod**, that is a body which can be
modelled as a straight line with its mass concentrated at its mid-point.
The point on a body at which its mass can be considered to be concentrated
is called the **centre of mass** of the body.
The centre of mass of a uniform rod is at its mid-point.

The pivot, P, of the seesaw is at its mid-point.

Suppose that Kieran sits at one end of the seesaw, that is 2 m from P,
and that Sasha's distance from P is x m.

Taking the seesaw and children as one composite object, the forces in newtons
acting on the object are

    the weight of the seesaw, $30g$ acting at its centre

    Kieran's weight, $20g$

    Sasha's weight, $25g$

    the upward reaction R of the pivot

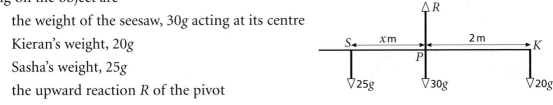

The force diagram for the seesaw is shown.

We need to find the value of x for which the seesaw is in equilibrium.

For equilibrium, the total anticlockwise moment about P must equal the total
clockwise moment about P.

The forces R N and $30g$ N go through P, so they have zero moment about P.

So $25g \times x = 20g \times 2$

     $\Rightarrow$ $x = \dfrac{40g}{25g} = 1.6$

So Sasha must sit 1.6 m from the pivot.

Additionally, for equilibrium, the resultant of the forces on the seesaw must be zero.

B2 Use the fact that the resultant force on the seesaw is zero to find R.

When a particle is in equilibrium, the resultant of the forces acting on it is zero.
This condition is not sufficient for a rigid body to be in equilibrium.
A rigid body is in equilibrium if the resultant force is zero and the total
moment is zero.

As the seesaw is in equilibrium, if the pivot is replaced by a force with the same magnitude as the reaction $R\,\text{N}$ the seesaw will remain in equilibrium.

The force diagram for the seesaw is unchanged.

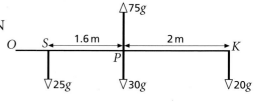

B3 (a) Find the total moment of the forces about S.

(b) Find the total moment of the forces about K.

(c) Find the total moment of the forces about O.

(d) Comment on your results.

K A rigid body is in equilibrium if the resultant force is zero and the total moment about any point is zero.

B4 A uniform rod of weight $50\,\text{N}$ rests horizontally in equilibrium on two smooth supports at A and B as shown.

The force diagram for the rod is shown.

The rod is in equilibrium, so the total moment about any point is zero.

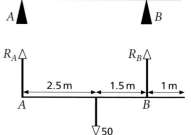

(a) Use the fact that the total moment of all the forces about A is zero to write down an equation involving R_B. Hence find the value of R_B.

(b) Now do the same for the total moment about B, and hence find the value of R_A.

(c) Find the resultant of the forces vertically to check that they are in equilibrium.

Finding the total moment about a point A is usually called 'taking moments about A'. This can be abbreviated to $\text{M}(A)$.

If the total moment about A is zero, it follows that the sum of the anticlockwise moments about A is equal to the sum of the clockwise moments about A.

B5 The supports are moved to the positions shown and the rod remains in equilibrium.

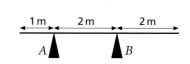

(a) By taking moments about B, find the reaction at A.

(b) By taking moments about A, find the reaction at B.

(c) What effect has moving the support had on the reactions?

B6 A particle of weight 10 N is positioned on the rod, 1 m from B as shown. The rod remains in equilibrium.

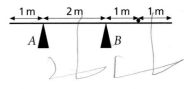

(a) Draw a force diagram for the rod.

(b) Find the reaction at A.

(c) Find the reaction at B.

A **non-uniform rod** is a body which can be modelled as a straight line with its mass concentrated at some point other than its mid-point.
The centre of mass of a non-uniform rod is generally not at its mid-point.

B7 A non-uniform rod PQ of length 6 m and weight 75 N is resting horizontally on supports at P and Q. The centre of mass of the rod is 2 m from P.

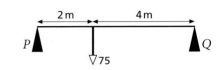

(a) Draw a force diagram for the rod.

(b) Find the reaction at P.

(c) Find the reaction at Q.

B8 A particle of weight 30 N is positioned at the centre of rod PQ.

(a) Find the reaction at P.

(b) Find the reaction at Q.

> **K** A problem about a rigid body in equilibrium can be solved by recognising that the total moment about an appropriate point equals zero and that the forces resolved in any direction equal zero.
> Taking moments about a point through which an unknown force acts can eliminate the need to find that force.

Example 2

A uniform rod has weight 30 N and length 4 m. It is suspended from point C by a light string. The rod is held in equilibrium by a vertical force applied at the end B as shown.

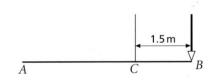

Find the magnitude of the applied force.

Solution

Sketch a force diagram showing all the forces in newtons acting on the rod.

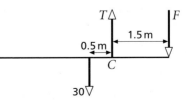

The question does not require the tension to be found, so take moments about C to set up an equation without T.

Take moments about C.

$$\text{M}(C): 30 \times 0.5 = 1.5 \times F$$
$$\Rightarrow \quad F = 10$$

The magnitude of the applied force is 10 N.

Example 3

A non-uniform rod of weight 40 N rests horizontally in equilibrium on two smooth supports at A and B as shown. The reaction on the rod at A is three times the reaction at B. Find the position of the centre of mass of the rod.

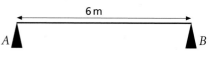

Solution

Sketch a force diagram showing all the forces acting on the rod. The reaction at A is three times the reaction at B, so label these forces 3R and R.

The rod is non-uniform, so the centre of mass may not be at its mid-point. The distance in metres between A and the centre of mass of the rod is labelled x.

Take moments about A.

$$\mathrm{M}(A): \quad 40 \times x = R \times 6$$
$$\Rightarrow \quad 40x = 6R \qquad (1)$$

Take moments about B.

$$\mathrm{M}(B): \quad 3R \times 6 = 40 \times (6 - x)$$
$$\Rightarrow \quad 18R = 240 - 40x \qquad (2)$$

Multiply (1) by 3.
$$18R = 120x \qquad (3)$$

Subtract (3) from (2).
$$0 = 240 - 160x$$
$$x = 1.5$$

The centre of mass is 1.5 m from A.

Alternatively take moments through the centre of mass of the rod, so only one equation is needed.

Exercise B (answers p 157)

1 Each diagram below shows a light rod in equilibrium under the action of coplanar parallel forces in newtons. Find the values of the lettered forces.

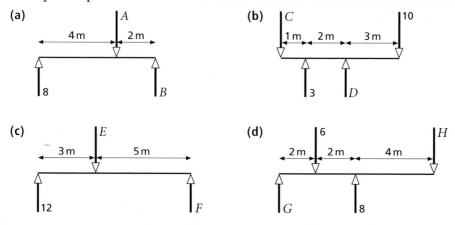

2 A seesaw of length 6 m is pivoted at its mid-point *P*.
Khyle sits on one side of the seesaw, 3 m from the pivot, and Jack sits on the
other side, 2.4 m from the pivot. The seesaw is in equilibrium and is uniform.
Given that Khyle has mass 32 kg, find the mass of Jack.

3 A uniform rod of weight 12 N and length 6 m hangs
in equilibrium in a horizontal position.
It is held in position by two light vertical cables attached
at *A* and *B* as shown.

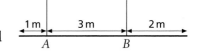

(a) Draw a force diagram for the rod.

(b) Find the tension in the cable at *A*.

(c) Find the tension in the cable at *B*.

4 A uniform rod of weight 14 N rests in equilibrium
on supports at *X* and *Y* as shown.

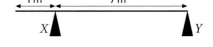

(a) Find the reaction at *X*.

(b) Find the reaction at *Y*.

5 A non-uniform rod *AB* of length 5 m and weight
100 N rests horizontally in equilibrium on supports
at *X* and *Y* as shown.
The centre of mass is 2 m from *B*.

(a) Draw a force diagram for the rod.

(b) Find the reaction at *X*.

(c) Find the reaction at *Y*.

6 A non-uniform rod *AD* of length 2 m and weight 25 N
hangs in equilibrium in a horizontal position.
It is held in position by two light vertical cables
attached at *B* and *C* as shown.
The centre of mass of the rod is 0.6 m from *A*.

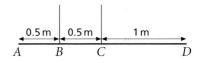

(a) Find the tension in the cable at *B*.

(b) Find the tension in the cable at *C*.

7 A non-uniform rod of weight 60 N rests horizontally in
equilibrium on supports at *P* and *Q* as shown.
The reaction at *P* is four times the reaction at *Q*.
Find the position of the centre of mass of the rod.

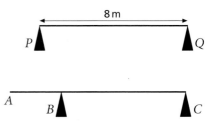

8 A uniform plank *AC* of mass 55 kg and length 10 m
rests horizontally in equilibrium on supports at
B and *C* as shown.
A child of mass 20 kg stands on the plank at *A*. The plank remains in equilibrium.
The reaction on the plank at *B* is now twice the reaction at *C*.
Find the distance *AB*.

C Tilting (answers p 157)

C1 A uniform beam rests horizontally in equilibrium on two smooth supports as shown. Tim stands on the beam.

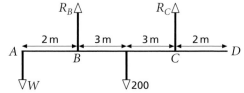

Describe what might happen to the beam if Tim stands between

(a) A and B (b) B and C (c) C and D

The beam may or may not remain in equilibrium depending on several factors including Tim's weight, the weight of the beam, the length of the beam and where the supports are placed.

The beam AD is of length 10 m and weight 200 N. The supports at B and C are positioned symmetrically 2 m from A and D respectively.
Tim stands on the beam at A.

The force diagram for the beam is shown.

The reactions at the supports B and C will vary depending on Tim's weight, W N.

C2 (a) By taking moments about B, find an equation that links W and R_C.

(b) Describe what happens to R_C as W increases.

(c) What is the maximum value of W for the beam to remain in equilibrium?

(d) Describe what happens to R_B as W increases.

(e) Write down the values of R_B and R_C as the beam is about to tilt.

C3 The supports for the beam are moved and it now rests horizontally in equilibrium as shown. Neeta stands on the beam at D and it just remains in equilibrium.

(a) Which of the supports will be the pivot if the beam tilts?

(b) By taking moments about this pivot, find Neeta's weight.

(c) Find the magnitudes of the reactions at B and C.

K When a rod or beam is about to tilt about one support, the reaction of the other support on the rod is zero.

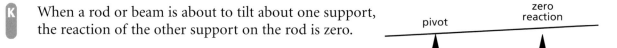

Example 4

A non-uniform rod rests horizontally in equilibrium on supports at P and Q as shown.

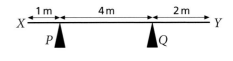

When a vertically upward force of 200 N is applied at X, the rod is about to tilt about Q.

When a vertically upward force of 100 N is applied at Y, the rod is about to tilt about P.

Find the weight of the rod and the distance of the centre of mass from X.

Solution

Draw a force diagram with the force applied at X.

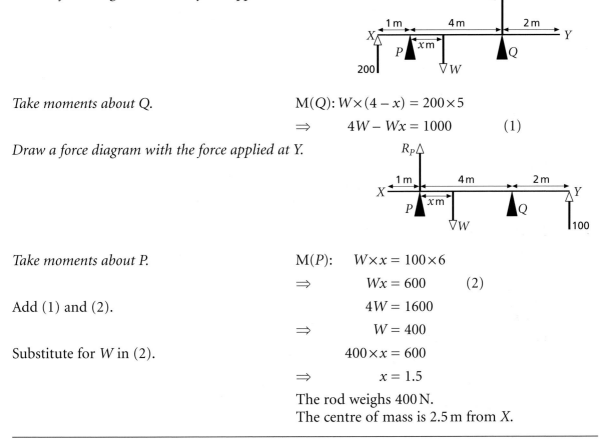

Take moments about Q.

$$M(Q): W \times (4 - x) = 200 \times 5$$
$$\Rightarrow \quad 4W - Wx = 1000 \qquad (1)$$

Draw a force diagram with the force applied at Y.

Take moments about P.

$$M(P): \quad W \times x = 100 \times 6$$
$$\Rightarrow \quad Wx = 600 \qquad (2)$$

Add (1) and (2).

$$4W = 1600$$
$$\Rightarrow \quad W = 400$$

Substitute for W in (2).

$$400 \times x = 600$$
$$\Rightarrow \quad x = 1.5$$

The rod weighs 400 N.
The centre of mass is 2.5 m from X.

Exercise C (answers p 158)

1 A uniform rod of weight 60 N and length 8 m rests horizontally in equilibrium on supports at B and C as shown. A force, F N, is applied at A so that the rod is just about to tilt.

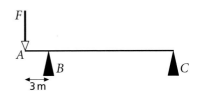

(a) What is the reaction at C?

(b) Find the magnitude of F.

(c) Find the reaction at B.

2 A uniform beam AD of length 8 m and weight 400 N rests in equilibrium on supports at B and C as shown. When Peter stands on the beam 2.2 m from D it just remains in equilibrium.

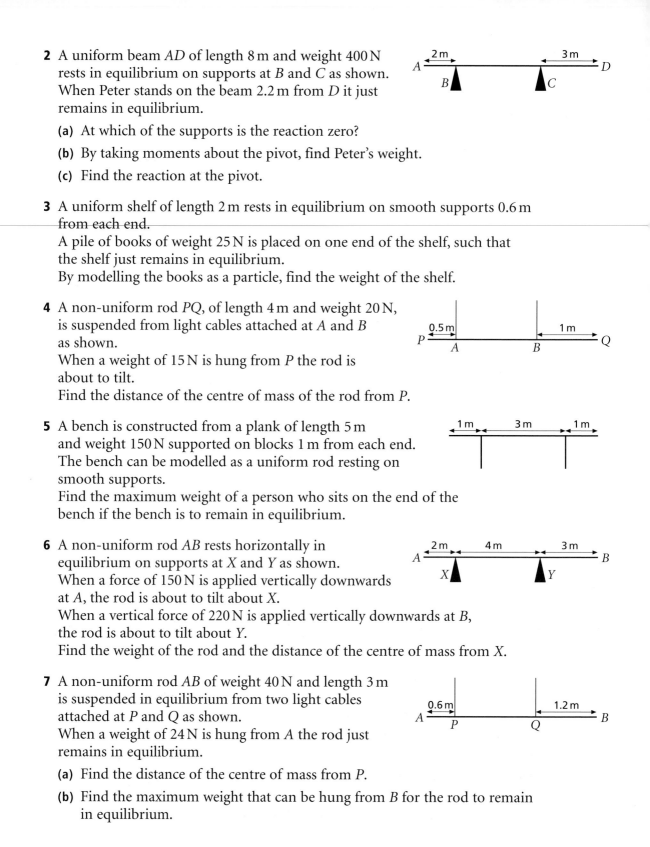

(a) At which of the supports is the reaction zero?

(b) By taking moments about the pivot, find Peter's weight.

(c) Find the reaction at the pivot.

3 A uniform shelf of length 2 m rests in equilibrium on smooth supports 0.6 m from each end.
A pile of books of weight 25 N is placed on one end of the shelf, such that the shelf just remains in equilibrium.
By modelling the books as a particle, find the weight of the shelf.

4 A non-uniform rod PQ, of length 4 m and weight 20 N, is suspended from light cables attached at A and B as shown.
When a weight of 15 N is hung from P the rod is about to tilt.
Find the distance of the centre of mass of the rod from P.

5 A bench is constructed from a plank of length 5 m and weight 150 N supported on blocks 1 m from each end. The bench can be modelled as a uniform rod resting on smooth supports.
Find the maximum weight of a person who sits on the end of the bench if the bench is to remain in equilibrium.

6 A non-uniform rod AB rests horizontally in equilibrium on supports at X and Y as shown.
When a force of 150 N is applied vertically downwards at A, the rod is about to tilt about X.
When a vertical force of 220 N is applied vertically downwards at B, the rod is about to tilt about Y.
Find the weight of the rod and the distance of the centre of mass from X.

7 A non-uniform rod AB of weight 40 N and length 3 m is suspended in equilibrium from two light cables attached at P and Q as shown.
When a weight of 24 N is hung from A the rod just remains in equilibrium.

(a) Find the distance of the centre of mass from P.

(b) Find the maximum weight that can be hung from B for the rod to remain in equilibrium.

Key points

- The moment of a force about a point is the product of the magnitude of the force and the perpendicular distance from the point to the line of action of the force.

  Moment of F about $O = Fd$

  Anticlockwise moments are taken as positive and clockwise moments as negative.

  The units of a moment are newton metres ($N\,m$). (p 123)

- If the line of action of a force acts through a point then the moment of the force about that point is zero. (p 123)

- If a rigid body is in equilibrium the resultant force is zero and the total moment about any point is zero. (pp 126, 127)

- When a rod resting on two supports is about to pivot about one of the supports then the reaction at the other support is zero. (p 130)

Mixed questions (answers p 158)

1 A uniform beam AB of weight $150\,N$ and length $3\,m$ rests on a smooth pivot at C, where $AC = 2.5\,m$.

A load of weight $800\,N$ is placed on the beam at B. The beam is held in equilibrium by a force F applied at A.

(a) Find the magnitude of F.

(b) The pivot is moved so that a force of magnitude $250\,N$ must be applied at A for the beam to remain in equilibrium. Find the new distance AC.

2 A bench is constructed from a beam AB of length $6\,m$ and mass $20\,kg$ resting horizontally in equilibrium on supports at X and Y as shown.

A child of mass $25\,kg$ sits on the bench, $2\,m$ from the end A. The child is modelled as a particle and the bench as a uniform rod. The bench and child are in equilibrium.

(a) Calculate the magnitude of the reaction force exerted by the support on the beam at X.

(b) Calculate the magnitude of the reaction force exerted by the support on the beam at Y.

(c) A man now sits on the bench at the end B. The child is still on the bench. The bench just remains in equilibrium. Calculate the mass of the man.

3 A non-uniform rod AD of length 10 m and weight 120 N rests in equilibrium on supports at B and C as shown.

(a) Given that the reaction at C is three times the reaction at B, find the distance of the centre of mass from B.

(b) A particle of weight WN is positioned on the rod at D and the rod just remains in equilibrium.
Find the value of W.

4 A non-uniform rod AB has length 5 m and weight 80 N.
The rod hangs in equilibrium in a horizontal position, held by two light vertical strings attached to the rod at points C and D as shown.
When a particle P of weight 140 N is attached to the rod at B, the rod just remains in equilibrium.

(a) Find the distance of the centre of mass of the rod from A.

(b) Find the tension in the string at D.

(c) Another particle, Q, is attached to the rod, 2 m from A.
The rod remains in equilibrium with P and Q attached.
Given that the tension in the string at D is now three times the tension at C, find the weight of the particle Q.

5 A non-uniform rod AD of length 10 m and weight 50 N rests horizontally in equilibrium on supports at B and C as shown.
The centre of mass of the rod is 4 m from A.
A particle of weight W newtons is attached to the rod at a point E, where E is x metres from A.
The rod remains in equilibrium and the magnitude of the reaction at B is now three times the magnitude of the reaction at C.

(a) Show that $W = \dfrac{50}{7 - 2x}$.

(b) Hence deduce the possible range of values of x.

Test yourself (answers p 158)

1 A uniform rod AD of length 5 m and weight 90 N rests in equilibrium on two smooth supports at B and C as shown.
The reaction on the rod at B has magnitude 30 N.

(a) Find the magnitude of the reaction at C.

(b) Find the distance CD.

2 A beam AB of length $10\,\text{m}$ is resting horizontally in equilibrium on supports at P and Q as shown. A load of weight $250\,\text{N}$ is placed on the beam at A and a load of weight $900\,\text{N}$ is placed on the beam at B. The beam remains in equilibrium on the point of tilting about Q. The beam is modelled as a uniform rod and the loads as particles.

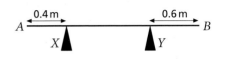

(a) Draw a diagram showing all the forces acting on the beam.

(b) Find the magnitude of the reaction at Q.

(c) Find the weight of the beam.

(d) Explain how you have used the fact that the beam is uniform.

3 A uniform rod has length $2\,\text{m}$. It rests horizontally in equilibrium on two supports at X and Y as shown. A particle of weight $20\,\text{N}$ is attached to the rod at A and the rod remains in equilibrium. The reaction on the rod at X has magnitude $40\,\text{N}$.

(a) Find the weight of the rod.

(b) Find the magnitude of the reaction at Y.

(c) The support at Y is now moved to a point Z on the rod and the rod remains in equilibrium with the particle at A.
Given that the reaction at X is now three times the reaction at Z, find the distance AZ.

4 A non-uniform plank of wood AB has length $6\,\text{m}$ and mass $90\,\text{kg}$. The plank is smoothly supported at its two ends A and B, with A and B at the same horizontal level.

A woman of mass $60\,\text{kg}$ stands on the plank at the point C, where $AC = 2\,\text{m}$, as shown.

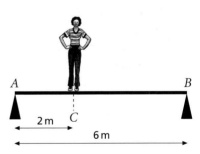

The plank is in equilibrium and the magnitudes of the reactions on the plank at A and B are equal.
The plank is modelled as a non-uniform rod and the woman as a particle.
Find

(a) the magnitude of the reaction on the plank at B

(b) the distance of the centre of mass of the plank from A

(c) State briefly how you have used the modelling assumption that

    (i) the plank is a rod

    (ii) the woman is a particle

Edexcel

Answers

1 Kinematics in one dimension

A Velocity and displacement (p 6)

A1 (a) 60 m

(b) You need to know the direction he was walking and his starting point.

A2 (a) 120 m

(b) They walked in different directions.

A3 (a) 240 m   (b) −240 m   (c) 480 m

A4 (a) 4 km   (b) 2 km

A5 (a) 420 m   (b) 240 m

(c) 180 m in the positive direction

A6 (a) $7.5\,\mathrm{m\,s^{-1}}$

(b) The gradient of the graph

(c) The graph is a straight line.

A7 (a) March: gradient = 7.09 (to 2 d.p.)
June: gradient = 7.41 (to 2 d.p.)
The units for the gradients are metres per second.

(b) The velocity of each athlete

(c) The graph is steeper, which means that the gradient and thus the velocity is greater.

(d) She ran with constant velocity on both occasions.

(e) Straight lines are unrealistic. The athlete starts from rest and increases her velocity, then runs at constant velocity for most of the race, possibly increasing it at the end of the race.

A8 (a) $5\,\mathrm{m\,s^{-1}}$ (b) $-3.3\,\mathrm{m\,s^{-1}}$ (to 1 d.p.)

(c) 150 m

A9 $1.875\,\mathrm{m\,s^{-1}}$

A10 350 m

A11 $4.375\,\mathrm{m\,s^{-1}}$

Exercise A (p 10)

1 (a) $10\,\mathrm{m\,s^{-1}}$ (b) $12.5\,\mathrm{m\,s^{-1}}$

(c) $15\,\mathrm{m\,s^{-1}}$ (d) $20.8\,\mathrm{m\,s^{-1}}$ (to 1 d.p.)

2 $\dfrac{150+150}{30+75} = 2.9\,\mathrm{m\,s^{-1}}$ (to 1 d.p.)

3 $\dfrac{150+60}{30+30} = 3.5\,\mathrm{m\,s^{-1}}$

4 $2.5 \times 60 + 1.7 \times 120 = 354\,\mathrm{m}$

5 (a) 810 m   (b) −90 m

(c) $10.8\,\mathrm{m\,s^{-1}}$ (d) $-1.2\,\mathrm{m\,s^{-1}}$

6 (a) $\dfrac{480+300}{180} = 4.3\,\mathrm{m\,s^{-1}}$ (to 1 d.p.)

(b) $\dfrac{480-300}{180} = 1\,\mathrm{m\,s^{-1}}$

7 Total time $= \dfrac{360}{80} = 4.5$ hours
Time for first half $= \dfrac{180}{75} = 2.4$ hours
Average speed for second half $= \dfrac{180}{4.5-2.5}$
$= 85.7\,\mathrm{km\,h^{-1}}$ (to 1 d.p.)

8 (a) He stopped for 20 s.   (b) $2\,\mathrm{m\,s^{-1}}$

(c) $1.5\,\mathrm{m\,s^{-1}}$ (d) $1.3\,\mathrm{m\,s^{-1}}$ (to 1 d.p.)

9 (a)

(b) $200 \div 75 = 2.7\,\mathrm{m\,s^{-1}}$ (to 1 d.p.)

(c) $0\,\mathrm{m\,s^{-1}}$

10 Tracy overtakes Simon after about 86 minutes, about 5 miles from Aycliffe.

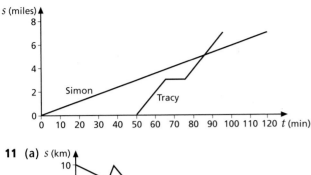

11 (a)

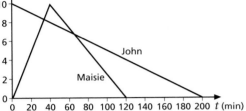

(b) They pass each other at about 12:33, 8.3 km from Blakesfield and about 13:07, 6.7 km from Blakesfield.

(c) 12:40

B Graphs of motion (p 11)

B1 (a) 0.25

(b) Metres per second per second

(c) The rate of increase of velocity, namely the acceleration, of the car

B2 The rate of decrease of velocity, or deceleration, of the car

B3 (a) $2\,\mathrm{m\,s^{-1}}$ **(b)** $4\,\mathrm{m\,s^{-1}}$ **(c)** $20\,\mathrm{m\,s^{-1}}$ **(d)** $40\,\mathrm{m\,s^{-1}}$

B4 $15\,\mathrm{m\,s^{-1}}$

B5 $0.1\,\mathrm{m\,s^{-2}}$

B6 (a) (i) A straight line

(ii) A line parallel to the t-axis

(b) (i) A steeper line

(ii) A line higher above the t-axis

(c) (i) A horizontal line

(ii) A line along the t-axis

B7 No, because the acceleration is zero through each phase of the cyclist's motion. There is no way to represent the instantaneous changes at t_1 and t_2.

B8 (a) The velocity is increasing at a constant rate from zero to $V\,\mathrm{m\,s^{-1}}$ at $T\,\mathrm{s}$. The acceleration is constant.

(b)

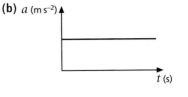

(c) The displacement is increasing at a faster and faster rate.

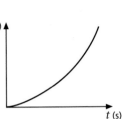

B9 A: constant velocity of $10\,\mathrm{m\,s^{-1}}$

B: velocity $10\,\mathrm{m\,s^{-1}}$, starts to decrease at constant rate

C: velocity $5\,\mathrm{m\,s^{-1}}$, constant deceleration of $0.25\,\mathrm{m\,s^{-2}}$

D: velocity $0\,\mathrm{m\,s^{-1}}$, constant deceleration of $0.25\,\mathrm{m\,s^{-2}}$

E: velocity $-5\,\mathrm{m\,s^{-1}}$, constant deceleration of $0.25\,\mathrm{m\,s^{-2}}$

F: velocity $-10\,\mathrm{m\,s^{-1}}$, now remains constant

G: constant velocity of $-10\,\mathrm{m\,s^{-1}}$

Exercise B (p 14)

1 (a) $0.2\,\mathrm{m\,s^{-1}}$ **(b)** $0.4\,\mathrm{m\,s^{-1}}$ **(c)** $2\,\mathrm{m\,s^{-1}}$

(d) $12\,\mathrm{m\,s^{-1}}$

2 Deceleration of $0.5\,\mathrm{m\,s^{-2}}$

3 (a) $0.2\,\mathrm{m\,s^{-2}}$ **(b)** $0\,\mathrm{m\,s^{-2}}$ **(c)** $-0.4\,\mathrm{m\,s^{-2}}$

4 (a) The displacement increases at a steady rate until t_1, it is constant until t_2 and then it decreases at a faster steady rate until it reaches zero.

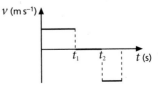

(b) The displacement is decreasing at a steady rate throughout the motion; the object passes through the origin at time t_1.

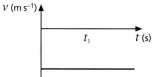

5 (a) The velocity is decreasing at a constant rate throughout the motion.

(b) The velocity is constant and negative until time t_1, then it increases at a steady rate until time t_2, when it is positive. After t_2 the velocity remains constant.

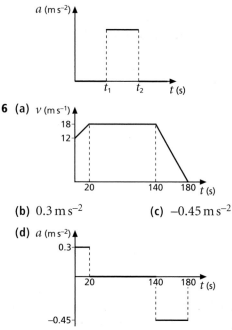

6 (a)

(b) $0.3\,\mathrm{m\,s^{-2}}$ **(c)** $-0.45\,\mathrm{m\,s^{-2}}$

(d)

C Area under a velocity–time graph (p 15)

C1 (a) 180   **(b)** 180   **(c)** Metres

    (d) Aisha's displacement

C2 (a) 120   **(b)** −120   **(c)** $0\,\mathrm{m}$

C3 $195\,\mathrm{m}$

C4 (a) The velocity increases at a steady rate from zero until it reaches its maximum of $15\,\mathrm{m\,s^{-1}}$ after $45\,\mathrm{s}$. It then continues at this constant value for a further $75\,\mathrm{s}$.

    (b) $337.5\,\mathrm{m}$ **(c)** $1462.5\,\mathrm{m}$

Exercise C (p 17)

1 $2250\,\mathrm{m}$

2 (a) $60\,\mathrm{m}$ **(b)** $300\,\mathrm{m}$

3 (a)

    (b) $1602\,\mathrm{m}$

4 (a)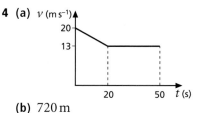

    (b) $720\,\mathrm{m}$

5 $1170\,\mathrm{m}$

6 Displacement of car at time $T\,\mathrm{s}$
$$= \tfrac{1}{2} \times T \times (0.25T)$$
Displacement of van at time $T\,\mathrm{s}$ $(T > 30)$
$$= \tfrac{1}{2} \times 30 \times 10 + (T - 30) \times 10$$
The car overtakes the van when the displacement of the car is equal to the displacement of the van.
$$\Rightarrow \frac{T^2}{8} = 10T - 150$$
$$\Rightarrow T^2 - 80T + 1200 = 0$$
$$\Rightarrow T = 20, 60$$
As $T > 30$, the car overtakes the van after $60\,\mathrm{s}$.

7 (a) The area under the velocity graph for $0 < t < T$ is equal to the area under the graph for $T < t < 9$.

So $4T = 2(9 - T) \Rightarrow T = 3$

    (b) $24\,\mathrm{m}$

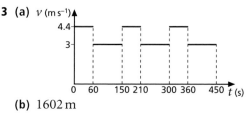

D Motion with constant acceleration (p 18)

D1 $a = \dfrac{v-u}{t} \Rightarrow at = v - u \Rightarrow v = u + at$

D2 $15\,\text{m s}^{-1}$

D3 $14\,\text{m s}^{-1}$

D4 $277.5\,\text{m}$

D5 $20\,\text{s}$

Exercise D (p 20)

1 $10\,\text{m s}^{-1}$

2 $12\,\text{m s}^{-1}$

3 $210\,\text{m}$

4 $0.2\,\text{m s}^{-2}$

5 $20\,\text{m s}^{-1}$

6 $4\,\text{m s}^{-1}$

7 (a) $11\,\text{m s}^{-1}$ (b) $375\,\text{m}$

8 (a) $120\,\text{m}$ (b) $0.07\,\text{m s}^{-2}$ (to 2 d.p.)

9 (a) $40\,\text{s}$ (b) $320\,\text{m}$

E Constant acceleration equations (p 21)

E1 $s = \frac{1}{2}(u + v)t \Rightarrow s = \frac{1}{2}(u + u + at)t$
$\Rightarrow s = \frac{1}{2}(2u + at)t \Rightarrow s = ut + \frac{1}{2}at^2$

E2 $120\,\text{m}$

E3 (a) $u = v - at$

    (b) $s = \frac{1}{2}(u + v)t \Rightarrow s = \frac{1}{2}(v - at + v)t$
    $\Rightarrow s = \frac{1}{2}(2v - at)t \Rightarrow s = vt - \frac{1}{2}at^2$

E4 (a) $t = \dfrac{v - u}{a}$

    (b) $s = \frac{1}{2}(u + v)t \Rightarrow s = \frac{1}{2}(u + v)\left(\dfrac{v - u}{a}\right)$
    $\Rightarrow s = \dfrac{v^2 - u^2}{2a}$
    $\Rightarrow v^2 = u^2 + 2as$

E5 $20.6\,\text{m s}^{-1}$ (to 1 d.p.)

E6 $15.8\,\text{m s}^{-1}$ (to 1 d.p.)

Exercise E (p 22)

1 $7.5\,\text{m s}^{-1}$

2 $26.0\,\text{m s}^{-1}$ (to 1 d.p.)

3 Acceleration $= 2.4\,\text{m s}^{-2}$ (to 1 d.p.),
    distance $= 189\,\text{m}$

4 Distance $= 440\,\text{m}$, final speed $= 30\,\text{m s}^{-1}$

5 Deceleration $= 1.722\,\text{m s}^{-2}$, time $= 12.2\,\text{s}$ (to 1 d.p.)

6 (a) Area of rectangle $= ut$
      Area of triangle $= \frac{1}{2}at \times t = \frac{1}{2}at^2$
      $\Rightarrow s = ut + \frac{1}{2}at^2$

    (b) Area of large rectangle $= vt$
      Area of triangle $= \frac{1}{2}at^2$
      $\Rightarrow s = vt - \frac{1}{2}at^2$

7 (a) $0.4\,\text{m s}^{-2}$ (b) $36\,\text{m s}^{-1}$

8 (a) Substituting into $v = u + at$ gives $18 = 5 + 25a$
      $\Rightarrow 13 = 25a \Rightarrow a = 0.52$

    (b) $287.5\,\text{m}$ (c) $13.2\,\text{m s}^{-1}$

9 $61.2\,\text{s}$ (to 1 d.p.)

10 (a) $1.27\,\text{m s}^{-1}$ (to 2 d.p.)   (b) $v = \dfrac{u}{\sqrt{2}}$

F Vertical motion under gravity (p 24)

F1 (a) The stone starts from rest and moves vertically
      downwards with constant acceleration until it
      hits the water.

    (b) The motion is not affected by the weight of
      the stone: the stone will move with the same
      constant acceleration.

F2 $19.6\,\text{m s}^{-1}$ downwards

F3 (a) $5.2\,\text{m s}^{-1}$ upwards
    (b) $4.6\,\text{m s}^{-1}$ downwards
    (c) $14.4\,\text{m s}^{-1}$ downwards
    (d) $24.2\,\text{m s}^{-1}$ downwards

F4 (a) The velocity decreases at a constant rate from
      its original value to zero and continues to
      decrease, finishing with a negative value.

    (b) Zero

    (c) The velocity has the same magnitude but it is
      acting downwards rather than upwards.

    (d)   (e)

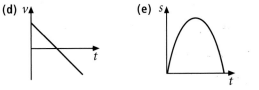

Exercise F (p 25)

Answers are given to three significant figures where appropriate

1 $19.6\,\mathrm{m\,s^{-1}}$ downwards

2 (a) $29.4\,\mathrm{m\,s^{-1}}$ downwards

   (b) $44.1\,\mathrm{m}$ (c) $122.5\,\mathrm{m}$

3 $24.8\,\mathrm{m\,s^{-1}}$

4 $9.9\,\mathrm{m}$

5 (a) $5.10\,\mathrm{m}$ (b) $2.04\,\mathrm{s}$

6 (a) $24.2\,\mathrm{m\,s^{-1}}$ (b) $4.95\,\mathrm{s}$

7 (a) $0.30\,\mathrm{s},\ 3.37\,\mathrm{s}$ (b) $3.07\,\mathrm{s}$

8 $3.12\,\mathrm{s}$

9 (a)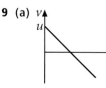

   (b) $v^2 = u^2 - 2gs$, and $v = 0$ at maximum height
   $$\Rightarrow s = \frac{u^2}{2g}$$

   (c) $v = u - gt$, and $v = 0$ at maximum height
   $$\Rightarrow t = \frac{u}{g}$$

   (d) The only force acting on the ball is its weight; air resistance is negligible.

10 (a) The coin hits the ground when $s = -1.2$, so $-1.2 = 2t - 4.9t^2$. The time is positive when the coin hits the ground, so take the positive root of this equation.
   The coin hits the ground after 0.74 seconds.

   (b) $5.25\,\mathrm{m\,s^{-1}}$

Mixed questions (p 27)

1 (a) The gradient of the speed–time graph is negative and constant for $0 \le t \le 5$ indicating that the car has constant deceleration.

   (b) $1.2\,\mathrm{m\,s^{-2}}$ (c) $345\,\mathrm{m}$ (d) $23\,\mathrm{m\,s^{-1}}$

2 (a) $0.8\,\mathrm{m\,s^{-2}}$ (b) $150\,\mathrm{m}$

3 (a) $16.3\,\mathrm{m}$ (to 1 d.p.)   (b) $17.9\,\mathrm{m\,s^{-1}}$ (to 1 d.p.)

   (c) $2.33\,\mathrm{s}$ (to 2 d.p.)

4 (a) $0.16\,\mathrm{m\,s^{-2}}$ (b) $0.13\,\mathrm{m\,s^{-2}}$

   (c) Distance travelled while accelerating $= 8\,\mathrm{m}$
   Distance travelled while decelerating $= 9.6\,\mathrm{m}$
   So distance at constant speed $= 22.4\,\mathrm{m}$
   Time at constant speed $= 22.4 \div 1.6 = 14\,\mathrm{s}$
   So total time $= 36\,\mathrm{s}$

5 (a) $4.5\,\mathrm{s}$ (b) $-10\,\mathrm{m\,s^{-2}}$ (c) $202.5\,\mathrm{m}$

6 (a) $10\,\mathrm{s}$

   (b)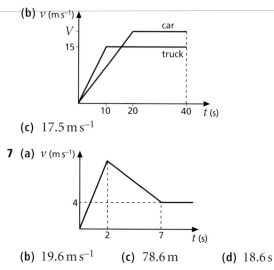

   (c) $17.5\,\mathrm{m\,s^{-1}}$

7 (a)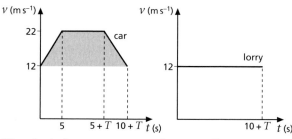

   (b) $19.6\,\mathrm{m\,s^{-1}}$ (c) $78.6\,\mathrm{m}$ (d) $18.6\,\mathrm{s}$

   (e) Air resistance or wind could be taken in to account.

8 The car travels at constant velocity for time T s. When overtaking the car has to travel $(50 + 16 + 50 + 4) = 120\,\mathrm{m}$ further than the lorry. The velocity–time graphs for the car and the lorry are as shown.

The shaded area represents the extra distance travelled by the car.
So $120 = \frac{1}{2}(10 + T + T) \times 10$
$\Rightarrow 24 = 2T + 10 \Rightarrow T = 7$
The car takes $17\,\mathrm{s}$ to get from its initial to its final position.
In this time the lorry has travelled $12 \times 17 = 204\,\mathrm{m}$. The car has travelled a total of $324\,\mathrm{m}$.

Test yourself (p 29)

1 (a) $39.2\,\text{m s}^{-1}$ (b) $78.4\,\text{m}$

2 (a) $0.4\,\text{m s}^{-2}$ (b) $10\,\text{m s}^{-1}$

3 (a) $467.5\,\text{m}$

  (b) (i) $0.73\,\text{m s}^{-2}$ (to 2 d.p.) (ii) $0\,\text{m s}^{-2}$

  (iii) $-0.55\,\text{m s}^{-2}$

4 (a) $5\,\text{m s}^{-2}$ (b) $40\,\text{m}$

5 (a)

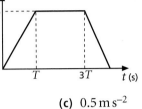

  (b) $T = 12$ (c) $0.5\,\text{m s}^{-2}$

6 (a) After 10 seconds, $v = 0 + 1.2 \times 10 = 12$.
    In the next 24 s, $u = 12$, $a = 0.75$, $t = 24$,
    so $v = 12 + 0.75 \times 24 = 30$.
    So 34 s after leaving A the speed is $30\,\text{m s}^{-1}$.

  (b)

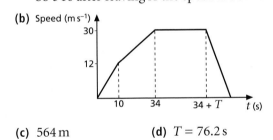

  (c) $564\,\text{m}$ (d) $T = 76.2\,\text{s}$

7 $T = 6$

2 Kinematics in two dimensions

Answers are given to three significant figures where appropriate.

A Displacement (p 31)

A1 Alexia's possible finishing points lie on a circle of radius $50\,\text{m}$, centred on her starting point.

A2 (a) x-component $= 36 \sin 30° = 18.0\,\text{m}$
    y-component $= 36 \cos 30° = 31.2\,\text{m}$

  (b) $\begin{bmatrix} 18.0 \\ 31.2 \end{bmatrix} \text{m}$

A3 (a) $60\mathbf{i} + 80\mathbf{j}$

  (b) $\sqrt{80^2 + 60^2} = 100\,\text{m}$

  (c) $\tan^{-1}\left(\frac{80}{60}\right) = 53.1°$ to the x-direction

A4 (a) $20°$

  (b) x-component $= 30 \cos 20° = 28.2\,\text{m}$
    y-component $= -30 \sin 20° = -10.3\,\text{m}$

  (c) $(28.2\mathbf{i} - 10.3\mathbf{j})\,\text{m}$

Exercise A (p 34)

1 (a) $(20\mathbf{i} + 15\mathbf{j})\,\text{km}$ (b) $(-20\mathbf{i})\,\text{km}$
  (c) $(18\mathbf{i} - 6\mathbf{j})\,\text{km}$ (d) $(-5\mathbf{i} + 10\mathbf{j})\,\text{km}$

2 (a) $8\mathbf{i} + 3\mathbf{j}$

  (b) Magnitude $= \sqrt{8^2 + 3^2} = 8.54$
    Direction $= \tan^{-1}\left(\frac{3}{8}\right) = 20.6°$ to the direction of the $\mathbf{i}$ vector

3 (a) $\sqrt{15^2 + 12^2} = 19.2\,\text{m}$

  (b) $\tan^{-1}\left(\frac{12}{15}\right) = 38.7°$ clockwise from the vector $\mathbf{i}$

4 $(100 \sin 70° \mathbf{i} + 100 \cos 70° \mathbf{j})\,\text{m} = (94.0\mathbf{i} + 34.2\mathbf{j})\,\text{m}$

5 $(35.4\mathbf{i} - 35.4\mathbf{j})\,\text{m}$

6 Distance $= \sqrt{15^2 + 20^2} = 25\,\text{m}$
  $\tan^{-1}\left(\frac{20}{15}\right) = 53.1°$, so bearing is $323.1°$

B Resultant displacement (p 34)

B1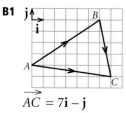

$\overrightarrow{AC} = 7\mathbf{i} - \mathbf{j}$

B2 (a) $(6\mathbf{i} + 4\mathbf{j}) + (\mathbf{i} - 5\mathbf{j}) = (6 + 1)\mathbf{i} + (4 - 5)\mathbf{j}$
$= 7\mathbf{i} - \mathbf{j}$

(b)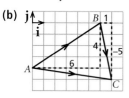

Total displacement in x-direction $= 6 + 1 = 7$
Total displacement in y-direction $= 4 - 5 = -1$

B3 (a) $\sqrt{7^2 + 1^2} = 7.07\,\text{m}$

(b) $\sqrt{6^2 + 4^2} + \sqrt{1^2 + 5^2} = 12.3\,\text{m}$

Exercise B (p 36)

1 $150\mathbf{i} - 30\mathbf{j}$

2 (a) $2\mathbf{i} + 2\mathbf{j}$

(b) 2.83 units at an angle of 45° to the vector $\mathbf{i}$

3 Let fourth vector be $a\mathbf{i} + b\mathbf{j}$.
$(-2 + 5 + 16 + a)\mathbf{i} + (-3 - 7 + 4 + b)\mathbf{j} = 10\mathbf{i} - 2\mathbf{j}$
$\Rightarrow (19 + a)\mathbf{i} + (b - 6)\mathbf{j} = 10\mathbf{i} - 2\mathbf{j}$
Hence the fourth vector is $-9\mathbf{i} + 4\mathbf{j}$.

4 (a) $(5\mathbf{i} + 8\mathbf{j})\,\text{m}$ (b) $\sqrt{5^2 + 8^2} = 9.43\,\text{m}$
(c) $\sqrt{8^2 + 2^2} + \sqrt{3^2 + 10^2} = 18.7\,\text{m}$

5 The resultant displacement is $(80\mathbf{i} + 10\mathbf{j})\,\text{m}$.
The displacement is 80.6 m at an angle of 7.1°
with the vector $\mathbf{i}$.

C Position vector (p 36)

C1 $\mathbf{r}_B = 5\mathbf{i} - \mathbf{j}$

C2 $\mathbf{s} = \mathbf{i} - 3\mathbf{j}$

C3 $(6\mathbf{i} - 2\mathbf{j}) + (-3\mathbf{i} + \mathbf{j}) = 3\mathbf{i} - \mathbf{j}$

C4 (a) $\mathbf{r}_C = 3\mathbf{i} + 2\mathbf{j}, \mathbf{r}_D = \mathbf{i} + 3\mathbf{j}$ (b) $-2\mathbf{i} + \mathbf{j}$

C5 $(\mathbf{i} + 3\mathbf{j}) - (3\mathbf{i} + 2\mathbf{j}) = -2\mathbf{i} + \mathbf{j}$

C6 $(4\mathbf{i} + 3\mathbf{j}) - (-2\mathbf{i} + 5\mathbf{j}) = (4 + 2)\mathbf{i} + (3 - 5)\mathbf{j}$
$= 6\mathbf{i} - 2\mathbf{j}$

C7 (a) When $t = 0, \mathbf{r} = 20\mathbf{j}$
When $t = 10, \mathbf{r} = 300\mathbf{i} - 20\mathbf{j}$

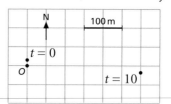

(b) $300\mathbf{i} - 40\mathbf{j}$

(c) 303 m

(d) The speedboat is due east when the
$\mathbf{j}$-component of the position vector is zero.
$20 - 4t = 0 \Rightarrow t = 5$

Exercise C (p 38)

1 $12\mathbf{i} - \mathbf{j}$

2 (a) $(4\mathbf{i} + 2\mathbf{j})\,\text{km}$ (b) 4.47 km

3 $(4\mathbf{i} - 2\mathbf{j}) - (-3\mathbf{i} + 6\mathbf{j}) = 7\mathbf{i} - 8\mathbf{j}$

4 $(25\mathbf{i} - 40\mathbf{j}) - (40\mathbf{i} - 30\mathbf{j}) = (-15\mathbf{i} - 10\mathbf{j})\,\text{m}$

5 (a) $-2\mathbf{j}$ (b) $300\mathbf{i} + 38\mathbf{j}$
(c)

$$300\mathbf{i} + 38\mathbf{j} \quad t = 10$$

(d) $(300\mathbf{i} + 38\mathbf{j}) - (-2\mathbf{j}) = (300\mathbf{i} + 40\mathbf{j})\,\text{m}$

6 (a) $18\mathbf{i} + 3.1\mathbf{j}$

(b) The ball hits the ground when the
$\mathbf{j}$-component of the position vector is zero.
$8t - 4.9t^2 = 0 \Rightarrow t(8 - 4.9t) = 0$
$\Rightarrow t = 0, t = 1.63$
$t = 0$ when the ball is kicked, so the ball hits
the ground when $t = 1.63$.

(c) The horizontal distance covered is the
$\mathbf{i}$-component of the position vector.
The ball has covered $18 \times 1.63 = 29.3\,\text{m}$.

7 (a) When $2t - 10 = 0$, hence when $t = 5$

(b) $\mathbf{r} = 31\mathbf{j}$, so the particle is 31 m from its starting
point at this time.

8 (a) The object is south-east of the origin when
$8t - 12 = -(t^2 - 8) \Rightarrow t^2 + 8t - 20 = 0$
$\Rightarrow (t + 10)(t - 2) = 0 \Rightarrow t = -10, t = 2$
When $t = 2$, $\mathbf{r} = 4\mathbf{i} - 4\mathbf{j}$
When $t = -10$, $\mathbf{r} = -92\mathbf{i} + 92\mathbf{j}$
The object is south-east of the origin when
$t = 2$.

(b) 5.66 km

D Velocity (p 39)

D1 (a) $4\mathbf{i} + 2\mathbf{j}$ **(b)** $20\mathbf{i} + 10\mathbf{j}$
(c) $10\mathbf{i} + 5\mathbf{j}$ **(d)** $\mathbf{r} = 4t\mathbf{i} + 2t\mathbf{j}$

D2 (a) $4.47\,\mathrm{m\,s^{-1}}$ **(b)** $\theta = 26.6°$

D3 (a)

(b) 45°
(c) $\mathbf{i}$-component $= 55\cos 45° = 38.9$
$\mathbf{j}$-component $= -55\sin 45° = -38.9$
(d) $(38.9\mathbf{i} - 38.9\mathbf{j})\,\mathrm{m\,s^{-1}}$

D4 (a) $(15\mathbf{i} + 25\mathbf{j})\,\mathrm{m}$ **(b)** $\dfrac{15\mathbf{i} + 25\mathbf{j}}{5} = (3\mathbf{i} + 5\mathbf{j})\,\mathrm{m\,s^{-1}}$

D5 (a) $3\mathbf{i}\,\mathrm{m}$ **(b)** $(63\mathbf{i} + 240\mathbf{j})\,\mathrm{m}$
(c) $(60\mathbf{i} + 240\mathbf{j})\,\mathrm{m}$ **(d)** $\dfrac{60\mathbf{i} + 240\mathbf{j}}{30} = (2\mathbf{i} + 8\mathbf{j})\,\mathrm{m\,s^{-1}}$

D6 (a) $(5t\mathbf{i} - 2t\mathbf{j})\,\mathrm{m}$ **(b)** $\big((5t - 10)\mathbf{i} + (4 - 2t)\mathbf{j}\big)\,\mathrm{m}$

Exercise D (p 41)

1 (a) $20\mathbf{j}\,\mathrm{m\,s^{-1}}$ **(b)** $-5\mathbf{i}\,\mathrm{m\,s^{-1}}$

2 (a) $(3\mathbf{i} + \mathbf{j})\,\mathrm{m}$ **(b)** $(30\mathbf{i} + 10\mathbf{j})\,\mathrm{m}$
(c) $(3t\mathbf{i} + t\mathbf{j})\,\mathrm{m}$

3 (a) $14.4\,\mathrm{m\,s^{-1}}$
(b) 33.7° below the vector $\mathbf{i}$

4 $20\sin 65°\mathbf{i} + 20\cos 65°\mathbf{j} = (18.1\mathbf{i} + 8.5\mathbf{j})\,\mathrm{m\,s^{-1}}$

5 $(12\mathbf{i} + 9\mathbf{j})\,\mathrm{m\,s^{-1}}$

6 (a) $(-30\mathbf{i} + 240\mathbf{j})\,\mathrm{m}$
(b) $\dfrac{-30\mathbf{i} + 240\mathbf{j}}{60} = (-0.5\mathbf{i} + 4\mathbf{j})\,\mathrm{m\,s^{-1}}$

7 When $t = 0$, $\mathbf{r} = 10\mathbf{i} + \mathbf{j}$
When $t = 30$, $\mathbf{r} = -80\mathbf{i} + 151\mathbf{j}$
Displacement $= -90\mathbf{i} + 150\mathbf{j}$
Average velocity $= \dfrac{-90\mathbf{i} + 150\mathbf{j}}{30} = (-3\mathbf{i} + 5\mathbf{j})\,\mathrm{m\,s^{-1}}$

8 (a) $200\mathbf{i} - 22\mathbf{j}$ **(b)** $800\mathbf{i} - 52\mathbf{j}$
(c) $\dfrac{600\mathbf{i} - 30\mathbf{j}}{10} = (60\mathbf{i} - 3\mathbf{j})\,\mathrm{m\,s^{-1}}$

9 (a) $4t\mathbf{i} - 3t\mathbf{j}$ **(b)** $(20 + 4t)\mathbf{i} + (30 - 3t)\mathbf{j}$
(c) $260\mathbf{i} - 150\mathbf{j}$

10 $\mathbf{r} = (10t - 30)\mathbf{i} + (12 - 3t)\mathbf{j}$
When $t = 20$, $\mathbf{r} = 170\mathbf{i} - 48\mathbf{j}$

11 (a) $\mathbf{r} = (6 - 2t)\mathbf{i} + (10 + 3t)\mathbf{j}$
(b) The particle is moving parallel to the vector $\mathbf{j}$
when the $\mathbf{i}$ term is zero.
$\Rightarrow 6 - 2t = 0 \Rightarrow t = 3$

E Resultant velocity (p 43)

E1 $0.1\,\mathrm{m\,s^{-1}}$

E2 (a) $0.361\,\mathrm{m\,s^{-1}}$ **(b)** $33.7°$

E3 (a)

(b) Scale drawing leading to resultant of
$0.46\,\mathrm{m\,s^{-1}}$ at 27° to the direction of motion of
the tray.

E4 $3\,\mathrm{m\,s^{-1}}$

E5 (a)

(b) $-1\,\mathrm{m\,s^{-1}}$, taking the direction of the current as
positive

E6 (a) $2.24\,\mathrm{m\,s^{-1}}$ **(b)** 63.4° to the bank

E7 (a)

(b) $1.41\,\mathrm{m\,s^{-1}}$ at 45° to the river bank.

E8 $1.80\,\mathrm{m\,s^{-1}}$ at 56.3° to the river bank.

Exercise E (p 45)

1 $(50\mathbf{i} + 5\mathbf{j})\,\mathrm{m\,s}^{-1}$

2 $(-3\mathbf{i} + 2\mathbf{j}) + (2\mathbf{i} - \mathbf{j}) = (-\mathbf{i} + \mathbf{j})\,\mathrm{km\,h}^{-1}$

3 (a)

(Diagram: vector triangle with $1.5\,\mathrm{m\,s}^{-1}$ along top, $1\,\mathrm{m\,s}^{-1}$ up left side, and *resultant*)

   (b) $1.80\,\mathrm{m\,s}^{-1}$ (c) $33.7°$

4 (a) $(\mathbf{i} + 6\mathbf{j})\,\mathrm{m\,s}^{-1}$ (b) $6.08\,\mathrm{m\,s}^{-1}$

   (c) $80.5°$ with the vector $\mathbf{i}$

5 (a) $3.20\,\mathrm{m\,s}^{-1}$ at $51.3°$ to the bank

   (b) $3.91\,\mathrm{m\,s}^{-1}$ at $39.8°$ to the bank

6 Velocity of water $= v\,\mathrm{m\,s}^{-1}$

Resultant velocity downstream $= 2.4 + v$

Time taken to row downstream $= \dfrac{50}{2.4 + v}$

Resultant velocity upstream $= 2.4 - v$

Time taken to row upstream $= \dfrac{50}{2.4 - v}$

$\dfrac{50}{2.4 + v} + \dfrac{50}{2.4 - v} = 75$

$50(2.4 - v) + 50(2.4 + v) = 75(2.4 + v)(2.4 - v)$

$240 = 432 - 75v^2$

$v = 1.6$

F Acceleration (p 46)

F1 (a) (i) $(2\mathbf{i} + \mathbf{j})\,\mathrm{m\,s}^{-1}$ (ii) $(4\mathbf{i} + 2\mathbf{j})\,\mathrm{m\,s}^{-1}$

     (iii) $(10\mathbf{i} + 5\mathbf{j})\,\mathrm{m\,s}^{-1}$

   (b) $\mathbf{v} = 2t\mathbf{i} + t\mathbf{j}$

F2 (a)

(Diagram: vector with components 5 and 2, labelled $(-2\mathbf{i} + 5\mathbf{j})\,\mathrm{m\,s}^{-2}$)   (b) $5.39\,\mathrm{m\,s}^{-2}$

   (c) $68.2°$ to the negative $\mathbf{i}$-direction

F3 $-2\mathbf{i} - \mathbf{j}$

F4 (a) $(-20\mathbf{i} + 30\mathbf{j})\,\mathrm{m\,s}^{-1}$

   (b) $(-\mathbf{i} + 1.5\mathbf{j})\,\mathrm{m\,s}^{-2}$

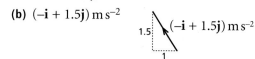

(Diagram: vector with components 1.5 and 1, labelled $(-\mathbf{i} + 1.5\mathbf{j})\,\mathrm{m\,s}^{-2}$)

Exercise F (p 48)

1 (a) $(\mathbf{i} - \mathbf{j})\,\mathrm{m\,s}^{-1}$ (b) $(5\mathbf{i} - 5\mathbf{j})\,\mathrm{m\,s}^{-1}$

2 $(-\mathbf{i} + \mathbf{j}) + 3(2\mathbf{i} - \mathbf{j}) = (5\mathbf{i} - 2\mathbf{j})\,\mathrm{m\,s}^{-1}$

3 (a) $(2\mathbf{i} + 6\mathbf{j})\,\mathrm{m\,s}^{-1}$ (b) $(0.2\mathbf{i} + 0.6\mathbf{j})\,\mathrm{m\,s}^{-2}$

4 $\dfrac{(-10\mathbf{i} - 5\mathbf{j})}{5} = (-2\mathbf{i} - \mathbf{j})\,\mathrm{m\,s}^{-2}$

5 The acceleration is $2.24\,\mathrm{m\,s}^{-2}$ at $63.4°$ clockwise from the vector $\mathbf{i}$.

6 $\dfrac{4\mathbf{i} + 2\mathbf{j}}{4} = (\mathbf{i} + 0.5\mathbf{j})\,\mathrm{m\,s}^{-2}$

7 $12\mathbf{i} + 2\mathbf{j} - 3(4\mathbf{i} - \mathbf{j}) = 5\mathbf{j}\,\mathrm{m\,s}^{-1}$

8 Acceleration $= (-3\mathbf{i} + 4\mathbf{j})\,\mathrm{m\,s}^{-2}$

Magnitude $= 5\,\mathrm{m\,s}^{-2}$ at $53.1°$ to the negative $\mathbf{i}$-direction

9 (a) $\mathbf{v} = (t\mathbf{i} - t\mathbf{j})$ (b) $11.3\,\mathrm{m\,s}^{-1}$

10 (a) $\mathbf{v} = (8 - 2t)\mathbf{i} + (2 + t)\mathbf{j}$ (b) $t = 4$

11 At time t, $\mathbf{v} = (2t - 4)\mathbf{i} + (t + 3)\mathbf{j}$

P moves parallel to $(\mathbf{i} + \mathbf{j})$ when $2t - 4 = t + 3$

$\Rightarrow t = 7$

Mixed questions (p 50)

1 (a) $\mathbf{r} = -5t\mathbf{j}$, $\mathbf{s} = (5t + 200)\mathbf{i} + 8t\mathbf{j}$

   (b) $262\,\mathrm{m}$

   (c) $(5t + 200)\mathbf{i} + 13t\mathbf{j}$

   (d) $t = 25$

2 (a) $(3\mathbf{i} - \mathbf{j})\,\mathrm{m\,s}^{-2}$

   (b) $18.4°$ below the vector $\mathbf{i}$

   (c) $27.9\,\mathrm{m\,s}^{-1}$

3 (a) (i) $090°$ (ii) $104°$

   (b) $\mathbf{a} = 6t\mathbf{i}$, $\mathbf{b} = 4t\mathbf{i} + (5 - t)\mathbf{j}$

   (c) $t = 5$

   (d) The displacement of B from A is

$\mathbf{b} - \mathbf{a} = (4t - 6t)\mathbf{i} + (5 - t)\mathbf{j} = -2t\mathbf{i} + (5 - t)\mathbf{j}$

The distance is the magnitude of the displacement.

$d^2 = (-2t)^2 + (5 - t)^2$

$\quad = 4t^2 + 25 - 10t + t^2$

$\quad = 5t^2 - 10t + 25$

(e) The ships are 5 km apart when
$25 = 5t^2 - 10t + 25 \Rightarrow 5t^2 - 10t = 0$
$\Rightarrow 5t(t - 2) = 0 \Rightarrow t = 0, t = 2$
Initially $t = 0$, so they are again 5 km apart after 2 hours.

4 $21\mathbf{i} + 7\mathbf{j}$

Test yourself (p 51)

1 (a) $(4\mathbf{i} + 11\mathbf{j})\,\mathrm{m\,s^{-1}}$ **(b)** $t = 5.5$
 (c) $35.2\,\mathrm{m\,s^{-1}}$

2 (a) $(60\mathbf{i} - 120\mathbf{j})\,\mathrm{km\,h^{-1}}$
 (b) $\mathbf{p} = (20 + 60t)\mathbf{i} + (35 - 120t)\mathbf{j}$
 (c) $\mathbf{q} = 96t\mathbf{i} - 72t\mathbf{j}$ **(d)** $80\,\mathrm{km}$

3 (a) $33.7°$ clockwise from the vector $\mathbf{i}$
 (b) $(2\mathbf{i} - \mathbf{j})\,\mathrm{m\,s^{-2}}$
 (c) $\mathbf{v} = (2 + 2t)\mathbf{i} - (3 + t)\mathbf{j}$
 (d) $10\,\mathrm{m\,s^{-1}}$

4 (a) $256°$
 (b) $\mathbf{r} = (2 - 16t)\mathbf{i} + (6 - 4t)\mathbf{j}$
 (c) $(-15\mathbf{i} - \mathbf{j})\,\mathrm{km\,h^{-1}}$

3 Forces

A Forces as vectors (p 52)

A1 D

A2 (a)
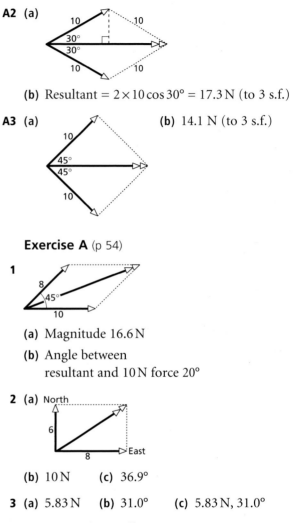

 (b) Resultant $= 2 \times 10\cos 30° = 17.3\,\mathrm{N}$ (to 3 s.f.)

A3 (a) **(b)** $14.1\,\mathrm{N}$ (to 3 s.f.)

Exercise A (p 54)

1

 (a) Magnitude $16.6\,\mathrm{N}$
 (b) Angle between resultant and $10\,\mathrm{N}$ force $20°$

2 (a)

 (b) $10\,\mathrm{N}$ **(c)** $36.9°$

3 (a) $5.83\,\mathrm{N}$ **(b)** $31.0°$ **(c)** $5.83\,\mathrm{N}, 31.0°$

4 (a) $7520\,\mathrm{N}$ (to 3 s.f.)
 (b) Along the line bisecting the angle between the forces

5 (a)
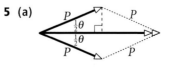

 (b) Magnitude of resultant
 $= $ length of diagonal
 $= P\cos(\tfrac{1}{2}\theta) + P\cos(\tfrac{1}{2}\theta)$
 $= 2P\cos(\tfrac{1}{2}\theta)$

B Resolving a force (p 55)

B1 5.14 N in direction p
6.13 N in direction q

B2 (a) 19.0 N   (b) 6.18 N

B3 (a) 9.85 N   (b) 24.0°

B4 (a) 8.66... N   (b) 4.69... N

(c) $8.66... + 4.69... = 13.359$ (to 3 d.p.)

(d) 5 N   (e) $-1.71...$ N

(f) $5 - 1.71... = 3.290$ (to 3 d.p.)

(g) (i) 13.8 N   (ii) 13.8°

Exercise B (p 57)

1 (a) 10 N   (b) 17.3 N

2 (a) 9.64 N   (b) 11.49 N

3 (a) 4.915 N   (b) 3.441 N   (c) 8.915 N

(d) 9.556 N   (e) 21.1°

4 (a) $(4\mathbf{i} + \mathbf{j})$ N   (b) 4.12 N, 14.0°

5 10.2 N, 68.3°

6 7.08 N, 72.3°

C Resolving coplanar forces in equilibrium (p 58)

C1 (a) (i) $P\cos 35°$ (ii) $P\sin 35°$

(b) The total component in direction Ox is zero, so $P\cos 35° - 10\cos 75° = 0$.

(c) The total component in direction Oy is zero, so $P\sin 35° + 10\sin 75° - Q = 0$.

(d) 3.16   (e) 11.47

C2 (a) The total component in direction Ox is zero, so $U\cos 40° - V\cos 70° = 0$.

(b) $U\sin 40°$, $V\sin 70°$

(c) The overall component in direction Oy is zero, so the total y-components of U and V must be 5 N.

(d) $U = 1.82$, $V = 4.08$

Exercise C (p 59)

1 (a) $P\cos 25° = Q\cos 25°$, so $P = Q$

(b) Resolve in direction Oy:
$$P\sin 25° + Q\sin 25° = 5$$
$$\Rightarrow P\sin 25° + P\sin 25° = 5$$
$$\Rightarrow 2P\sin 25° = 5$$
$$\Rightarrow P = \frac{5}{2\sin 25°} = 5.92$$

2 (a) $10\sin 60° = P\sin 45°$
$$\Rightarrow P = \frac{10\sin 60°}{\sin 45°} = 12.2 \text{ (to 3 s.f.)}$$

(b) 13.7

3 (a) $5\cos 30° = 8\cos\theta$
$$\Rightarrow \cos\theta = \frac{5\cos 30°}{8} = 0.541...$$
$$\Rightarrow \theta = 57.2°$$

(b) 9.22

4 (a) 36.9°   (b) 9

(c) 12 N in direction opposite to removed force

5 (a) Resolve in direction Ox:
$$P\cos\theta + 6\cos 60° = 10$$
$$\Rightarrow P\cos\theta + 3 = 10$$
$$\Rightarrow P\cos\theta = 7$$

(b) Resolve in direction Oy:
$$P\sin\theta = 6\sin 60°$$

(c) $\dfrac{P\sin\theta}{P\cos\theta} = \dfrac{6\sin 60°}{7}$
$$\Rightarrow \tan\theta = \frac{6\sin 60°}{7}$$
$$= 0.742...$$
$$\Rightarrow \theta = 36.6°$$

(d) 8.72

6 $p = 5$, $q = 1$

7 $P = 4.48$, $Q = 3.66$

D Weight, tension and thrust (p 61)

D1 (a)   (b)

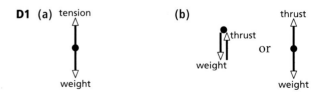

D2 (a)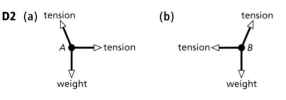
tension

A →tension

weight

(b) tension

tension◁ B

weight

D3 (a) If the ends are at the same height, the bead hangs symmetrically between them. The tension is the same throughout the string.

$T \diagdown \alpha | \alpha \diagup T$

$\downarrow W$

(b) If the ends are at different heights the bead hangs such that the angle between the string and the vertical is the same for both parts of the string. This is because tension is still the same throughout the string.

$T \diagdown \alpha | \alpha \diagup T$

$\downarrow W$

Exercise D (p 63)

1 (a)

15

25°

T

$\downarrow W$

(b) (i) 6.34 N   **(ii)** 13.6 N

2 (a) 6.39 N   **(b)** 2.18 N

3 (a) 22.4 N   **(b)** 27.5 N

4 (a) 59.0°   **(b)** 23.3 N

5 71.8°

6 (a) Resolve vertically: $T\cos\alpha + T\cos\alpha = W$

$\Rightarrow \qquad 2T\cos\alpha = W$

$\Rightarrow \qquad T = \dfrac{W}{2\cos\alpha}$

(b) As α increases, $\cos\alpha$ decreases, so T increases.

(c) As α approaches 90°, T gets larger and larger, without limit.

7 18.1 N (upper), 11.5 N (lower)

E Friction (p 64)

E1 The object remains stationary at first, but eventually it moves.

E2 (a)

R

F ◁— —▷ 8

$\downarrow$ 20

(b) (i) 8 N   **(ii)** 20 N

(c) 0.4

E3 4.2 N

E4 (a) Resolve vertically

(b) 7.5 N

(c) $F \le \mu R$

$\Rightarrow \quad 7.5 \le 0.3W$

$\Rightarrow \quad W \ge \dfrac{7.5}{0.3} = 25$

E5

normal reaction

tension

friction force ◁

weight

E6

normal reaction

weight

normal reaction

pulling force

friction force ◁

weight

The vertical component of the pulling force plus the normal reaction equals the weight, so the normal reaction is less than the weight.

E7 (a)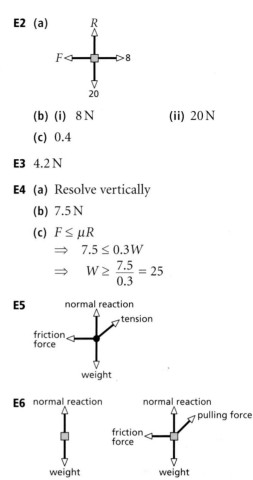

R

20

F ◁ 25°

40

(b) Resolve vertically: $R + 20\sin 25° = 40$

So $R = 40 - 20\sin 25° = 31.5$

(c) Resolve horizontally: $F = 20\cos 25° = 18.1$

(d) $18.1 \le 31.5\mu$, so $\mu \ge \dfrac{18.1}{31.5} = 0.57$

Exercise E (p 67)

1 (a)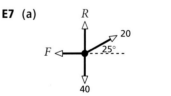

R

μR ◁— —▷ 12

15

(b) 0.8

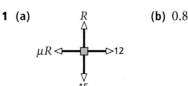

2 3.6

3 (a) 8 N

(b) F (friction) $= 4\cos 30° = 3.464$

$F \le \mu R$, so $3.464 \le 8\mu$

so $\mu \ge \dfrac{3.464}{8} = 0.433$

4 Resolve horizontally: $F = 6\cos 50° = 3.857$
Resolve vertically: $R = 9 + 6\sin 50° = 13.596$

$F = \mu R$ so $\mu = \dfrac{3.857}{13.596} = 0.28$ (to 2 d.p.)

5 (a) Resolve horizontally: $F = 1.5\cos 40°$
$= 1.15$

(b) 2.87 N   **(c)** 3.84 N

6 (a) Resolve vertically: $R + P\sin 45° = 7$
so $R = 7 - P\sin 45°$
$= 7 - 0.707P$

(b) F (friction) $= P\cos 45° = 0.707P$
$F \le \mu R \quad \Rightarrow \quad 0.707P \le 0.25\times(7 - 0.707P)$
$\Rightarrow \quad 0.707P \le 1.75 - 0.177P$
$\Rightarrow \quad 0.884P \le 1.75$
$\Rightarrow \quad P \le \dfrac{1.75}{0.884} = 1.98$

7 (a) 3.40 N

(b) $F = 3\cos 60° = 1.5$
$F \le \mu R \quad \Rightarrow \quad 1.5 \le 3.40\mu$
$\Rightarrow \quad \mu \ge \dfrac{1.5}{3.40} = 0.44$

8 Friction force to left:

Resolve horizontally: $F + P = 6\cos 45°$
$\Rightarrow \quad F = 6\cos 45° - P = 4.243 - P$
Resolve vertically: $R + 6\sin 45° = 10$
$\Rightarrow \quad R = 10 - 6\sin 45° = 5.757$
$F \le \mu R \Rightarrow 4.243 - P \le 0.2\times 5.757$
$\Rightarrow P \ge 4.243 - 0.2\times 5.757 = 3.09$ (to 2 d.p.)

Friction force to right

Resolve horizontally: $F + 6\cos 45° = P$
$\Rightarrow \quad F = P - 6\cos 45° = P - 4.243$

Resolve vertically: $R + 6\sin 45° = 10$
$\Rightarrow \quad R = 10 - 6\sin 45° = 5.757$
$F \le \mu R \Rightarrow P - 4.243 \le 0.2\times 5.757$
$\Rightarrow P \le 4.243 + 0.2\times 5.757 = 5.39$ (to 2 d.p.)

F Friction: inclined surfaces (p 68)

F1 As the angle α increases, the component of the weight down the plane, $W\sin\alpha$, increases and R decreases. As the component $W\sin\alpha$ increases, so the friction force F increases until it reaches its limiting value μR. If the angle increases further, then the object will start to move down the plane.

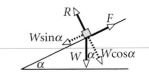

F2

As the plane is tilted, the normal to the plane rotates from a vertical position to 35° from the vertical.

Alternatively,
$\beta = 90° - 35° = 65°$
so $\alpha = 90° - \beta = 35°$

F3

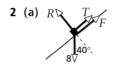

F4 $\mu R = 5\sin 35°$

F5 $R = 5\cos 35°$

F6 (a) $\mu \times 5\cos 35° = 5\sin 35°$
$\Rightarrow \mu = \tan 35° = 0.700$

(b) $R = 5\cos 35° = 4.10$ (to 3 s.f.)

Exercise F (p 70)

1 (a)

(b) 4.33 N (to 2 d.p.)   **(c)** $\mu = 0.58$ (to 2 d.p.)

2 (a)

(b) (i) 6.13 N (to 2 d.p.) **(ii)** 3.61 N (to 2 d.p.)
(c) (i) 6.13 N (to 2 d.p.) **(ii)** 6.67 N (to 2 d.p.)

3 5.87 N (to 2 d.p.)

4 (a) 2.19 N (to 2 d.p.)   **(b)** 5.23 N (to 2 d.p.)

5 11.2 N (to 3 s.f.)

6 (a) Resolve perpendicular to plane:
$R = 10 \cos 40° = 7.66$

Resolve parallel to plane:
$F = 10 \sin 40° = 6.43$

For equilibrium $F \le \mu R$ and $\mu R = 0.2 \times 7.66$
$= 1.53$

$\Rightarrow F > \mu R$, so the particle cannot remain in equilibrium.

(b) Resolve parallel to plane:
$F + P = 10 \sin 40°$

Resolve perpendicular to plane:
$R = 10 \cos 40°$
$F \le \mu R$
$\Rightarrow 10 \sin 40° - P \le 2 \cos 40°$
$\Rightarrow P \ge 10 \sin 40° - 2 \cos 40°$

(c) Resolve parallel to plane:
$P = F + 10 \sin 40°$

Resolve perpendicular to plane:
$R = 10 \cos 40°$
$F \le \mu R$
$\Rightarrow P - 10 \sin 40° \le 2 \cos 40°$
$\Rightarrow P \le 10 \sin 40° + 2 \cos 40°$

(d) $P \ge 10 \sin 40° - 2 \cos 40° = 4.90$
$P \le 10 \sin 40° + 2 \cos 40° = 7.96$
$\Rightarrow 4.90 \le P \le 7.96$

7 (a) The component of the weight down the plane is $8 \sin 30° = 4$ N. The 3 N force acts up the plane.
For the particle to be in equilibrium, forces down the plane = forces up the plane, so the friction force acts up the plane with magnitude 1 N.

(b) Resolve parallel to plane:
$F + 3 = 8 \sin 30$
$\Rightarrow F = 1$
Resolve perpendicular to plane:
$R = 8 \cos 30$
For equilibrium
$F \le \mu R \Rightarrow 1 \le \mu \times 8 \cos 30$
$\Rightarrow \mu \ge \dfrac{1}{8 \cos 30} = 0.144$

Mixed questions (p 72)

1 (a) $(8\mathbf{i} + 2\mathbf{j})$ N   **(b)** 8.25 N, 14.0°

2 (a) 5.20 N   **(b)** 30°

3 (a) 38.8°   **(b)** 9.07

4 6.22 N (left), 4.06 N (right)

5 (a) 0.58 N   **(b)** 1.75 N

6 (a)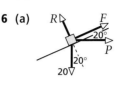

(b) 1.15 N   **(c)** 19.2 N

7 (a) Resolve vertically: $R + T \sin 30° = 5$
$\Rightarrow R = 5 - T \sin 30°$
$= 5 - 0.5T$

(b) $F = T \cos 30° = 0.866T$
$F \le \mu R \Rightarrow 0.866T \le 0.5 \times (5 - 0.5T)$
$\Rightarrow 0.866T \le 2.5 - 0.25T$
$\Rightarrow 1.116T \le 2.5$
$\Rightarrow T \le \dfrac{2.5}{1.116} = 2.24$

8 $\mu = 0.23$

Test yourself (p 74)

1 (a) $(7\mathbf{i} + 4\mathbf{j})$ N   **(b)** 8.06 N   **(c)** 60.3°

2 (a) 7.55 N   **(b)** 14.8°

3 $P = 17.3$ N, $Q = 10$ N

4 (a) 33.7°   **(b)** 3.61 N

5

(a) 13 N

(b) Resolve horizontally:
$F = P + 4 \cos 30°$
$= P + 3.464$
$F \le \mu R \Rightarrow P + 3.464 \le 0.3 \times 13$
$\Rightarrow P \le 3.9 - 3.464 = 0.436$

6 0.61

4 Newton's laws of motion 1

A Mass and momentum (p 75)

A1 The lighter ball will move faster.

A2 $2\,\mathrm{m\,s^{-1}}$

A3 $4\,\mathrm{kg}$

Exercise A (p 78)

1. (a) $17.5\,\mathrm{kg\,m\,s^{-1}}$
   (b) B is moving in the opposite direction to A. The momentum of B is $-7.5\,\mathrm{kg\,m\,s^{-1}}$.

2. $4\,\mathrm{m\,s^{-1}}$ forwards

3. $5\,\mathrm{m\,s^{-1}}$ forwards

4. $0.2\,\mathrm{m\,s^{-1}}$

5. $0.4\,\mathrm{m\,s^{-1}}$
   (There is no need to bother with the first collision. The total momentum after the second collision is equal to the original momentum.)

6. Total momentum before collision
$$= mU + 4m\left(\tfrac{1}{2}U\right)$$
$$= 3mU$$
   So if $V\,\mathrm{m\,s^{-1}}$ is the final velocity,
$$3mU = 5mV$$
$$\Rightarrow \quad V = \tfrac{3}{5}U$$

7. 1.2

B Force, momentum and impulse (p 79)

B1 (a) (i) The object accelerates.
   (ii) The object moves at a constant velocity.
   (b) (i) The object accelerates for twice as long and so reaches twice the velocity.
   (ii) The object accelerates at twice the rate and so reaches twice the velocity.

B2 The heavier object accelerates at a smaller rate than the lighter object, and reaches a lower velocity.

B3 $60\,\mathrm{N\,s}$

B4 (a) $40\,\mathrm{N\,s}$ (b) $40\,\mathrm{N\,s}$ (c) $8\,\mathrm{m\,s^{-1}}$

B5 (a) $20\,\mathrm{N\,s}$ (b) $6\,\mathrm{N\,s}$
   (c) $26\,\mathrm{N\,s}$ (d) $6.5\,\mathrm{m\,s^{-1}}$

B6 (a) The object decelerates.
   (b) The object comes to rest and then accelerates away from you.

Exercise B (p 82)

1. (a) $12\,\mathrm{N\,s}$ (b) $4\,\mathrm{m\,s^{-1}}$

2. (a) $30\,\mathrm{N\,s}$ (b) $12\,\mathrm{N\,s}$
   (c) $42\,\mathrm{N\,s}$ (d) $7\,\mathrm{m\,s^{-1}}$

3. $1.5\,\mathrm{m\,s^{-1}}$

4. $24\,\mathrm{N\,s}$

5. $3\,\mathrm{N\,s}$

6. $10.5\,\mathrm{m\,s^{-1}}$

7. (a) $-6\,\mathrm{N\,s}$ (b) $4\,\mathrm{m\,s^{-1}}$
   (c) $6\,\mathrm{N\,s}$
   The impulse exerted on the 3 kg object is equal and opposite to the impulse exerted on the 2 kg object. The total momentum of the two objects has remained constant during the collision due to the principle of conservation of momentum.

8. (a) $1.7\,\mathrm{m\,s^{-1}}$ (b) $3.2\,\mathrm{N\,s}$

9. (a) 0.75 (b) $0.375\,\mathrm{N\,s}$

C Force, mass and acceleration (p 83)

C1 $15\,\mathrm{N}$

C2 $8\,\mathrm{m\,s^{-2}}$

C3 $5\,\mathrm{kg}$

C4 (a) $450\,\mathrm{N}$ (b) $0.15\,\mathrm{m\,s^{-2}}$

Exercise C (p 85)

1. $0.8\,\mathrm{m\,s^{-2}}$

2. $124\,\mathrm{N}$

3. $2000\,\mathrm{N}$

4. (a) $0\,\mathrm{m\,s^{-2}}$ (b) $180\,\mathrm{N}$

5 (a) The direction of F is opposite to the direction of motion.

(b) $a = -0.375$ (deceleration)

6 $P = 1360$, $R = 160$

D Solving problems in one dimension (p 85)

D1 (a) $0.6\,\mathrm{m\,s^{-2}}$ **(b)** $5\,\mathrm{s}$

(c) $s = \frac{1}{2}(u + v)t = \frac{1}{2}(1.5 + 4.5) \times 5 = 15$

D2 (a) $0.5\,\mathrm{m\,s^{-2}}$ **(b)** $250\,\mathrm{N}$

Exercise D (p 87)

1 (a) $0.4\,\mathrm{m\,s^{-2}}$ **(b)** $12.5\,\mathrm{s}$ **(c)** $31.25\,\mathrm{m}$

2 (a) $0.8\,\mathrm{m\,s^{-1}}$ **(b)** 30

3 (a) $3600\,\mathrm{N}$ **(b)** $4.5\,\mathrm{m\,s^{-2}}$ **(c)** $25\,\mathrm{m}$

4 $9\,\mathrm{N}$

5 (a) 250 **(b)** $12\,\mathrm{s}$

6 (a) $0.4\,\mathrm{m\,s^{-2}}$ **(b)** $375\,\mathrm{m}$ **(c)** $1200\,\mathrm{N}$

E Vertical motion (p 88)

E1 $14.7\,\mathrm{N}$

E2 (a) $49\,\mathrm{N}$ **(b)** $9.3\,\mathrm{m\,s^{-2}}$

Exercise E (p 89)

1 (a)

(b) $5.8\,\mathrm{N}$ **(c)** $1.45\,\mathrm{m\,s^{-2}}$

2 (a) In the equation $F = ma$, $a = 0$ so the resultant force on the object is zero. The tension must be equal to the weight.

(b) $38.5\,\mathrm{N}$ **(c)** $4.49\,\mathrm{m\,s^{-2}}$

3 (a) $7380\,\mathrm{N}$ **(b)** $0.743\,\mathrm{m\,s^{-2}}$ (to 3 s.f.)

4 (a) $2.42\,\mathrm{N}$ **(b)** $6.05\,\mathrm{m\,s^{-2}}$ **(c)** $3.40\,\mathrm{s}$

5 (a) Resultant force $= -0.5g - 0.7 = -5.6\,\mathrm{N}$
Apply N2L: $-5.6 = 0.5a$
$\Rightarrow$ $a = -11.2$

(b) $8.4\,\mathrm{m\,s^{-2}}$ **(c)** $8.75\,\mathrm{m}$

6 (a) Resultant force $= 0.5g - 2.5 = 2.4\,\mathrm{N}$
Apply N2L: $2.4 = 0.5a$
$\Rightarrow$ $a = 4.8$

(b) $1.21\,\mathrm{s}$ (to 3 s.f.)   **(c)** $5.80\,\mathrm{m\,s^{-1}}$ (to 3 s.f.)

F Motion in two dimensions

Exercise F (p 90)

1 (a) $(20\mathbf{i} - 15\mathbf{j})\,\mathrm{N}$ **(b)** $(81\mathbf{i} - 59\mathbf{j})\,\mathrm{m\,s^{-1}}$

2 (a) $(15\mathbf{i} + 20\mathbf{j})\,\mathrm{m\,s^{-2}}$ **(b)** $(65\mathbf{i} + 78\mathbf{j})\,\mathrm{m\,s^{-1}}$

3 (a) $(1.6\mathbf{i} - 0.8\mathbf{j})\,\mathrm{m\,s^{-2}}$ **(b)** $4.47\,\mathrm{N}$ (to 3 s.f.)

(c) $(18\mathbf{i} - 5\mathbf{j})\,\mathrm{m\,s^{-1}}$

4 (a) $0.5\,\mathrm{N}$

(b) $36.9°$ below the vector $\mathbf{i}$

5 (a) $(6\mathbf{i} - 2\mathbf{j})\,\mathrm{N}$ **(b)** $(18\mathbf{i} - 6\mathbf{j})\,\mathrm{m\,s^{-1}}$

6 (a) $(2\mathbf{i} + 6\mathbf{j})\,\mathrm{N}$ **(b)** $12.6\,\mathrm{m\,s^{-2}}$ (to 3 s.f.)

(c) $(22\mathbf{i} + 59\mathbf{j})\,\mathrm{m\,s^{-1}}$

Mixed questions (p 92)

1 Let $v\,\mathrm{m\,s^{-1}}$ be the velocity of B after collision
$$mu - 4mu = -\tfrac{1}{2}um + 4mv$$
$$\Rightarrow \quad -3u = -\tfrac{1}{2}u + 4v$$
$$\Rightarrow \quad 4v = -2\tfrac{1}{2}u$$
$$\Rightarrow \quad v = -\tfrac{5}{8}u$$
So the speed of B is $\frac{5}{8}u\,\mathrm{m\,s^{-1}}$

2 (a) $515\,\mathrm{m}$

(b) The graph is a straight line with negative gradient between $t = 30$ and $t = 40$, when the brakes are applied. This shows that the van undergoes a constant deceleration, which means that it experiences a constant retarding force.

(c) $2250\,\mathrm{N}$

3 (a) $4.8\,\mathrm{m\,s^{-1}}$ **(b)** $2.4\,\mathrm{N\,s}$ **(c)** $1.6\,\mathrm{N}$

4 $v = \left(1.2t\mathbf{i} + (2 - 0.8t)\mathbf{j}\right)\,\mathrm{m\,s^{-1}}$

5 (a) At greatest height $v = 0$, $s = 25.6$, $a = -9.8$

$$v^2 = u^2 + 2as$$
$$0^2 = u^2 + 2 \times -9.8 \times 25.6$$
so $\quad u = \sqrt{501.76} = 22.4$

(b) 4.64

(c) 6370 or 6380

(d) Air resistance

Test yourself (p 93)

1 (a) 0.36 N s   **(b)** 2.7 m s^{-1} **(c)** 0.216 N s

2 (a) 2.5 m s^{-1} **(b)** 2.2 N s

3 (a) 1.5 m s^{-2} **(b)** 36.25 m   **(c)** 845 N

4 (a)
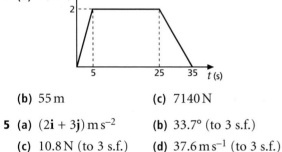

(b) 55 m   **(c)** 7140 N

5 (a) $(2\mathbf{i} + 3\mathbf{j})$ m s^{-2} **(b)** 33.7° (to 3 s.f.)

(c) 10.8 N (to 3 s.f.)   **(d)** 37.6 m s^{-1} (to 3 s.f.)

5 Newton's laws of motion 2

Answers are given to three significant figures where appropriate.

A Resolving forces (p 94)

A1 8.66 N

A2 0.217 m s^{-2}

A3 387

Exercise A (p 95)

1 (a)
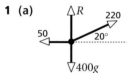

(b) Horizontal force $= 220 \cos 20° - 50 = 157$ N

(c) 0.392 m s^{-2}

2 (a) (i) 28.9 N   **(ii)** 868 N

  (b) (i) 80.8 N   **(ii)** 842 N

3 (a) 50.0   **(b)** 7700 N

4 0.120 m s^{-2}

5 (a) Resolve vertically (vertical acceleration = 0)
$T = 905$

(b) 5.66 m s^{-2}

B Friction (p 96)

B1 (a)
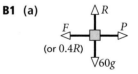

(b) Resolve vertically; no vertical acceleration

(c) 235 N   **(d)** 265 N

B2 (a)

  (b) 438 N

(c) 175 N   **(d)** 1.41 m s^{-2}

Exercise B (p 97)

1 0.3 m s^{-2}

2 157

3

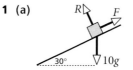

Resolve vertically: $R = 25g$
Maximum friction force $= 0.35 \times 25g = 85.75$
The push of 80 N does not exceed the maximum frictional force, so the block remains stationary.

4 (a) $3.92\,\mathrm{m\,s^{-2}}$ (b) $22.5\,\mathrm{m\,s^{-1}}$

5 (a) Resolve vertically:
$R + 20\sin 30° = 10g \Rightarrow R = 88$
(b) $8.8\,\mathrm{N}$ (c) $0.852\,\mathrm{m\,s^{-2}}$

6 (a) Resolve vertically:
$R = 20g + 70\sin 35° = 236$
(b) $47.2\,\mathrm{N}$ (c) $0.506\,\mathrm{m\,s^{-2}}$

7 (a) $86.0\,\mathrm{N}$ (b) $0.397\,\mathrm{m\,s^{-2}}$

8 (a) $0.4\,\mathrm{m\,s^{-2}}$ (b) 0.122 (c) $15.8\,\mathrm{s}$

C Smooth inclined surfaces (p 99)

C1 The block will accelerate down the plane.
The acceleration increases as the angle increases.
This is because the component of the weight acting down the plane increases as the angle increases.

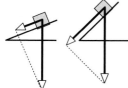

C2 (a) Resolve perpendicular to the plane: $R = 40.1$
(b) $5g\sin 35° = 5a$, so $a = 9.8\sin 35° = 5.6$

C3 (a)

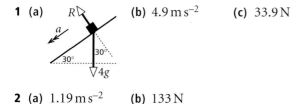

(b) (i) $13.3\,\mathrm{N}$
(ii) $4.14\,\mathrm{m\,s^{-2}}$

Exercise C (p 100)

1 (a)

(b) $4.9\,\mathrm{m\,s^{-2}}$ (c) $33.9\,\mathrm{N}$

2 (a) $1.19\,\mathrm{m\,s^{-2}}$ (b) $133\,\mathrm{N}$

---

3 $20.3\,\mathrm{N}$

4 (a) $5.34\,\mathrm{m\,s^{-2}}$ (b) $2.4\,\mathrm{s}$ (c) $98.6\,\mathrm{N}$

5 52.5

D Rough inclined surfaces (p 101)

D1 (a) Resolve perpendicular to the plane:
There is no acceleration in this direction, so
$R = 3g\cos 30°$.
(b) 5.09 (c) $3.20\,\mathrm{m\,s^{-2}}$

D2 (a)

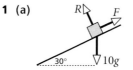

(b) Resolve perpendicular to the plane:
$R = 10g\cos 20° = 92.1$
(c) $27.6\,\mathrm{N}$
(d) (i) 61.1 (ii) 81.1

D3 (a) Resolve perpendicular to the plane:
$R = 5g\cos 25° = 44.4$
(b) Resolve parallel to the plane:
$F = 5g\sin 25° = 20.7$
(c) $F \le \mu R$, so $20.7 \le 44.4\mu$ so $\mu \ge \dfrac{20.7}{44.4} = 0.466$

Exercise D (p 102)

1 (a)

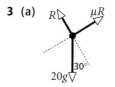

(b) Resolve perpendicular to the plane:
$R = 10g\cos 30° = 84.9$
So $F = 0.25R = 21.2$
Resolve down the plane, and use N2L:
$10g\sin 30° - 21.2 = 10a$
$\Rightarrow a = 2.8$ (to 2 s.f.)

2 (a) $276\,\mathrm{N}$ (b) $0.15 \times 276 = 41.4$
(c) $1.97\,\mathrm{m\,s^{-2}}$

3 (a)

Resolve perpendicular to the plane:
$R = 20g\cos 30° = 170$

(b) Resolve parallel to the plane:
$\mu R = 20g \sin 30°$
So $170\mu = 98 \Rightarrow \mu = 0.576$

4 (a) 368

(b) The box is a particle; the rope is light.

5 57.2 N

6 (a) 0.577　　　　**(b)** 0.342

7 (a) 15.0 N

(b) 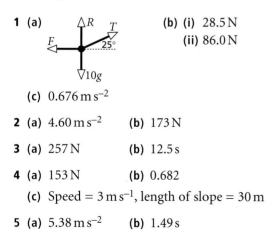 15.0

Resolve parallel to the plane:
If the block is at rest,
$F = 2g \sin 40° = 12.6$
$F \le \mu R$, so $12.6 \le 15.0\mu$
$\Rightarrow \mu = 0.84$

(c) $3.30\,\mathrm{m\,s^{-2}}$

8 (a) $0.978\,\mathrm{m\,s^{-2}}$　　**(b)** $1.71\,\mathrm{m\,s^{-1}}$

Mixed questions (p 104)

1 (a) $W = 20g = 20 \times 9.8 = 196\,\mathrm{N}$

(b) Resolve vertically:
$R + 70 \sin 25° = 196 \Rightarrow R = 166.4$

(c) 49.9　　　**(d)** $0.676\,\mathrm{m\,s^{-2}}$　　**(e)** 8.45 m

2 (a) 0.450　　　**(b)** 1.44 N

(c) It is not in equilibrium. The component of tension along the pole, 2 N, is greater than the maximum frictional force, $0.450 \times 1.44\,\mathrm{N}$.

3 (a) $7\,\mathrm{m\,s^{-1}}$　　**(b)** 4 N s　　**(c)** 0.5

Test yourself (p 105)

1 (a)

(b) (i) 28.5 N
(ii) 86.0 N

(c) $0.676\,\mathrm{m\,s^{-2}}$

2 (a) $4.60\,\mathrm{m\,s^{-2}}$　　**(b)** 173 N

3 (a) 257 N　　　**(b)** 12.5 s

4 (a) 153 N　　　**(b)** 0.682

(c) Speed = $3\,\mathrm{m\,s^{-1}}$, length of slope = 30 m

5 (a) $5.38\,\mathrm{m\,s^{-2}}$　　**(b)** 1.49 s

6 Newton's laws of motion 3

A Modelling (p 106)

A1 The cars would accelerate. Brakes are needed!

A2 It would not be appropriate.
The relative positions of different parts of the skater's body are important.

A3 For example, an elephant stepping on to an ocean-going oil tanker would not have a detectable effect.

A4 Air resistance in a tunnel cannot be ignored. Mass and speed of train, gradient and curvature of track, friction of rails, etc. need to be included.

A5 The dimensions of the diver are comparable with the distance fallen. As with the skater, the different positions of arms, legs and trunk are important.

B Newton's third law of motion (p 109)

B1 (a) $6000 - T = 1200a$

(b)

Reason: Newton's third law

(c) $T = 400a$　　　**(d)** $a = 3.75$, $T = 1500$

(e) It must be inextensible.

B2 (a) $6000 = 1600a$　　**(b)** $a = 3.75$

Exercise B (p 111)

1 (a) $0.8\,\mathrm{m\,s^{-2}}$　　　**(b)** 320 N

2 (a) $0.625\,\mathrm{m\,s^{-2}}$　　**(b)** 950 N

3 (a) 2400 N　　　**(b)** 300 N

4 (a) $0.8\,\mathrm{m\,s^{-2}}$　　　**(b)** 3840 N

5 (a) 100 N

(b) (i) 0 N　　　**(ii)** 100 N

6 (a) Crate　　Box

(b) 1485 N　　　**(c)** 297 N

(d) (i) $9.8\,\mathrm{m\,s^{-2}}$ downwards

(ii) $9.95\,\mathrm{m\,s^{-1}}$ (to 3 s.f.)

7 (a) $2.25\,\mathrm{m\,s^{-2}}$ **(b)** $1000\,\mathrm{N}$ **(c)** $80\,\mathrm{s}$

C Pulleys and pegs (p 113)

C1 (a) Both particles accelerate.

(b) What happens depends on

- the relative masses of the particles
- the roughness of the surface

The particles either remain stationary or accelerate.

C2 (a) $\triangle R$ **(b)** $T = 3a$ **(c)** $\triangle T$

$\quad T \qquad\qquad\qquad\qquad\qquad\qquad \bigtriangledown 2g$

$\bigtriangledown 3g$

(d) The string is inextensible.

(e) $2g - T = 2a$ **(f)** $a = 3.92$, $T = 11.76$

C3 (a)

$F \quad\longleftarrow\quad \triangle R \quad\longrightarrow\quad T$

$\bigtriangledown 3g$

(b) There is no vertical acceleration, so the normal reaction must be equal to the weight.

(c) $0.2 \times R = 0.2 \times 3 \times 9.8 = 5.88$

(d) $T - 5.88 = 3a$

(e) $\triangle T$

$\qquad 2g - T = 2a$

$\bigtriangledown 2g$

(f) $a = 2.74$, $T = 14.1$ (to 3 s.f.)

C4 (a) Acceleration $4.2\,\mathrm{m\,s^{-2}}$, tension $16.8\,\mathrm{N}$

(b) Acceleration $1.4\,\mathrm{m\,s^{-2}}$, tension $25.2\,\mathrm{N}$

C5 Both particles accelerate, A down and B up.

C6 (a) $\triangle T$ **(b)** $3g - T = 3a$

$\quad\downarrow a$

$\bigtriangledown 3g$

(c) $\triangle T$ **(d)** $T - 2g = 2a$

$\quad\uparrow a$

$\bigtriangledown 2g$

(e) $a = 1.96$, $T = 23.5$ (to 3 s.f.)

(f) The tension in the string is the same throughout its length. The downward force on the pulley is $T + T$ (see diagram). The downward force is $47\,\mathrm{N}$.

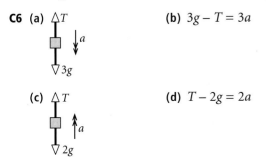

C7 (a) $1.4\,\mathrm{m\,s^{-2}}$ **(b)** $33.6\,\mathrm{N}$ **(c)** $2.8\,\mathrm{m}$ **(d)** $5.6\,\mathrm{m}$

C8 (a) This is difficult to guess! The correct answer comes out of the following working.

(b) $3g\sin 30° - T = 3a$

So $14.7 - T = 3a$

(c) $\triangle T$

$\qquad T - 2g = 2a$

$\bigtriangledown 2g$

(d) $a = -0.98$ (deceleration)

$T = 17.64$

A moves up the slope.

Exercise C (p 117)

All answers are to 3 s.f.

1 (a) (i) $3.27\,\mathrm{m\,s^{-2}}$ **(ii)** $13.1\,\mathrm{N}$

(b) (i) $6.53\,\mathrm{m\,s^{-2}}$ **(ii)** $13.1\,\mathrm{N}$

(c) (i) $3.68\,\mathrm{m\,s^{-2}}$ **(ii)** $18.4\,\mathrm{N}$

2 (a) (i) $3.27\,\mathrm{m\,s^{-2}}$ **(ii)** $26.1\,\mathrm{N}$ **(iii)** $52.3\,\mathrm{N}$

(b) (i) $2.45\,\mathrm{m\,s^{-2}}$ **(ii)** $36.8\,\mathrm{N}$ **(iii)** $73.5\,\mathrm{N}$

(c) (i) $3.92\,\mathrm{m\,s^{-2}}$ **(ii)** $20.6\,\mathrm{N}$ **(iii)** $41.2\,\mathrm{N}$

3 (a) (i) $2.61\,\mathrm{m\,s^{-2}}$ **(ii)** $14.4\,\mathrm{N}$

(b) (i) $5.88\,\mathrm{m\,s^{-2}}$ **(ii)** $15.7\,\mathrm{N}$

(c) (i) $0.638\,\mathrm{m\,s^{-2}}$ **(ii)** $27.7\,\mathrm{N}$

(d) (i) $1.4\,\mathrm{m\,s^{-2}}$ **(ii)** $25.2\,\mathrm{N}$

4 (a) (i) $1.4\,\mathrm{m\,s^{-2}}$ (up slope) **(ii)** $25.2\,\mathrm{N}$

(b) (i) $4.22\,\mathrm{m\,s^{-2}}$ (up slope) **(ii)** $22.3\,\mathrm{N}$

(c) (i) $0.656\,\mathrm{m\,s^{-2}}$ (down slope) **(ii)** $31.4\,\mathrm{N}$

(d) (i) $3.70\,\mathrm{m\,s^{-2}}$ (up slope) **(ii)** $24.4\,\mathrm{N}$

5 (a) $\mu \geq 0.4$ **(b)** 0.52

6 (a) $1.4\,\mathrm{m\,s^{-2}}$ **(b)** $1.7\,\mathrm{s}$ **(c)** $7.1\,\mathrm{m}$

7 (a) $5.88\,\mathrm{m\,s^{-2}}$ **(b)** $1.71\,\mathrm{m\,s^{-1}}$ **(c)** $0.292\,\mathrm{s}$

8 (a) $2.52\,\mathrm{m\,s^{-2}}$ **(b)** $0.891\,\mathrm{s}$ **(c)** $0.857\,\mathrm{m}$

9 (a) Acceleration $= 1.87\,\mathrm{m\,s^{-2}}$, tension $= 30\,000\,\mathrm{N}$

(b) $36.7\,\mathrm{m\,s^{-1}}$

(c) The braking system, the mass and elasticity of the cable, friction at the pulley, friction on the rails, etc. are all left out.

Mixed questions (p 119)

1 (a) $3.04\,\mathrm{m\,s^{-2}}$ **(b)** $10\,\mathrm{N}$

(c) $58.9\,\mathrm{m}$ (to 3 s.f.)

2 (a) $1.45\,\mathrm{m\,s^{-2}}$ **(b)** $0.596\,\mathrm{m\,s^{-2}}$ (to 3 s.f.)

3 (a) $\frac{3}{2}mg$ **(b)** 3

4 (a) N2L(A): $T - 6g\sin 30° = 6a$
  N2L(B): $8g - T = 8a$
  Add: $8g - 6g\sin 30° = 14a$
  $\Rightarrow$ $a = 3.5\,\mathrm{m\,s^{-2}}$

(b) $50.4\,\mathrm{N}$

5 (a) $\frac{12}{5}mg$ **(b)** $\frac{2}{5}$

6 (a) $2.45\,\mathrm{m\,s^{-2}}$ **(b)** $36.75\,\mathrm{N}$

(c) $1.38\,\mathrm{s}$ (to 3 s.f.)

Test yourself (p 120)

1 (a) $1.5\,\mathrm{m\,s^{-2}}$ **(b)** $1600\,\mathrm{N}$ **(c)** $54\,\mathrm{s}$

2 (a) N2L(A): $T - 2g = 2a$
      $T - 2\times 9.8 = 2\times 4.2$
    $\Rightarrow$ $T = 28\,\mathrm{N}$

(b) 5 **(c)** $56\,\mathrm{N}$

3 (a) $\frac{1}{2}g$ **(b)** mg

(c) $0.553\,\mathrm{s}$ (to 3 s.f.)

4 (a) N2L(A): $T - F = 2ma$
      $T - 2\mu mg = 2ma$
  N2L(B): $mg\sin 30° - T = ma$
  Add: $mg\sin 30° - 2\mu mg = 3ma$
    $\Rightarrow$ $\frac{1}{2}mg - 2\mu mg = 3ma$
    $\Rightarrow$ $\frac{1}{6}g - \frac{2}{3}\mu g = a$
    $\Rightarrow$ $a = \frac{1}{6}(1 - 4\mu)g$

(b) $\frac{7}{6}h$

(c) The mass of the string, the elasticity of the string, the friction on the pulley

7 Moments

A Moment of a force (p 122)

A1 In the first case the ruler remains stationary on the table.
In the second case the ruler rotates on the table.

A2 (a) The force will cause the spanner to turn anticlockwise and loosen the nut.

(b) The force will again cause the spanner to turn anticlockwise, but the turning effect will not be as great as in (a). The nut will again loosen.

(c) The force will cause the spanner to turn clockwise and tighten the nut.

A3 (a) $12\,\mathrm{N\,m}$ anticlockwise   **(b)** $20\,\mathrm{N\,m}$ clockwise
(c) $12\,\mathrm{N\,m}$ anticlockwise

A4 (a) $20\,\mathrm{N\,m}$ clockwise   **(b)** $0\,\mathrm{N\,m}$ **(c)** $0\,\mathrm{N\,m}$

A5 (a) $0\,\mathrm{N\,m}$ **(b)** $0\,\mathrm{N\,m}$
(c) $20\,\mathrm{N\,m}$ anticlockwise
(d) $20\,\mathrm{N\,m}$ anticlockwise

Exercise A (p 124)

1 (a) $8\,\mathrm{N\,m}$ anticlockwise   **(b)** $4.5\,\mathrm{N\,m}$ clockwise
(c) $17.5\,\mathrm{N\,m}$ anticlockwise

2 (a) $16\,\mathrm{N\,m}$ clockwise   **(b)** $16\,\mathrm{N\,m}$ clockwise
(c) $0\,\mathrm{N\,m}$ **(d)** $0\,\mathrm{N\,m}$

3 (a) $25\,\mathrm{N\,m}$ anticlockwise
(b) $15\,\mathrm{N\,m}$ anticlockwise
(c) $20\,\mathrm{N\,m}$ anticlockwise

4 (a) $8\,\mathrm{N\,m}$ anticlockwise   **(b)** $4\,\mathrm{N\,m}$ clockwise

5 6

B Equilibrium of a rigid body (p 125)

B1 (a) The seesaw will not balance. It will rotate so that Sasha's feet rest on the ground and Kieran is in the air.

(b) Sasha should move towards the pivot, or Kieran should move away from it, to make the seesaw balance.

B2 Resolve vertically: $R = 25g + 30g + 20g$
$$R = 75g = 735$$

B3 (a) Total moment about S
$$= 75g \times 1.6 - 25g \times 0 - 30g \times 1.6 - 20g \times 3.6$$
$$= 120g - 48g - 72g = 0\,\text{N m}$$

(b) Total moment about K
$$= 25g \times 3.6 + 30g \times 2 + 20g \times 0 - 75g \times 2$$
$$= 90g + 60g - 150g = 0\,\text{N m}$$

(c) Total moment about O
$$= 75g \times 2 - 25g \times 0.4 - 30g \times 2 - 20g \times 4$$
$$= 150g - 10g - 60g - 80g = 0\,\text{N m}$$

(d) The total moment of the forces is zero about each of the points. The seesaw is in equilibrium, so the total moment of the forces about any point will be zero.

B4 (a) Total moment about A
$$= R_B \times 4 - 50 \times 2.5 = 4R_B - 125 = 0$$
$$\Rightarrow R_B = 31.25$$

(b) Total moment about B
$$= 50 \times 1.5 - R_A \times 4 = 75 - 4R_A = 0$$
$$\Rightarrow R_A = 18.75$$

(c) Resolve vertically: $R_A + R_B = 50$
Substitute calculated values:
$18.75 + 31.25 = 50$, which is correct, so the forces are in equilibrium.

B5 (a) M(B): $50 \times 0.5 = R_A \times 2 \Rightarrow R_A = 12.5$
Reaction at $A = 12.5\,\text{N}$

(b) M(A): $R_B \times 2 = 50 \times 1.5 \Rightarrow R_B = 37.5$
Reaction at $B = 37.5\,\text{N}$

(c) Moving the supports has changed the magnitudes of the reactions, but the sum of the reactions must remain as $50\,\text{N}$ for the rod to remain in equilibrium.

B6 (a)

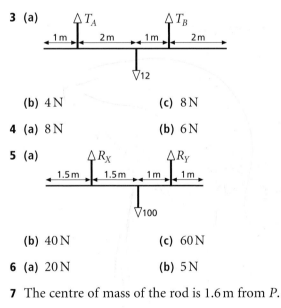

(b) M(B): $50 \times 0.5 = 10 \times 1 + R_A \times 2$
$$\Rightarrow R_A = 7.5$$
Reaction at $A = 7.5\,\text{N}$

(c) M(A): $R_B \times 2 = 50 \times 1.5 + 10 \times 3$
$$\Rightarrow R_B = 52.5$$
Reaction at $B = 52.5\,\text{N}$

B7 (a)

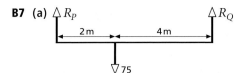

(b) M(Q): $75 \times 4 = R_P \times 6$
$$\Rightarrow R_P = 50$$
Reaction at $P = 50\,\text{N}$

(c) M(P): $R_Q \times 6 = 75 \times 2$
$$\Rightarrow R_Q = 25$$
Reaction at $Q = 25\,\text{N}$

B8 (a) M(Q): $75 \times 4 + 30 \times 3 = R_P \times 6$
$$\Rightarrow R_P = 65$$
Reaction at $P = 65\,\text{N}$

(b) M(P): $R_Q \times 6 = 75 \times 2 + 30 \times 3$
$$\Rightarrow R_Q = 40$$
Reaction at $Q = 40\,\text{N}$

Exercise B (p 128)

1 (a) $A = 24$, $B = 16$ (b) $C = 12$, $D = 19$
  (c) $E = 19.2$, $F = 7.2$ (d) $G = 0.5$, $H = 2.5$

2 $40\,\text{kg}$

3 (a)

(b) $4\,\text{N}$ (c) $8\,\text{N}$

4 (a) $8\,\text{N}$ (b) $6\,\text{N}$

5 (a)

(b) $40\,\text{N}$ (c) $60\,\text{N}$

6 (a) $20\,\text{N}$ (b) $5\,\text{N}$

7 The centre of mass of the rod is $1.6\,\text{m}$ from P.

8 $0.5\,\text{m}$

C Tilting (p 130)

C1 (a) The beam could remain in equilibrium or tilt with B as the pivot.

(b) The beam will remain in equilibrium.

(c) The beam could remain in equilibrium or tilt with C as the pivot.

C2 (a) $2W + 6R_C = 600$

(b) As W increases, R_C decreases.

(c) The maximum value of W for the beam to remain in equilibrium is 300.

(d) M(C): $8W + 600 = 6R_B$
As W increases, R_B increases.

(e) $R_C = 0$, $R_B = 500$

C3 (a) C

(b) M(C): $200 \times 3.4 = 1.6W \Rightarrow W = 425$
Neeta's weight is 425 N.

(c) $R_B = 0$, $R_C = 625$

Exercise C (p 131)

1 (a) 0 N **(b)** 20 N **(c)** 80 N

2 (a) B **(b)** 500 N **(c)** 900 N

3 37.5 N

4 0.875 m

5 225 N

6 The weight of the rod is 240 N. Its centre of mass is 1.25 m from X.

7 (a) 0.36 m **(b)** 28 N

Mixed questions (p133)

1 (a) 100 N **(b)** 2.1875 m

2 (a) 259 N **(b)** 182 N
(c) 61.7 kg (to 3 s.f.)

3 (a) 3.75 m **(b)** 75

4 (a) 2.25 m **(b)** 220 N **(c)** 132 N

5 (a) M(B): $W(x-2) + 100 = 6R$ (1)
M(C): $W(8-x) + 200 = 18R$ (2)
Subtract (2) from (1)$\times 3$:
$3W(x-2) + 300 - W(8-x) - 200 = 0$
$$14W - 4Wx = 100$$
$$\Rightarrow \quad W = \frac{50}{7-2x}$$

(b) $0 \leq x < 3.5$

Test yourself (p 134)

1 (a) 60 N **(b)** 2 m

2 (a)

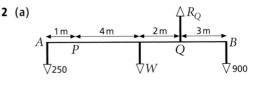

(b) 1625 N **(c)** 475 N

(d) The weight of the beam acts at its mid-point because the beam is uniform.

3 (a) 30 N **(b)** 10 N **(c)** 1.2 m

4 (a) 735 N **(b)** 3.67 m (to 3 s.f.)
(c) (i) The plank is rigid (does not bend).
(ii) The weight of the woman acts at C.

Index